BOURASSA

BOURASSA

Michel Vastel
translated by Hubert Bauch

Macmillan Canada
Toronto, Ontario, Canada

Canadian Cataloguing in Publication Data
Vastel, Michel
  Bourassa

Translation of: Bourassa
Includes bibliographical references and index.
ISBN 0-7715-9148-9

1. Bourassa, Robert, 1933-   . 2. Quebec (Province) – Politics and government –
1960-   . 3. Federal-provincial relations – Quebec (Province).*
4. Canada – Constitutional law – Amendments.   5. Prime ministers – Quebec
(Province) – Biography.   I. Title.

FC2925.1.B6V313 1991   971.4'04'092   C91-094529-2
F1053.25.B6V313 1991

Macmillan Canada
A Division of Canada Publishing Corporation
Toronto, Ontario, Canada

1 2 3 4 5 95 94 93 92 91

Printed in Canada

TABLE OF CONTENTS

To Robert Bourassa,
a Québécois

Acknowledgements

I would like to thank my superiors at *Le Devoir, L'Actualité, La Presse,* and the three papers in the Edimédia Group (*Le Soleil, Le Droit,* and *Le Quotidien*), who allowed me over the years of my career in Ottawa to visit the capitals of the country to gather the comments of all the provincial premiers and to measure the pulse of public opinion in Canada with regard to Robert Bourassa and Quebec's evolution.

I am also indebted to Antoine del Busso, of Les Éditions de l'Homme, who patiently awaited the manuscript which was late in coming, and who helped in refining the first version of this work. I would also like to thank Nicole Bureau-Lévesque, Nicole Raymond, and Katherine Sapon, who stayed with me throughout the process of putting out the final version of the French edition.

I am very happy to have had Hubert Bauch, my translator for *The Outsider*, apply his lively style and eye for detail to the translation of *Bourassa*. The English edition was also extensively revised to take account of recent events in 1991 and to incorporate information from interviews with Bourassa that took place after the publication of the French edition. Jennifer Glossop, freelance editor, and Philippa Campsie, editor-in-chief at Macmillan, also helped to make the book more accessible to an English-Canadian audience.

Finally, I would like to thank my family, for whom, for innumerable evenings, I was only a back bent over a computer keyboard.

PREFACE

The hard thing is to be moderate without being weak.

Alain

Robert Bourassa is a walking paradox. Whereas other premiers of Quebec have aroused extremes of emotion—Maurice Duplessis aroused indignation; Jean Lesage, irritation; Daniel Johnson, enthusiasm; and René Lévesque, vast outpourings of emotion— Robert Bourassa never inspired rebellion, hostility, admiration, or any other passion. Yet this does not mean he is destined to join the likes of Adélard Godbout as a footnote in tomorrow's history books. For despite Bourassa's lack of charisma, the Quebec electorate has renewed its confidence in him more than once, something that cannot be said of the unlauded Adélard.

Many of Quebec's great political leaders have left office with little warning. Their heirs-apparent—Paul Sauvé, who inherited the Duplessis mantle; Jean-Jacques Bertrand, who became premier after Johnson died suddenly; and Pierre-Marc Johnson, who slipped into the Parti Québécois leadership after Lévesque's sudden resignation—had no time to assess their inheritance and make their mark. Premier Robert Bourassa had no successor but himself. Thus he had a unique chance for a replay, matured and transformed as he was.

The first time I met Bourassa was in November 1970, on the top floor of the Queen Elizabeth Hotel in Montreal. His slightly stooped posture made him look frail beside his hefty bodyguards. We had agreed in advance to talk about economic matters, but he had to excuse himself shortly after our session began: he was expected at another cabinet meeting—the October Crisis was wearing on.

Since then we have met in Quebec City, in the corridors of power, then in Montreal, in the city's business circles, and finally in Ottawa and in the capitals of the other provinces. Everywhere he was the same person: attentive (it's amazing what he can hear), silent (is he shy or afraid of compromising himself?), tolerant (he never bears a grudge), and impassive (he distrusts all passions). He never lets others get close to him. When he opens up at all, he does so in fits and starts—and never completely. Secretive, protective of his private life, he seldom makes a fuss and always avoids expressing his feelings. That is why he does not inspire emotions. One can only formulate "opinions" about him.

Obviously, Robert Bourassa does not have former prime minister Pierre Trudeau's panache, nor René Lévesque's exceptional personality. Nor does he have the self-assurance of a Jacques Parizeau, still less the passionate impulses of a Lucien Bouchard. Nevertheless, it's hard not to admire his obsession with Quebec, his sense of civic duty, his modesty, and the caution that guides his relations with others. At the same time, there's the feeling that he will jinx anyone who gets too close. The October Crisis, his electoral humiliation in 1976, and the Oka confrontation are not easily forgotten. Does bad luck dog his footsteps, or does his chronic indecision inevitably push him towards political pitfalls?

Some say Robert Bourassa is ordinary and lacks ability. Hardly. As a student, he won the most prestigious scholarships open to him. Later, he was the youngest premier in Quebec's history, and he has remained on the political scene for twenty-five years and made French Quebec's official language.

In many ways, the premier's life has mirrored his people's recent history: for the past twenty-five years the trajectory of his political life has paralleled Quebec's repeated attempts to assert its identity without jeopardizing the armistice it made long ago with English Canada.

But this achiever must still overcome one difficulty: he must rid himself of the idea that the province he governs needs others—the rest of Canada in particular—to develop, prosper, and flourish.

Ever since I started observing him, I have been fascinated by the extent to which this man, who is said to be obsessed with his image, has been impervious to criticism and scorn. It is as though he was unaware that by remaining indifferent to slurs he is damaging

Quebeckers' own self-esteem, since they cannot help but share their leader's humiliations.

Today he stands at a critical juncture in Quebec's history. His antennae must be fully extended to sense what his people expect of him. For although Quebeckers clearly hold him in considerable esteem, and even occasionally discreetly express their respect for him, they have never fully let down their guard with him. Indeed, Quebec people who, along with Papineau, kept changing course under the hail of English bullets, are no different from their Bourassa hedging his bets under a shower of Canadian gibes.

After writing about Pierre Trudeau's relationship with Quebec in *The Outsider*, I was drawn to the idea of examining Robert Bourassa and his relations with English Canada. Trudeau and Bourassa represent, to me, the two faces of a coin that has been rolling on its edge for 124 years, without finally falling on one side or the other.

The first time I spoke to Mr. Bourassa about my book idea was at his home in Outremont on April 29, 1990, the twentieth anniversary of his first election as head of Quebec's government. He didn't reproach me for having forgotten the anniversary, but he expressed a few reservations about the project, saying he considered it premature. We did, however, agree on one point: now, twenty-three years after the October 1967 convention of his party, and following the clash between his attempt to maintain federalism in Quebec and his compatriots' desire to establish sovereignty, he had arrived—as had Quebec—at a turning point in his life.

Without knowing exactly what we were up to, we finally started work on the book. Had the Meech Lake Accord been ratified, had Bourassa died from cancer, the story would have stayed unfinished. For there remains a chapter of this book to be written, inspired by Quebeckers themselves.

Once he finally agreed to take the risk of being misunderstood, even betrayed, Mr. Bourassa cooperated generously in the production of this book, responding to my questions and clarifying points for me. Two members of his immediate entourage, Ronald Poupart and Sylvie Godin, kindly gave me access to the premier and left me alone with him.

In writing *The Outsider: The Life of Pierre Elliott Trudeau,* I was struck by the relentless intensity with which Trudeau opposed his provincial counterpart. Taking a closer look, I discovered in Robert Bourassa a pretty hard nut to crack, but also an extremely engaging man. Fragile, to be sure, and desperately calculating, but basically worthy of a great destiny. And therefore of Quebec.

CHAPTER ONE

Just As He Is...

No matter what anyone says or does, Quebec has always been, is now, and will always be a distinct society, free and capable of taking responsibility for its destiny and its development.

Robert Bourassa

Robert Bourassa's first major political decision was made in the basement of his house on Brittany Street in Ville Mont-Royal during the summer of 1967. There, he broke with René Lévesque and isolated his party from the nationalist wave that was rising in Quebec at the time. But nowadays Bourassa is more claustrophobic: before making a decision on a delicate question, he retires alone to the roof of Complex J. There he paces, as though waiting for the stiff wind rising from the St. Lawrence below to bring him, along with the sounds of the city, the latest reading of the pulse of public opinion.

Complex J, the government building in Quebec City that houses the premier's office, is a squat, concrete construction known locally as the Bunker, a legacy of the October Crisis of 1970. Obsessed by the prospect of a terrorist attack, the government's architects designed, at the foot of the Grande Allée, a sprawling blockhouse with heavy grey walls pierced by narrow windows, much like the loopholes of the nearby Citadel, except that the windows in the Bunker are bulletproof, and the walls of the cabinet room are filled with lead.

On the roof of the Bunker, Bourassa has had a little terrace built, furnished with two garden chairs and a small table; only Zeller's knows how much they cost the public purse. From this wooden platform to the helipad overlooking the Plains of Abraham, a narrow walkway winds between the building's ventilation outlets.

Even at his home on Maplewood Avenue in Outremont, which is also of solid concrete construction, Bourassa likes to spend his weekends outdoors on the narrow strip of ground between his house and his neighbour's. In the wall there, as on the roof of the Bunker, a small wooden niche conceals the beige telephone linked directly to his office switchboard.

On the morning of June 22, 1990, after a phone call from Brian Mulroney suggested that time was running out for the Meech Lake Accord, Bourassa, true to his habit, went upstairs to pace across the roof of Complex J. He had promised to deliver a five-minute speech to the National Assembly that evening, and he wanted to take full advantage of the opportunity. "All things considered," he told himself, "I can't accept the rejection of the distinct society without some dramatic gesture. I'm not going to content myself with saying, 'I'm sorry.' "[1]

Suddenly he remembered that it was also on June 22, in 1960, that Jean Lesage's government had been elected for the first time. The day was therefore the thirtieth anniversary of the Quiet Revolution. "It's a good omen," he told himself. Then he reviewed the five conditions—"neither more nor less, without second thoughts about haggling"—that Quebec had placed on its acceptance of a constitutional agreement in April 1987. He had to prevent the opposition leader, Jacques Parizeau, from suggesting that Quebec had offered itself cheaply in the negotiations.

"I need a conclusion that will carry the day," he told himself as he paced the length of his little wooden walkway one more time.

He hadn't expected the Meech adventure to end like this. Barely ten days before, the prime minister had boasted to three journalists from the *Globe and Mail* that he had pulled off a replay of 1867. Referring to the Fathers of Confederation, Brian Mulroney had said, "The boys . . . spent a lot of time in places other than the library." Mulroney went on to describe various hard-drinking, tough-talking constitutional sessions. "This is the way Confederation came about . . . It's become a kind of tradition."[2]

Bourassa knew that Mulroney was neither a scholar nor an expert in government systems, but Mulroney had obviously read the standard history books. His concept of constitutional conferences was like that of Robert Rumilly, Quebec's leading historian of the Duplessis era. According to Rumilly, constitutional conferences interested only a few intellectuals and political groups. They generated no popular trends, and most of the populace knew little about them.[3] This idea appealed to Mulroney, who disliked open debates, preferring to negotiate behind closed doors. The parallel between the conferences of 1864 and those of 1987 was striking.

Indeed, between the initial conference in 1864 and the proclamation of the new Canadian constitution in 1867, everything had nearly come apart. It took two conferences, one month apart, the first at Charlottetown, the second at Quebec, to adopt the first set of resolutions that would make up the British North America Act.

In 1864, the *rouges*, complaining about the secrecy surrounding the Act that gave birth to Canada, had demanded a popular vote. Others suggested that the act be adopted in bits and pieces, article by article. Then John A. Macdonald had laid down the law: it was better, he said, that the document be adopted as a whole, and judged on its necessity rather than its omissions.[4]

Bourassa mentally reviewed the events that followed: the Quebec Conference; the New Brunswick provincial election, where for the first time the Confederation proposal was submitted, albeit indirectly, to the voters; the defeat of the government; the reaction of the Protestant minority in Lower Canada and that of the Catholic minority in Upper Canada (which would be denied what it sought); Macdonald's retreat; the thumping Protestant backlash; their complaints and their threats to pull out . . . [5]

When he was elected, 120 years later, Mulroney dreamed, as had John A. Macdonald, of reconstituting the sacrosanct alliance between Ontario's Anglo-Protestant Conservatives and Quebec's Franco-Catholic bourgeoisie. (As he reviewed the events, Bourassa imagined an odd sort of dialogue spanning 123 years of history: "Any proposal which entails the absorption of Lower Canada's individuality will not be greeted with favour by the people of this region," Macdonald had said in 1865; "We will make it distinct," proposed Mulroney in 1985. "No arrangement other than the federal system is possible," George-Étienne Cartier had maintained; "I have always supported economic federalism for Canada: it is highly advantageous for Quebeckers," echoed Bourassa.[6])

But soon Mulroney's dream turned into a nightmare. For if in 1867 the real Quebec federalists sat in Ottawa and the autonomists in Quebec, the reverse was true in 1987. On the Commons benches, in the offices of federal ministers, and even in the embassies abroad, were sovereignist survivors from the "Yes" camp of the 1980 referendum who had allowed themselves to be swept up in the "great adventure" of the Tory party, an adventure made all the more attractive because it entailed all the trappings of power. Bourassa, along with the veterans of the "No" campaign, found himself in the National Assembly, hemmed in on all sides: by the Parti Québécois, which was waiting to head him off at the pass the next time he made a federalist turn; by the Quebec "*bleus,*" who accused him of cashing in on their humiliation following the 1982 patriation;[7] and by his Liberal cousins in Ottawa, who blamed him for their electoral defeat in 1984.

It seemed as though Mulroney's designated Quebec lieutenant was not Lucien Bouchard, as many said, but Robert Bourassa himself. But English Canadians had never fully trusted Bourassa. They were suspicious of him and of his language policies. And Bourassa, for his part, neither knew English Canada well nor cared what its people thought of him. To Mulroney this indifference might have seemed an asset as well as a handicap. Bourassa, recalling the epidemic of loathing that his Bill 178, which banned English from outdoor commercial signs in Quebec, had provoked among the members of the Alliance for the Preservation of English, had sneered, "So they don't like me, eh?"[8]

On the morning of April 30, 1987, the ones who didn't like Bourassa had come from his own province. When the cortege of limousines set out on the dirt road leading up to Meech Lake in Gatineau Park, a band of about thirty (at most) militant members of the Mouvement Québec Français gathered to demonstrate their resistance to any pact with the English. "You see," said David Peterson, premier of Ontario, shaking Bourassa's hand, "ten years ago there would have been 25,000 people waiting for us here. We can't let an occasion like this go by."[9]

The meeting that day of the prime minister and the premiers was held on the second storey of Willson House, a building perched on a huge rock outcropping that dominates Meech Lake. The atmosphere there was rather more sober than the one in Charlottetown had been in 1864: there was orange juice for some, ginger ale or milk for others. The only remaining vice left to the premiers was tobacco: Peterson's du Mauriers and the cheap cigars smoked by Brian Peckford of Newfoundland and William Vander Zalm of British Columbia. But the eleven hours of debate that followed had the same effect on their state of mind as had the hard drinking that accompanied the birth of Confederation.

Peterson, who at times appeared to be taking the role of George Brown, the publisher of the *Globe* who in 1864 had been Upper Canada's chief spokesman, emerged from the meeting satisfied. Wasn't it extraordinary what they had done? Surely Quebeckers were not going to kick up a fuss over a deal like this.

Twenty-eight days later, the leader of the latter-day "rouges" fired a warning shot across their bows: Mulroney was both a "poltroon" and a lousy negotiator, and the premiers of the English Canadian provinces were "eunuchs." Trudeau had returned to reawaken the age-old anxieties of the ethnic minorities, who felt excluded from this pact among Canada's great white fathers, and the fears of the Maritimers, Confederation's permanent welfare cases who jealously guarded Ottawa's "spending power." (And Ottawa did indeed spend a lot on them.)

Peterson had feared a barrage from the Quebec nationalists. But the opposition to the Meech Lake Accord, whose rationale was worked out in a law office on de Maisonneuve Boulevard in midtown Montreal, came instead from the rest of the country—as it had in 1867. In comfortable exile in his chancellery in the Faubourg Saint-Honoré in Paris, Lucien Bouchard kept his opinions to himself. Only certain members of the Parti Québécois leadership seemed put out by the agreement reached at Meech Lake.

When the first ministers met again on the night of June 2 and into the early morning of June 3, 1987, to finalize the Meech Lake draft, it was not, as expected, Robert Bourassa who imposed conditions, requirements, and demands. Instead, a strange coalition of Ontario Liberals and western New Democrats provided what resistance there was. Even so, at 5:29 a.m., Mulroney emerged from his office with an agreement signed by all the provincial leaders. He was the only one who had taken the time to shave and change his shirt before venturing out to face the cameras.

"Canada is saying yes to Quebec," he said. Canada maybe, but not necessarily Canadians.

Those were the salad days of "national reconciliation," a time of acts of faith, a state of grace. Bourassa had warm memories of that wonderful morning in June 1987.

Bourassa aroused the wrath of anglo-Canadian intellectuals on two occasions during the fall of 1988. The first was his campaign in favour of free trade with the United States. When Bourassa's Parti Québécois adversaries suggested that free trade would make the eventual break with English Canada that much easier, the rest of the country saw Bourassa's support of free trade as serving Quebec's interests. Nonetheless, his popularity at the time was at its zenith, and the province was fully behind him on Meech Lake. Then came Bill 178 and the prohibition of English on outdoor signs. As might have been expected, every last one of English Canada's democrats and defenders of civil liberties joined in a chorus of indignation. (To make things worse, Bourassa's use of the "notwithstanding" clause in the 1982 constitution in passing this legislation made people suspicious of what Quebec might do with its "distinct society" clause.)

In the other provinces, things weren't going much better. After Richard Hatfield's defeat in New Brunswick, it was Manitoba premier Howard Pawley's turn to be turfed out by his electorate. No one apparently ventured to suggest that popular opposition to the Meech Lake Accord had anything to do with these upsets. By then the deal was headed towards an impasse anyway, and the election of

Clyde Wells in Newfoundland put the cat among the pigeons. But from Ottawa there was no reaction.

The good judges of the Supreme Court of Canada made a futile, timid offer of their services, hoping to alleviate English Canada's anxiety over the recognition of Quebec society's distinct character: still no reaction.

Barely two months before the end of the Meech Lake saga, Mulroney attempted a final manoeuvre: a tripartite committee headed by Jean Charest, a Quebec MP and former minister for youth and fitness, would tour the country in the space of a few days to allow the major players—New Brunswick, Manitoba, Newfoundland, the Liberal Party of Canada, the New Democratic Party, and the Assembly of First Nations—to draw up a "shopping list" of requirements that would be delivered the day after the ratification of the Meech Lake Accord.

Bourassa chose not to intervene at the time; he had already repeated too often that the recognition of Quebec's distinct character was of capital importance. He did not want to compromise the ratification of the accord by refusing a few last-minute adjustments. His minister of Canadian intergovernmental affairs, Gil Rémillard, was a bit restive, but since Bourassa's popularity had never been greater, even among the sovereignists, Rémillard realized it was the wrong moment to defy Bourassa's authority overtly. He, too, kept quiet.

The Quebeckers in Ottawa therefore took it upon themselves to organize the resistance. In May 1990, Lucien Bouchard told Paul Tellier, the clerk of the Privy Council, that he would accept no changes to the accord. Tellier wanted Bouchard to try to convince the Quebec parliamentary caucus to accept a proviso that the federal Parliament should promote linguistic duality in Quebec. But Bouchard himself was firmly opposed to any such notion.

Bouchard was even more opposed to Tellier's idea of making a deal with Jean Chrétien. While a candidate to the leadership of his party, Chrétien had made it clear that the Charter of Rights and Freedoms should always prevail over the "distinct society" clause. Tellier argued that Chrétien had a significant role in the federal strategy and that Mulroney was applying a lot of pressure on him to get the accord nailed down. It came as no surprise that Tellier wanted to bring Chrétien in on the initiative; the two had know each other well ever since Tellier had served in the Trudeau government. In addition, Tellier felt it was his responsibility to make sure the accord was ratified, even if he had to make a pact with the devil.

Some Liberals had accused Lucien Bouchard of being a traitor. Chrétien was manoeuvring to water down the Meech Lake Accord to score points with Wells, McKenna, and Manitoba's opposition leader, Sharon Carstairs. All this, combined with the federal bureaucracy's compromises, pushed Bouchard to counterattack. Shortly before he left for Europe, he had promised the organizers of a PQ meeting, scheduled to be held during his absence in Lac St. Jean near the end of May, that he would send them a welcoming telegram. It was from Paris that he finally dispatched the missive to his Quebec compatriots. In it he evoked the memory of René Lévesque and the inalienable right of Quebeckers to determine their own destiny.[10]

Bouchard, who had always dealt directly with Mulroney, had also come to realize that he was being kept from his old university friend by a hostile bureaucracy, something that irked him all the more because Bourassa still enjoyed direct access to the prime minister. For his part, Bourassa, well aware that the rupture between Bouchard and Mulroney was complete, let Mulroney convene the last-ditch conference, to roll the dice one more time, as it were, and to prepare the most splendid scenario for failure in the country's constitutional history.

For a month the country grew impatient, then fearful, then panicky. Mulroney played for time; Bourassa temporized. All that counted now was to make sure Quebec wasn't forced into saying no, and to find a scapegoat as closely associated with Jean Chrétien as possible. Because after June 23, 1990, the Conservatives would have to think about getting ready for the next election.

Meanwhile, Parti Québécois leader Jacques Parizeau was playing with English Canada's nerves. Acting as though the failure of the Meech Lake Accord would lead his party directly to power and Quebec to independence, he began talking about the division of the national inheritance: a quarter of the assets for a quarter of the debt, and a common currency. The English Canadian columnists were beside themselves with incoherent hysteria.

Lucien Bouchard, in turn, almost derailed the federal leader's strategy with his resignation (which Mulroney had foreseen but had hoped to hold off until after June 24). Bouchard immediately found every finger in English Canada pointed at him: he was the one whittling down the slim margin of manoeuvrability remaining to Bourassa; he was the real reason for the failure of the Meech Lake Accord, this separatist who had bitten the very hand that had signed the papers naming him ambassador to Paris.

During this long month of May, Mulroney made every effort to ensure that no Quebecker—not Lucien Bouchard or Jacques Parizeau, still less Bourassa himself—would be held responsible for the failure of the constitutional negotiations. For better or worse he succeeded. He also managed, with the help of a formidable propaganda campaign conceived in the halls of the Canadian Broadcasting Corporation, to maintain the suspense until the evening of June 2, when he decided to "roll the dice." Brian Mulroney convened his colleagues at a private dinner at the National Museum of Civilization.

It turned out to be a long evening. The next morning, Monday, June 3, Ontario's Attorney General Ian Scott advised his colleagues and some of the journalists to beef up their wardrobes. The salesclerks in the stores at Ottawa's Rideau Centre who happily sold fresh underwear, shirts, and socks to these eleven would-be Fathers of Confederation as the week wore on, could later tell their grandchildren they had played a part in history.

Though it was a week of considerable agitation (Bourassa threatened to walk out, Wells was booed by some and cheered by others), it ended without too much drama. On the evening of June 9, at 10:31 p.m., a five-page constitutional agreement was finally signed with great pomp and circumstance. Mulroney would be able to maintain that he had attempted, until the very last minute, to pull off the impossible. As for Bourassa, he had not been forced to say no.

The prime minister was generally thought of as the most coldly calculating political leader Ottawa had seen for a long time, but on that day he surpassed himself. After a week of bargaining, he had succeeded in convincing all the provincial premiers to sign a document that would preserve—if only for another two weeks—the illusion that the Meech Lake Accord could be saved. And he was proud of pulling it off!

He had also set up his constitutional scapegoats in the persons of Gary Filmon of Manitoba and Clyde Wells of Newfoundland. Their "yes-maybe" responses could easily become a "no," making them, not Quebec, the dismantlers of Meech Lake.

Bourassa's thoughts had brought him back to the present, to the morning on June 22. Mulroney's phone call had worried him. He recalled the "balcony scene" General Charles de Gaulle had played on the world's TV screens. Not the one in 1967 at Montreal City Hall, but the one in Algiers in 1958. At the time, Bourassa had been studying in Europe. "No matter what anyone says or does ... has always been, is now, and will always be ... " the General had declared as he promised to keep Algeria French. "I'd found the perfect formula," Bourassa recalled later.[11]

From one end of the country to the other, the TV networks opened half a dozen "windows" on their satellites. In St. John's, Quebec City, Ottawa, Winnipeg, and Calgary, they were poised to transmit live from Toronto or Montreal the unfolding of an implausible chain of events.

Legislators were on standby, ready to ratify any last-minute proposal. The cabinet was closeted with Brian Mulroney on the third floor of Centre Block on Parliament Hill in Ottawa. Even the Supreme Court was on call to deal with any forthcoming federal cabinet recommendations. Never before in the country's history, not even on the eve of a declaration of war, had the entire power structure—legislative, judicial, and executive—remained on alert for a full day.

The last paragraphs of the Meech Lake saga were being written, one after the other across the country's time zones. Within the next twelve hours, English Canada would dare to say no to Quebec. "As though it was up to them to tell us, in a way, 'You are free!'" Bourassa later said.[12]

In St. John's, Newfoundland, Clyde Wells went back on his

promise to leave the final word to his Liberal members and to opposition leader Tom Rideout's Conservatives. "I hope it passes," he had been heard to murmur to the other first ministers in Ottawa on June 9. "He said it, but I think it just kind of slipped out," recalls his colleague from New Brunswick, Frank McKenna.[13]

It was already noon in Newfoundland, as the premier impatiently waited for the Manitoba legislature to begin its daily session. Elijah Harper mounted the steps of the legislature in Winnipeg, borne along on the resentment of his people and the belligerence of the Manitoba capital's multicultural groups. One woman proffered a red rose. "Thank you very Meech," he told her with a smile.[14]

For several hours, Winnipeg and St. John's took turns saying, "You first," as though reluctant to decide who would be the first to say no. But Clyde Wells was bound to lose at this game, since his timeclock was running two and a half hours ahead of Gary Filmon's.

In Calgary, the sun was half a day behind Newfoundland time. There, 5,000 Liberals, gathered for their leadership convention, were recovering from the effects of a long festive evening in honour of outgoing leader John Turner. The convention co-chairs, Serge Joyal and Ethel Blondin, had already warned the leadership candidates that the timetable for the speeches they were to give that night might well be disrupted by the speech Bourassa was scheduled to make in the National Assembly the same evening.

In Ottawa, Brian Mulroney gathered his senior ministers around him in the Privy Council room. The English Canadians looked solemn and a few of the Quebeckers had tears in their eyes.

In Quebec, Bourassa had already decided that no matter what happened elsewhere, he was not going to play along meekly. Early in the morning, Gil Rémillard had warned Lucien Bouchard.[15] Bourassa rose to address the Assembly.

"No matter what anyone says or does, Quebec has always been, is now, and will always be a distinct society, free and capable of taking responsibility for its destiny and development." From a distance of thirty-two years, the General had inspired one of the most incisive phrases ever uttered by a Quebec premier in the National Assembly.

The phrase had the desired effect. The people of Quebec held their collective breath: did this mean that Bourassa, the "doubtful federalist" had become, in spite of himself, a "convinced sovereignist"? A flabbergasted Jacques Parizeau went so far as to congratulate the premier and to offer his cooperation. During the night, a great sense of solidarity began to knit together the Quebec people. Quebeckers were already looking forward to St. Jean Baptiste Day on June 24, to the parades, the songs, the dancing in the streets amid a tide of fleur-de-lys banners.

Rebroadcast across the country, the speech burst on Canada like a bomb. "Free and capable of taking responsibility for its own destiny." The words marched across the front pages of the major newspapers the next day. They echoed across the province over the radio stations. For the first time in a political career that had spanned a quarter of a century, Bourassa was left without an alibi: he was the leader of the government, the head of state of Quebec. The powerful wave of enthusiasm that he had provoked, had carried him, in spite of himself, back towards that crossroads where twenty-three years earlier his itinerary had diverged from René Lévesque's.

As though stricken with vertigo, Bourassa nevertheless—already—tried to postpone his rendezvous with history. At a press conference the following day, he settled back into the tone of a government leader who has trouble making up his mind. In fact, he even gave the impression that he was backing off. Later he explained, "It was necessary to straighten things out a bit." As usual, Bourassa didn't dare follow through on his convictions.

CHAPTER TWO

The Child Prodigy of Parthenais Street

My interest has always been to serve at the Quebec level.
Robert Bourassa

Robert Bourassa was born on Bastille Day, July 14, 1933. The time of his birth could be said to have foreshadowed his destiny. For the young lad who awoke to the world of politics by listening to the speeches of France's leaders on the radio, July 14 was indeed a powerful symbol. As for 1933, it was the year of the Regina Manifesto, the gospel of Canadian socialism according to James Shaver Woodsworth, founder of the Co-operative Commonwealth Federation, the forerunner of the New Democratic Party. All his adult life, Bourassa would remain the same: a militant for French and a social democrat.

In Quebec that year, the unemployment rate rose to 26.4 percent, a peak never equalled since. The government's response was to launch a vast rural settlement campaign to bring people back to the land. The idea was to kill two birds with one stone: to staunch the haemorrhage of the thousands of Quebeckers to the U.S., and to ease the burden that the hordes of unemployed had become in the cities. In Montreal, the soup kitchens served at least a million meals during the Depression. Those who were lucky enough to have jobs often had to content themselves with a salary of three dollars for a seventy-two-hour work week. The Commission des Assurances Sociales du Quebec, headed by Édouard Montpetit, outlined a program that would stand as an inspiration for a whole generation of political leaders, including Bourassa: allowances for needy mothers, old age pensions, unemployment insurance, and health insurance.

Young Robert's family, for better or worse, largely escaped the worst of the Dirty Thirties. His father, Aubert Bourassa, was a documents clerk for the National Harbours Board. Though his salary was modest, it was nevertheless sufficient to shelter his family from the harsh realities of the Depression. "It wasn't luxurious, but it wasn't poor. I'd say that the neighbourhood was lower middle class,"[1] explained the premier, in a rare moment of openness about his private life.

The Bourassa family occupied the ground floor of a grey stone triplex on Parthenais Street at the corner of Saint Joseph Boulevard in Montreal's East End. It was a typical French-Canadian neighbourhood. Young Robert attended the nearby Saint Pierre Claver parish school.

Early on he noticed that when his father went to work every morning, he left the French language at home. The federal administration of maritime transport was conducted in English at all levels of its organization. Like thousands of other French Canadians, Aubert Bourassa had no choice but to submit to the injustice of this situation, without realizing that it engendered a deep sense of insecurity in his son.

The modest habits and lifestyle ("monastic," even, according to a friend) for which Bourassa is famous are products of his childhood. "We mustn't pay too much for the wine," he still says to the few intimates whose restaurant invitations he accepts.[2]

His mother, Adrienne Courville, as well as his two sisters—Marcelle, the eldest, and Suzanne, the baby—spared him the burden of domestic chores. Even after his father's death, when, at age seventeen, he might have been expected to assume the responsibilities of a "head of the family," Robert Bourassa remained buried in his books. "There was nothing to prevent me from studying," he said. "I wasn't needed in the kitchen. I would have been the fourth and last in there."[3]

It may seem surprising that in 1945 Bourassa found himself at the storied Collège Brébeuf, which at the time had a reputation as a rich boys' school. It is often forgotten, however, that the college took in many young Quebeckers of modest means; the list of its most illustrious graduates proves this point. Its fees for day students were, in fact, within the means of the families of junior functionaries.

Bourassa did not mix much with the other children. If he drew attention to himself at all, it was usually for his excellent marks, particularly in mathematics. "He was timid, cheeky, sarcastic, funny. He was exceptionally generous with his colleagues who needed help catching up with their schoolwork,"[4] said Jacques Godbout, one of his closest friends, who got to know him on the hard benches of little Saint Pierre Claver school and later at Brébeuf.

Some years later Pierre Bourgault would also note this quality in Bourassa:

> I was once in a desperate way. I joked to my friends that I was going to call Bourassa. Then, one morning, I couldn't take it any more; I was at the end of my rope. I phoned Bourassa, who was premier at the time, to ask him if he could find me some work. And the next day, Jean Paul l'Allier [then minister of communications] offered me a translation contract. It has to be emphasized that Bourassa is a generous guy, and what he did for me he also did for others. Even as premier, he's always been concerned with individuals and their problems.[5]

What writings have survived from Bourassa's college and university years betray a great preoccupation with money matters, but suggest that the young French-language militant, who was president of the France-Canada association at the University of Montreal, had no particular gift for syntax or style.

In 1956, while he was finishing his law studies, Bourassa campaigned in favour of the creation of a Canadian French-language student federation. For the previous two years, the University of Montreal student association had snubbed the National Federation of Catholic University Students because the Quebeckers could not identify with the national organization: communications were mostly in English, and it was a constant struggle to ensure that francophones occupied the presidency or the vice-presidency as often as anglophones. Denying any allegation of chauvinism—a kind of behaviour he called "long outmoded"—Bourassa nevertheless argued in favour of the formation of an association for French-language students that they could call their own.

> It is only natural that an association whose common denominator would be its language of origin exist, if such a group constitutes a minority: it's simple logic that a minority group feels a greater need to create its own framework in order to work together.[6]

Otherwise, he devoted the rare pieces he published in the university paper, *Le Quartier latin*, to the financial difficulties that plagued many students. "We tend to forget this," he wrote, "probably because students themselves are discreet about their personal problems." For this reason, he urged that students be given an extra week off before Christmas.

> It is not out of caprice, as some would believe, that students have been asking for this early holiday year after year. The few dozen dollars earned working for the post office or elsewhere represent for many the only opportunity to defray school and other expenses, which are subject to constant increases ...
> One might understand the irrevocable refusal on the part of the authorities if the students were demanding free courses or even a pre-salary, as there is in Europe, which is nevertheless poorer than our "prosperous" province.[7]

A few weeks later, the tone grew more demanding. Christmas was fast approaching, and the end of classes had still not been announced. For once, Bourassa allowed himself to indulge in polemics.

> There has been a lot of talk these days about the needs of universities, and much less about the needs of the students themselves. Yet it can be said without exaggeration that it profits the national interest to have its elite educated under the best possible conditions so as to eliminate mediocrity. Why this paradox? Some, who have their eyes wide open, would reply that it exists because the electoral value of students is nil, or at least less than that of road-building contractors![8]

The debate surrounding this question awoke in Robert Bourassa the social democrat with a strong sense of egalitarianism.

> It is hard to imagine that university administrators have a great deal to gain from the kind of social equity whereby everyone would have equal access to the university, and money would cease to be an obstacle for those who have the talent and desire to acquire a professional skill.[9]

Thus the handful of articles he wrote during his university days emphasized the need for members of the francophone minority to show solidarity and the theme of economic security. "I'm a convinced social democrat," Bourassa volunteered during one interview. "For me, egalitarianism in society is a fundamental and irreplaceable objective."[10]

With his excellent grades, Robert Bourassa qualified for scholarships and bursaries that allowed him to finance his studies in law at the University of Montreal, in economics at Oxford, and in tax law at Harvard. Supplementary income came from a variety of summer jobs. One year he collected tolls on the Jacques Cartier Bridge, which links the Island of Montreal to the South Shore. Another time he worked in a bank.

Among the awards Bourassa won were the Mackenzie King Scholarship (conferred by the Royal Society), the Governor General's Medal, and a Ford Foundation bursary. Bourassa's head-of-the-class academic performance also caught the attention of Jean-Louis Gagnon, editor of *La Réforme*, the Quebec Liberal party's house organ:

> He gave the impression of being self-effacing and timid. He seemed to me to be discreet, studious, and respectful of his elders. Since he didn't talk much and seemed to enjoy listening to us air our views, I took it for granted that he was a true Liberal.[11]

Four years later, when Bourassa visited him after he had moved on to *La Presse*, the same Jean-Louis Gagnon, a close friend of

Pierre Trudeau and future vice-chairman of the Commission on Bilingualism and Biculturalism, saw in him the ideal candidate for a career in the federal government: "I got the impression that budgetary equilibrium interested him more than the ideological issues that were troubling the public order."[12]

It was at the University of Montreal that Bourassa met Andrée Simard, who was enrolled in the family studies program. She was the assistant secretary of AGEUM, the University of Montreal student union, and the muse of the class of '56. "O sweet Judith, o chaste Abigail, bring to AGEUM the honey of your presence and the balm of your word. Happy is the executive that has known the days when its ranks were blessed to receive a woman who is everything a man could want, the kind of woman that the family studies school knows how to turn out," her classmates rhapsodized in *Le Quartier latin*.[13]

The young woman came from a family of rich industrialists—the Sorel Simards—whose shipyards had prospered handsomely from the Second World War. Already well off at the outbreak of the war, the three Simard brothers went on to amass a colossal fortune building ships, artillery, and tanks for the Canadian armed forces.

Had Bourassa never become premier, no one would have thought to dig out the clippings from the society columns of August 23, 1958, or the yellowed photographs of the sumptuous wedding reception on the immense lawn of the Simard family estate on the St. Lawrence riverbank at Sorel. Afterwards, some people saw the marriage as a coldly calculated move by an ambitious young lawyer. They assumed that Bourassa, hungry for power, had deliberately set out to marry a rich heiress to finance his political career. In reality, however, the union caused Bourassa's career more problems than it solved.

After his marriage, he continued to seek bursaries to finance his studies in London, England; the young couple's apartment on Victoria Road, heated by gas jets and a coal fire, was notably lacking in creature comforts. By the time Bourassa entered politics for good, the Simard empire was being dismantled; the family fortune consisted mainly of some sumptuous properties and a few sound investments. The Simards of Sorel had become paper entrepreneurs, and though this situation left little scope for nepotism,

Bourassa nevertheless wound up being accused of conflict of interest in relation to his in-laws.

On the other hand, the marriage did give Bourassa the opportunity to mix with the French-Canadian captains of industry. Through them he discovered that not only lowly functionaries like his father had to work in English; even Édouard Simard, for all his wealth and power, had to use the language of "les autres" to negotiate contracts with the Department of National Defence or even to write memos to his own employees.

In 1963—and Bourassa would have a front-row seat for the event—the Quebec government, through its General Investment Corporation, took over the Simard empire, which had been shaken by an ill-prepared succession and the difficult transition to postwar production. Marine Industries Ltd. would become more than a Crown corporation, it would become a truly francophone enterprise, and an incubator for a new generation of Quebec entrepreneurs. Though he never admitted it, the boy from St. Pierre Claver (which is something he has basically remained all his life—he even longed to be the member of the National Assembly for the district) no doubt recognized a victory of intelligence over fortune in what became of his in-laws' empire.

To this day the premier is protective of his family life. "It's true that people are interested in the way we live, but I see political life differently."[14] He avoids society gatherings with such zeal that some of his advisers have accused him of being antisocial. The Bourassas rarely entertain at home, and when they do, the event is hardly relaxed. "Only six of us, and we are all squeezed up in the dining room of his house on Maplewood Avenue," said one of the privileged few who have been invited to dinner at the premier's.[15]

Though the house is handsomely situated on the flank of Mount Royal in the fashionable part of Upper-Outremont, the premier continues to lead the discreet life of a modest French Canadian. One sunny springtime afternoon, while "le tout Outremont" was traipsing off to garden parties or up to Laurentian chalets, he was in his backyard, reading through a pile of cabinet documents, oblivious to the growl of the traffic going up Côte-Ste.-Catherine. "I'm not very big on social events," he explained. (That weekend he had passed up a sparkling reception thrown by Paul Desmarais, the president of Power Corp., at his chateau at La Malbaie, attended by just about everyone who was anyone in Canadian politics.) "There isn't anybody who can boast of having had him over for a weekend," confirmed one of Bourassa's friends with a certain note of regret in his voice.[16]

One might think that Bourassa would have developed a taste for high-rent neighbourhoods during his passage from Parthenais Street to Maplewood Avenue (one block from Pierre Trudeau's boyhood home), by way of Brittany Street in upper-middle-class Ville Mont-Royal. But even though he is financially well off, he has never been one to flaunt his wealth.

He lives like a recluse, and insists he finds it boring to talk about himself. It is for the solitude as much as the exercise that he keeps up his daily regimen of twenty or so lengths in the swimming pool. "Let's say tennis was my sport," he says to explain why he prefers swimming to other sports. "It's not so easy to find tennis partners. And I don't want to make anyone feel obliged to play tennis just because the premier wants to play."[17]

As head of the government, with all manner of demands on his time, he needs his family as an insurance policy against the futility of public affairs and the ingratitude of politics. "I work with my family's presence, its warmth, and its support," he says. "I spend a lot of time at home; I do my telephoning there, I have my associates over. My children are there, my wife is there; to be sure they've had to adapt to my life, but in the end we always wind up together."[18]

It was a sign of Bourassa's destiny that the first article he wrote for *Le Quartier latin* in 1953 recounted an exclusive interview he and his pal Jacques Godbout had wangled with none other than Quebec Premier Maurice Duplessis. The article, which appeared in the November 19 edition, was entitled: "An Interview with Uncle Maurice." The two students were obviously impressed by Duplessis, and somewhat intimidated by the presence of photographers and reporters from the big dailies.

No, he didn't read *Le Quartier latin*, Duplessis informed the two of them. The solution to the problem of university financing? "We'll have to make do with the solutions we have at hand," he

said. Bourassa asked him if it was really necessary to add a fourth
year to the course leading to a law degree, as had been done a few
years before. "You're certainly just as intelligent as people were in
my day," responded Uncle Maurice, "and in my day there were
only three years."

"Did students work in your day, Mr. Duplessis?" he was asked.

"Sure we worked . . . I earned four bucks a week, and I paid two
for my room; and later I made sixty bucks a month, but seeing as I
smoked cigars, I never had any left over. I don't have to tell you that
I'd go to the theatre on foot and that when I got there you would
have found me in the pit."

"So you think the authorities should give students a chance to
work?" Bourassa pressed on.

"Yes, they need to earn money."

Bourassa and Godbout may not have won a Pulitzer Prize for
their article, but the meeting with Le Chef had an impact.
Bourassa, only twenty years old at the time, was already entertain-
ing his first political ambitions.

According to Godbout, those ambitions were not new. All premiers have their own legend. Someone will always emerge to testify
that at a precocious age the future leader predicted his destiny.
Bourassa is no exception. He was all of twelve years old, according
to Godbout, when he stopped on the corner of De Lorimier Street
and St. Joseph Boulevard one day and said, "Someday I will be
premier!" Once Bourassa was head of the Quebec government, he
confirmed the anecdote, but he also denied its accuracy. "It would
surprise me if I'd said, 'I will be,' but I certainly said, 'I'd like to
be.'"[19]

Bourassa's political aims diverted him from what would certainly
have been a successful career in high finance, and most likely
deprived the federal bureaucracy of a brilliant francophone manager, which it greatly needed at the time. With a bachelor's degree
in his pocket at the age of twenty, admission to the bar at twenty-
four, a master's degree from Oxford and another from Harvard at
twenty-seven, Bourassa had an academic record that was more
precocious and more complete than that of Pierre Trudeau, who
came away from a six-year tour of Harvard, the Sorbonne, and the
London School of Economics without a diploma of any sort.

Newly married and loaded down with diplomas, Bourassa got his first job as a financial adviser with the federal revenue department in 1960. At the same time he taught economics at the University of Ottawa. But he was never really at ease, and never would be, in an English-Canadian milieu.

> My interest has always been to serve at the Quebec level, to work to strengthen Quebec, especially in the economic sector, because it is an essential prerequisite to the question of identity.[20]

He therefore offered his services to Marcel Bélanger, who was at the time the leading fiscal wizard in Quebec, and the head of a commission assigned to study Quebec's fiscal structure. Bourassa was appointed the commission's secretary, and he took advantage of the opportunity to get close to Jean Lesage, with whom he worked on provincial budgets. When he became a member of the Liberal party, his patron promised to find him a safe riding. Lesage obviously recognized the young Bourassa's raw political talent. In 1966, the first time Bourassa ran in an election, Lesage assigned him to represent the party in a televised debate on the English CBC network against André d'Allemagne of the separatist Rassemblement pour l'Indépendance Nationale, and Michel Chartrand of the Parti Socialiste.[21]

No one expected the election to turn into a disaster for the Liberal government. Bourassa, who was just short of his thirty-third birthday, was primarily concerned with learning the political ropes, expecting someday to be revenue minister, or finance minister, a position that would allow him to apply the directives of the Bélanger Commission's report, which he had just finished writing. Above all, he hoped to work with the man he most admired in Lesage's special team of young, bright politicians and bureaucrats, the group known as the ''équipe de tonnerre''—René Lévesque himself.

Bourassa got his seat in the National Assembly but the Liberals lost their majority. The young member for Mercier would have to settle for the job of finance critic on the opposition benches. But, as the party hierarchy would decide, he would soon reach the top job.

CHAPTER THREE

The Missed Opportunity

I must say that between Daniel Johnson, René Lévesque, and Pierre Trudeau, there wasn't much room left for me.

Robert Bourassa

Before he became a member of the National Assembly at the age of thirty-three, Bourassa had spent more time in European institutions than in Canadian ones. His idea of a federation, a concept to which he was first introduced while studying in London in 1958, is that of a voluntary association of sovereign and equal states, a notion that was difficult to apply back home at the time. But then, as now, Bourassa knew little about English Canada. In fact, all he really knew of the other provinces was the federal capital, where he had worked for three years, and which is about as representative of the rest of the country as St. Pierre and Miquelon are of France.

It was therefore with some naiveté as well as a touching candour that the young member for the Montreal riding of Mercier told his colleagues, "One doesn't have to be a prophet to foresee that among the options available to it, Quebec will choose a special status, in keeping with its own characteristic traits, within a renewed Canadian federation."[1] At the time René Lévesque warned him that in committing himself to such a course, he was engaging in "the old defensive battle, the skirmishes in which we wear ourselves down while losing sight of the main goal; the half-victories of by-elections between two defeats; the false consolations of verbal nationalism, and above all, above all—it has to be said, said again, and shouted if necessary—this incredible waste of energy, which is surely for us the most disastrous aspect of the system.''[2]

The year 1967 nevertheless began well for Bourassa, Lévesque, Trudeau, and others. On the first of April, Bourassa joined a small circle of Liberals who were trying to draft a nationalist manifesto for the party. A sojourn on the opposition benches is usually a propitious time for reflection, and the Liberals had been making the most of the opportunity since the party had lost its majority in the election the previous year.

But time was short, and Liberal reformers were spurred on even more by the fact that Daniel Johnson, who was now premier, had already laid out his basic ideas in his manifesto, *Égalité ou indépendance* (Equality or Independence). These ideas had been formulated in 1964 after an interprovincial conference in Jasper, at which the federal Liberal government had had the audacity to revoke Quebec's right to self-determination. Premier Lesage had, in effect, accepted an amending formula—the Fulton-Favreau formula, named after the two justice ministers who conceived it— which subjected all transfers of new powers to Quebec to the approval of the nine other provinces. An irate Daniel Johnson, then leader of the Union Nationale party, railed:

> Can you see the leader of the State of Quebec undertaking a pilgrimage to each provincial capital to humbly beseech each of the other premiers to have a law passed in his legislature that would allow us, for example, to regulate French-language radio and television?

Johnson went on for eight more paragraphs to ridicule the Quebec Liberal party's flabby platform. ''In the end,'' he thundered, ''are we really masters in our own house when Ottawa alone regulates everything that concerns radio and television, media that in our age are perhaps the most effective instruments of culture? Are we masters at home, if we have absolutely no idea when Lesage will finally get back provincial powers over things like tariff policy, immigration, monetary policy, corporate taxation, succession duties, natural resources development? Are we masters at home, finally, when the Supreme Court, whose judges are all named by Ottawa, is the ultimate interpreter of francophone law, and the only tribunal to which grievances against the federal government can be submitted?"

To René Lévesque, who had coined the "Maîtres chez nous" (Masters in our own house) slogan, and who was becoming more and more uncomfortable within the Liberal party, these were embarrassing home truths. One can only imagine what went through his mind on March 19, 1965, when Daniel Johnson wrapped up his speech to 2,000 delegates at a Union Nationale convention by saying: "Canada or Quebec, wherever the French-Canadian nation finds freedom, there will be its homeland."[3]

A year later, Daniel Johnson was premier of Quebec. The Liberals, whose caucus now included the new member for Mercier, Robert Bourassa, could finally do some catching up and bring their platform up to date. Unfortunately, the reformers within the party found themselves distracted by the backroom intrigues aimed at displacing Jean Lesage.[4]

Ideas and ambitions are to the members of a political party as the two poles of a magnet are to a handful of pins: one attracts, the other repels. The small group of reformers who gathered at Mont-Tremblant on April 1, 1967, represented all three of the main currents of thought within the Liberal party. There were the orthodox federalists, like party president Eric Kierans and Jean-Paul Lefebvre, a Trudeau disciple, who were there to keep an eye on things. There were those who were quickly labelled the "independentists" (all the better to provoke them so they could then be thrown out), who on Saturday, October 14, would follow René Lévesque to the basement of the Victoria Hotel in Quebec City for the first official meeting of the Sovereignty-Association Movement. Finally, there were those who claimed to be "half pregnant" (as Jean Chrétien would say)— the members of the party's constitutional affairs committee, headed by former Lesage minister Paul Gérin-Lajoie, as well as all the partisans of some form of "special status."

The three groups had at least one thing in common: they were all anxious to make up for lost time and to rejuvenate the Liberal party platform. The exercise was rendered all the more auspicious by the fact that René Lévesque was the one wielding the pen.

When the president of France came to visit Quebec on June 24, 1967, Robert Bourassa was there, alongside René Lévesque, as part of the Montreal VIP delegation. The chairman of his party's policy committee, Jean Lesage's anointed successor, a young intellectual respected by all the Liberal factions of the day, Bourassa was holding nothing but high cards at the time. Canada was celebrating its centennial that year. The prime minister, Lester B. Pearson, had recently asked his new justice minister, Pierre Elliott Trudeau, to prepare a plan for the revision of the 1867 constitution. But with the enthusiastic reception that they lavished upon the French head of state, Quebeckers were revisiting an even more distant past. Already the clocks in Quebec and the rest of Canada weren't keeping the same time.

The General's fateful cry, "*Vive le Québec libre!*"—delivered from the City Hall balcony in Montreal—was that of an old patriot. De Gaulle felt borne along by "an immense wave of faith and French hope."

> From Quebec to Montreal, for the length of the 250 kilometres of road that followed the St. Lawrence ... millions of men, women and children were assembled ... and these millions of people held aloft hundreds of thousands of French tricolors and Quebec fleur-de-lys banners to the near total exclusion of all other emblems.[5]

The reunion was so enthusiastic that people even forgot to hoist the new Canadian maple leaf flag, which had been adopted only two years earlier, after a memorably venomous national debate. The general was not surprised by this omission; for him the Canadian federation was nothing more than an accident of history, a territory clumsily cobbled together after the wars of colonization and the peace treaties that followed them. Which centennial was being celebrated here anyway? He behaved as though he didn't know the reason for the festivities, or even his visit, preferring instead to step back into Quebec's past to 1763 and the Treaty of Paris between France and England, "after the inconsolable sovereignty of France had been torn from this land."

Above and beyond any Gaullian emphasis, the reference to the Treaty of Paris allowed the French president to note that the

"French of Canada are unanimously convinced that after the century of oppression that followed the British conquest, a second century spent under the system defined by the British North America Act of 1867 has not ensured them of liberty, equality, and fraternity in their own country."[6]

One hundred years of oppression. One hundred years of disappointment. Surely the general was piling it on a bit thick, especially, as René Lévesque noted, when he went on to compare his triumphant journey in Quebec to the liberation of Paris, which he led in 1944.

De Gaulle's visit resulted in a further deterioration in the relations between Ottawa and Quebec, and between Lester Pearson and Daniel Johnson. To Johnson's "Equality or Independence" ultimatum, the federal government replied that equality would be affirmed in Ottawa, and that independence was, in the words of Pierre Trudeau, "utter stupidity." Within the Quebec Liberal party, de Gaulle's visit also had its effect: Jean Lesage was increasingly incapable of containing the nationalist, even independentist elements within his own ranks.

In the eyes of visitors to Expo '67 in Montreal, Quebec was rediscovering itself. Timidly. People spoke only (even then) of a "distinct society." After a century of placid submission, it was time, declared Johnson, to examine the "problem of Quebec's distinct identity, and its immense efforts toward self-affirmation."[7] At the interprovincial "Confederation of Tomorrow" conference on November 27, 1967, Quebec insisted on the adoption of a new constitution that would "recognize the existence in Canada of two nations, linked by history and enjoying equal collective rights." Within this Canada, which would "enjoy absolute sovereignty," Quebec would have its own "internal constitution." "This is not to say," added Johnson, "that we would for any reason be opposed to any other provinces that claimed exactly the same powers as Quebec."[8] (This expression of goodwill strongly resembled the attitude that Robert Bourassa would bring to the negotiating table at Meech Lake twenty-three years later. It makes one wonder: will Quebec forever be doubtful of its negotiating strength? Will it always, until the end of time, feel obliged to share its political gains?)

A single sovereign country. Two constitutions. "And what else?"

asked Pierre Trudeau. Quebeckers, along with the rest of the country, would shortly provide him with a chance to lay down the law. De Gaulle, who never left anything to chance, chose November 27 of that year, the very day the Confederation of Tomorrow conference opened in Toronto, to explain himself once and for all at a press conference in Paris. Though in the end his statement had few repercussions in Quebec, the General was nevertheless unrepentant, four months after the "balcony incident."

"As things stand now, the resolution of this question will require a complete change in the Canadian structure, as it resulted from the act approved by the Queen of England one hundred years ago that created this federation. I believe it must result in the accession of Quebec to the rank of a sovereign state, master of its national existence, as has been the case with so many other peoples, so many other states which are not even as well founded or as well populated as this one."[9]

De Gaulle knew whereof he spoke. For the past ten years he had been presiding—though admittedly he was somewhat behind England in his initiative—in the dismantling of the French colonial empire. Everywhere in Africa, frontiers that crossed rivers or skirted mountains were being redrawn to reunite peoples, to respect religious traditions, and to cement cultures. If he had received any encouragement, the president would probably have been willing to sit down with Elizabeth II—as Louis XV had with George III—and write a new Treaty of Paris.

English Canada was insulted: the General's logic reduced Canada to the level of a colony, and Pearson to the status of governor of a British Crown possession. The reaction was heated in some quarters (these were "unacceptable statements"), petty in others ("Canadians don't need to be liberated . . . thousands of Canadians gave their lives for the liberation of France"), high-handed in others ("Some of the president's statements tend to encourage the small minority of our population whose goal is the destruction of Canada").[10]

Bourassa was uncomfortable with de Gaulle's incendiary declarations and with the wave of enthusiasm they provoked. Flights of oratory embarrassed him, and strong crowd reactions frightened him. He was further disillusioned by de Gaulle's stance in Europe.

France wasn't playing the federalist game, as Bourassa had hoped it would. "If only France had been willing," he sighed. "De Gaulle was offered a federal Europe in which France would have played a leading role."[11]

After having taken a head count of the handful of hard-core Liberals prepared to follow de Gaulle on the sovereignist road, Lévesque soon discovered that "Robert Bourassa's basement seemed large enough to accommodate those who remained."[12] For this is where those young Liberal reformers were going to meet in the months following de Gaulle's visit.

While Bourassa's wife cooked spaghetti for the group, they kept arguing the pace and the scope of the negotiations that Quebec should entertain with the rest of Canada. Too bad these young Turks had not read some pages of André Laurendeau's *Journal*, written three years earlier, and still kept secret in the files of the Royal Commission on Bilingualism and Biculturalism. Laurendeau wrote in 1964:

> The nationalists of yesteryear, like Henri Bourassa, constantly appealed to a sense of justice, whereas today's nationalists seek to establish a better balance of forces. It seems to me that history endorses the validity of the second attitude . . . because the English have a habit of dominating, something I had never before realized.[13]

Laurendeau had spent three years visiting every corner of Canada with the B&B Commission: like de Gaulle, he knew *les Anglais* and was aware that they would never give up anything that was not taken from them by force or threat. "A separatist living our current experience would come away more than ever convinced. A young nationalist would certainly be tempted by separatism," concluded Laurendeau.[14]

At the end of the summer of 1967, when the tempest stirred up by the de Gaulle visit had somewhat abated, Robert Bourassa went back to visiting one Liberal reform group after another, like the smartest kid in class whose company everyone seeks out on the eve of tough exam: the orthodox federalists had plans for him, the special-status crowd knew they would go nowhere without him, and the sovereignists thought he was tempted to throw in his lot with them.

In reality, the young member was instinctively drawn more to René Lévesque than to the others. Years later, he would recall with a note of regret in his voice the days when he used to host the sovereignists in his basement on Brittany Street, and the personal esteem in which he held his colleague.

> When you're young, and working for political personalities, you always have the impression that you're working to advance their careers. In Lévesque's case, it wasn't like that at all: I found that working for him, or with him, meant working for ideas, and not for ambitions. That's a rare thing to find in political life. With Lévesque you had the impression that you were working to advance his ideas, which were for the greater progress of Quebec.[15]

Nevertheless, when confronted with a choice between ideas and ambitions, Bourassa—out of some atavistic sense of caution—would choose the latter. "The caution I have today," he confided in July 1990, while the Mohawk crisis was going into its third week, "is the caution I had back then [in 1967]. There were uncalculated risks in [René Lévesque's] constitutional proposals that I wasn't ready to embrace. Particularly on the economic level."[16]

There was the same distance between Lévesque and Bourassa on one hand, as there was between de Gaulle and Johnson on the other: they were separated by "an immense wave of faith and French hope." Had Johnson and Bourassa let themselves be carried along by the wave, instead of breaking it, a great tide would have swept all that was "Canadian" from both banks of the St. Lawrence from Blanc Sablon to St. Regis, but at the time they still weighed the blessings of self-identity against the benefits of a common federal regime.

At the opening of the constitutional conference in Toronto in November 1967, Daniel Johnson declared:

> First, there are all the problems that have nothing directly to do with language and culture. In other words, those in which Quebec's interests coincide with those of the other provinces.

Federalism remains a valid formula for resolving such problems.

At about the same time, Bourassa told the members of the St. Laurent Kiwanis Club:

The economic aspect of a completely independent Quebec always leads to a stumbling block, no matter how you look at it, when it comes to the problem of suddenly instituting a Quebec currency.[17]

Neither appeared able to imagine for a moment, even as a hypothesis, a Quebec outside the Canadian space, as though Canada's future and Quebec's were inextricably linked. De Gaulle and Lévesque, on the other hand, were fired by the miracle of French Canada's survival, and had no fear of the unknown. What a waste to have come this far and not want to go farther, they seemed to be saying in unison. De Gaulle urged them on:

Your resolve to survive as an unshakable and compact community, after having so long cloaked your character under a passive sort of resistance, opposed to everything that risked compromising your cohesion, has taken on an active vigour, becoming the ambition to seize upon all means of emancipation and development that the modern era offers to a strong and enterprising people.[18]

And Lévesque echoed:

Among ourselves, it is essentially a matter of maintaining and developing a personality that has endured for three and a half centuries. At the heart of this personality is the fact that we speak French. Everything else is connected to this essential element. Everything flows from it and everything inevitably carries us back to it.[19]

It is unclear whether Lévesque and Bourassa could ever have been reconciled. The misunderstandings between them were largely a matter of vocabulary. They did not use the same language: when one spoke to the voters of ''a sovereign Quebec within a Canadian economic union,'' the other would attack with "independence-association." The eventual "divorce" between the two can be attributed to the in-laws, the father-in-law in particular, Eric Kierans, an anglo-Quebecker whose apocalyptic warnings carried all the more weight in that he had once been chairman of the Montreal Stock Exchange. He breathed down Bourassa's neck, preventing him from associating too closely with the sovereignists.

René Lévesque took for granted (and promised as much to his followers) that English Canada would accept his offer in the end: a monetary union, a common market, and coordinated fiscal policies. Time "should bring us together at the same table without too much delay in the end," he said in 1967.[20] Robert Bourassa doubted, as did Lévesque deep down, that Quebec would really have to establish its own currency. However, undoubtedly as a result of Kierans's blackmail, he feared that Quebec would be forced to do so, in spite of itself. The prospect of a brutal separation terrified Bourassa, and still does. In 1990, at the time of the historic vote on German reunification, he said:

> The German example shows I was right after all. The two Germanys separated when their money became different after the Americans arrived in 1948 with suitcases full of deutschmarks to replace the reichsmark, and they validated these deutschmarks in West Germany only. A few years later, the Berlin Wall went up. And when did the two Germanys reunite? When they started using the same money again![21]

In recalling the series of events that almost tore the Quebec Liberal party apart and led to the founding of the Sovereignty-Association Movement (Lévesque's short-lived precursor to the Parti Québécois), Bourassa once again brought his version of the facts up to date:

> The German situation shows I was right about the importance of the currency question. Lévesque was always asking me, "What does currency have to do with the destiny of a people? Will you quit bothering me with that?" But I told him it's fundamental. Regimes have fallen because of currency, and I can give you a lot of examples. I think that Lévesque took a lot of uncalculated risks in that area.[22]

Lévesque undoubtedly did go too far at the time, particularly since he would not articulate his point, still groping around for a name for his vision: "independence-association," "sovereignty-association." (One day political science treatises will be written about the critical importance of the hyphen.)

As chairman of his party's policy committee, Bourassa next faced the question of what to do with the report of the constitutional affairs committee,[23] which he received in October 1967. The report went as far as Daniel Johnson's manifesto, but did not impose a final ultimatum on English Canada. In terms that presaged the Allaire Report of 1991, the committee, which had been chaired by Paul Gérin-Lajoie, categorically rejected the status quo:

> Concentrated on a given territory, distinct from all other communities in North America, endowed for the first time with a proper government, [Quebeckers] have maintained what they have succeeded in preserving under all the political regimes they knew before 1867, that is to say a distinct identity and their particular aspirations . . . They have progressively developed an inexpugnable aspiration to be masters of their own destiny . . . Witnesses of a worldwide movement towards the emancipation of peoples . . . they are now convinced that their existence and their development are tied to a Quebec state, endowed with the powers essential to this end . . . If Quebec wishes to remain a distinct society, it can no longer accept the 1867 constitutional framework.

The committee's verdict was not subject to appeal: it rejected out of hand any patchwork solution, or any individual amendments to particular clauses. "Current imperatives require new documents, documents conceived here at home, written at home, and with the sanction of a sovereign people."

Aware of the need, no doubt, to get a leg up on the Union Nationale, the Liberal party drew up a list of "new powers necessary for the State of Quebec." (The list that Bourassa eventually presented at Meech Lake looks like a mere afterthought by comparison.) These were the "minimum powers that could not be left with an outside authority without endangering [Quebec's] collective personality," added Gérin-Lajoie.

The party proposed to get back all powers that, through educational institutions and the arts, touched directly on language and individual culture, as well as those dealing with the diffusion of mass culture (cinema, radio, and television). It also sought jurisdiction over immigration, social assistance and security, employment (including adult education and professional training), marriage and divorce, insurance companies, and commercial and financial institutions. Further demands added to this already substantial list included recognition of the new state as an international entity, capable of negotiating its own international agreements, and direct participation in the elaboration of monetary and tariff policies. Whew!

Would there still be a Canada? "This new federalism provides that one of its member states would have a distinct and different system from the others." This proposal went further than the one Daniel Johnson had made at the Toronto conference. Without overly insisting, the Quebec Liberals even ventured to suggest how federal institutions might be reformed, in particular the Supreme Court and the Senate, and timidly proposed replacing the monarchy with a "Federal Canadian Republic."

Unfortunately for the party reformers, whose ranks still included Robert Bourassa, the Liberal convention of October 14, 1967, turned into a settling of accounts. "We didn't come here to talk about René Lévesque's ideas, we're after his head!" declared a group of delegates from Abitibi.[24] And that is exactly what they got.

Lévesque had come with a manifesto of his own, the one written in Bourassa's basement but for which he had not been able to gather any support. The group had not met since September and all but a handful of Lévesque's supporters had decided to settle for the Gérin-Lajoie Report. Even before the convention rejected his "independentist" proposal by a vote of 1,500 to 4, René Lévesque had gone to the Hotel Victoria where he stayed with some sixty supporters, "his share of memories, and the regret that it had to end like this." After his departure, the Liberal party decided, for form's sake, to "reject separatism in all its guises." *Le Devoir*'s correspondent, Paul Cliche, described the end of the convention as follows:

To mark the new climate that reigned in the Liberal party, one conventioneer rose at the end of the meeting to ask that the Canadian flags, which had been kept out of sight up to then, be brought out to grace the hall along with the Quebec flags. His wish was granted, and yesterday [Sunday] morning, the maple leaf flew alongside the fleur-de-lys. The same delegate asked that the meeting be closed with the singing of the national anthem. Mr. Kierans joined in with pride. And it was with the final bars of "O Canada" that the Liberal party embarked on its new destiny.[25]

The anglo-Quebeckers, who had succeeded in pushing the Liberal party back into the federal corral, were ostentatious in their triumph. A clear message had been sent to anyone with ambitions of taking over the party leadership: don't frighten English Canada! But all was not lost. The Gérin-Lajoie report was nevertheless sent on to the policy committee, whose chairman was Robert Bourassa. As he says:

René Lévesque's departure completely changed the dynamic inside the party. It produced a polarization. As financial critic, I thought that the only issue that could maintain party unity was the economy.[26]

One wonders if Bourassa agreed at the time with the thrust of a report that insisted that Quebec be granted the essential attributes of a distinct society. A few weeks after the Meech Lake failure, he replied without hesitation:

Yes, I did. But I'm not sure that the federal Liberal party, which still played a big role in Quebec politics, was ready for it. You can't forget how popular Trudeau was ... So there wasn't a lot of room to manoeuvre with a program like that. I also remember that Gérin-Lajoie left a few months after René Lévesque.[27]

In fact, Gérin-Lajoie was "conscripted" by Trudeau for the federal Wages and Prices Commission. Not a bad way to bring him around.

"I must say that between Johnson, Lévesque, and Trudeau,

there wasn't much room left for me ... The only way we, the provincial Liberals, could stand out from the crowd was to talk about the economy," says Bourassa. In the end, the Gérin-Lajoie Report wound up on the top shelf in the Opposition finance critic's office at the National Assembly.

The economy was also the means Bourassa chose to set himself apart from Pierre Laporte and Claude Wagner, his future rivals in the upcoming race for the party leadership. "Once you become a leadership candidate, you have to be realistic," he explained with a discreet smile tugging at his lips.[28]

In Quebec, the stakes were becoming clearer. Trudeau, Johnson, and Lévesque had engaged in a constitutional guerrilla war. The Liberals needed a new theme.

> During the years 1968 and 1969, three-quarters of my speeches dealt with the economy. I'm not saying there wasn't an element of strategy in that: in amongst "equality or independence," "sovereignty-association," and "a bilingual Canada," the Liberal party's standing room on national issues was pretty narrow. How were we going to distinguish ourselves from Johnson, who was a conditional federalist, or from Trudeau or Lévesque? I told myself: we renounce nothing, we maintain our objectives, but we take the current circumstances into account.[29]

Bourassa had set himself and his party off on a great tangent that would continue until June 22, 1990. Henceforth, he would sing the praises of "profitable federalism."

In the spring of 1969, Jean Lesage received a voluminous study of the mood of the provincial electorate from the Chicago polling firm Social Research Inc. This document made him the only one, apart from his chief organizer, Paul Desrochers, to have in hand the information necessary to choose his successor. The composite portrait of the ideal new party leader, as sketched by the Chicago firm, closely resembled Robert Bourassa. The people of Quebec, it seemed, were yearning for a younger leader who would be a bridge between the generations but who had the clout necessary to deal with Ottawa and the heads of high finance on an equal footing. At the same time he had to be tuned in to the problems of the post-1960s world.

Bourassa corresponded so closely to the party's current needs that Paul Desrochers put himself at his service even before the convention date was announced. His first move was to draw up a list of the party's 77,000 members. By September 1969, the "Friends of Robert Bourassa" were ready with a bulk mailing that included a return card asking members if they were favourably disposed towards Bourassa's candidacy. By the time Bourassa officially announced that he would run, 16,000 names were lodged in the IBM 1130 computer at his campaign headquarters.

Desrochers was a highly talented organizer and a pitiless adversary. Twenty-four hours before the leadership race was officially open, and more than a month before Bourassa declared his candidacy, Desrochers rented some five dozen billboards at major intersections in the provincial capital where the convention would be held. He lined up all the available air time on the city's most popular TV channel for the night of January 16, the eve of the leadership vote, and slapped reservations on 2,264 hotel and motel rooms in town.

Claude Rouleau, a young consulting engineer who had made a name for himself on the Expo '67 construction project, took over fund-raising chores, targeting the very road-building contractors fingered by Bourassa in 1953 as having considerably more influence on the political process than impoverished university students.

Jean Lesage, meanwhile, made it clear he held his young recruit in high esteem; certainly the caucus members and party faithful who had remained loyal to him knew how he felt. "It was Lesage who decided it would be me," claimed Bourassa.[30]

Prominent Liberal lawyer Antoine Geoffrion, who ruled the roost on the Grande Allée, took it upon himself to bring around the orthodox federalists: "Laporte is too doctrinaire and Wagner is a fanatic. Bourassa is only a token nationalist. Once in power, he'll behave like a Liberal."[31]

Despite his comparatively tender age of thirty-six, and whatever one said of his adversaries, who were both older and more experienced than he, Bourassa was intellectually ready to contest his party's leadership. For the past year he had been working on a four-point program, based on the gains of the Quiet Revolution. He proposed that these should serve as a springboard for yet another leap forward, comparable to the one Quebec had made during the early 1960s. He emphasized especially the role of Quebec's younger generation, just then beginning to emerge from the modern new educational institutions founded during the Quiet Revolution. Bourassa was keenly aware that the universities and the CEGEPs, the newly created system of junior colleges, were producing 50,000 graduates a year. But the industrial restructuring then under way in the province's traditional industries was being accomplished at a cost of thousands and thousands of jobs. He must have already been toying with his future campaign slogan, "100,000 jobs," when he said:

> When I think that billions have been invested in training competent people! Quebec must find a way to profit from these people, and not let them go to other, richer provinces and countries. It is hard to accept that even though we have a weaker industrial structure than our southern and western neighbours, our own taxes are contributing to the widening of this gap. But this is what will happen if our young people leave the province for lack of opportunities.[32]

As for the "new social order" he was proposing, it consisted largely of a mish-mash of shopworn platitudes, somewhere between unfettered American capitalism and Soviet-style socialism. But objectives were less important to Bourassa than "government efficiency," which he promised to bring about using his own fiscal expertise and the help of the Bélanger report, "which Lesage had been preparing to implement [before his defeat] but which was now gathering dust on the shelves of the [new] government's offices."

From fiscal reform to the power struggles with Ottawa was only a short step, and one that Bourassa would take very quickly. The redistribution of powers between the two levels of government seemed to him "more necessary than ever," most notably in the area of family allowances and old-age pensions.

Bourassa could tip his hat to his friends in the party's nationalist wing—at least to those who hadn't left with René Lévesque—by showing that he was taking an interest in federal spending powers, the Pandora's box that Trudeau had dared to open ... "Quebec Liberals must be prepared," he added in a defiant tone, "to push the logic of federalism to its ultimate conclusion, and some of them could well catch their federal counterparts off guard."[33]

Considering these words, it is hardly surprising that the most serious opposition to Bourassa's candidacy came from his Liberal counterparts in Ottawa. "I don't think Trudeau was very happy about my nomination," Bourassa remembers. "My ties to René Lévesque called into the question the depth of my faith in federalism."[34]

The federal Liberals were so worried about the prospect of this brash young upstart getting his hands on the provincial party that they decided to take a hand in the matter. Senator Louis de Gonzague Giguère, the federal party's official "headhunter," even asked Jean Marchand to take the plunge into provincial politics. "Robert is too young," Giguère would tell people. "He's still a student."

Marchand, the hero of the great union battles against Duplessis and now a federal minister, was certainly still very popular in Quebec. But as the Social Research Inc. soundings had indicated, Quebec Liberals wanted a younger, more modern leader, preferably from Montreal, and capable of keeping some distance between himself and Ottawa.

> The polls showed that I was way ahead of Pierre Laporte and also ahead of Jean Marchand. The feds soon realized that they weren't getting anywhere and that they were bound to lose. Jean [Marchand] told me afterward: "Robert, we tried, but we realized we didn't stand a chance."[35]

On January 17, 1970, Robert Bourassa was all but crowned Liberal leader on the first convention ballot, with 843 votes (53 percent of the vote) against 455 votes for Claude Wagner and 288 for Pierre Laporte.

A good sport, Pierre Trudeau called to offer his congratulations. "He was cordial, nothing more," recalled Bourassa. But an election was looming, and the Trudeauites preferred the lukewarm friendship of the provincial Liberals to the outright hostility of the Union Nationale.

Since 1967 Robert Bourassa has, in a way, been condemned to be a federalist, sometimes in spite of himself. Often his act has been less than convincing—not convincing enough for Pierre Trudeau, who wanted him to sing the praises of the centralization of power in Ottawa, but much too convincing for René Lévesque, who had abandoned him—unless it was Bourassa who pushed him out—to found the Sovereignty-Association Movement.

Soon Bourassa would find himself caught even more tightly between the differing demands of Trudeau and Lévesque.

CHAPTER FOUR

The Holdout

*The heads of the Quebec government have always
had to fight, much more than the other heads of governments in Canada . . . At five million against
twenty million, I think we were born to fight.*[1]
Robert Bourassa

In order to distinguish himself from the other Liberal Party leadership candidates, Robert Bourassa promised to concentrate on the
economy. In the next provincial election, he used the same promise
every time he mounted a stump, and on April 29, 1970, the province
gave him a mandate to come up with the "100,000 jobs" he had
pledged to create.

No one knew it then, but among those who would benefit from
Bourassa's job creation initiative would be a goodly number of
constitutional experts. Since he came to power at roughly the same
time as Pierre Elliott Trudeau, Bourassa soon found he had no
choice but to mount a passive resistance to the prime minister's
"patriation" campaign, which seriously threatened Quebec's right
to self-determination. And he soon would have to deal with the
events surrounding the language crisis he himself had unleashed.
For a premier who had promised to make economic development
and the modernization of the state apparatus his foremost priorities,
none of this boded well.

The next five years of agitation on the constitutional front would
teach Bourassa a lesson he would remember for a long time—

especially since Trudeau never missed an opportunity to remind him. Both in 1970, when he campaigned with his line about "100,000 jobs," and in 1973, when his slogan was "Bourassa builds" (*Bourassa construit*), he won overwhelming majorities. But when Bourassa campaigned on the constitution, as he did in 1976, he lost miserably.

For Robert Bourassa, political stability and economic progress went hand-in-hand with constitutional agreement and linguistic equanimity. Traumatized by the schism the constitutional debate had caused within his party in 1967, alarmed by the rise of terrorist violence in Quebec, and keenly aware that the language issue constituted a veritable "powderkeg,"[2] the new premier of Quebec developed an abiding obsession with "social peace."

As a result of this obsession, Bourassa pursued foreign investment with a greater determination than any of his predecessors. The notorious "*coup de la Brinks*" (the convoy of armoured trucks that ostentatiously rolled towards the Ontario border from Montreal on the eve of the 1970 election as a warning to those who were considering voting for the separatists) was, in the end, nothing more than an admission of how vulnerable Quebec was to a flight of investment capital. Since he knew Hydro-Quebec would soon need money from New York brokers to finance his "project of the century," he had to avoid any semblance of a political crisis.

The constitution? "It was an important problem, but not an urgent one," Bourassa insisted some years later. "I didn't see why the new government, which was coming to grips with the economic situation and the financial situation, should immediately throw itself into that question."[3]

The 1970 election result was interpreted by Ottawa as a sign that things in Quebec were getting back to normal. In 1965 the Royal Commission on Bilingualism and Biculturalism had warned the country: "All we have seen and heard has convinced us that Canada is at the most critical point of its history since Confederation. We believe there is a crisis."[4] By the time of the commission's last meeting in February 1971, the members of the same commission were asking themselves if their final report should retain the "crisis'' diagnosis, or if they should even use the word at all. Only Paul Lacoste kept insisting that Trudeau should recognize the urgency of the situation.

How can this reversal be explained? André Laurendeau, one of the commission's co-chairmen, had died in 1968, but that in itself was not enough to explain such a change. Only the 1970 election could explain the reversal. At that 1971 meeting, commissioner Royce Frith, now a senator, said he was reluctant to include the slightest reference to a crisis "in light of the provincial election result of last April 29.''[5] For the commissioners, as for most English Canadians, the October Crisis was nothing more than an internal conflict, strictly a Quebec thing. As for the other crisis, the one that André Laurendeau had evoked in 1965—the crisis between the country's two majorities, the French in Quebec and the English in the rest of Canada—it seemed to be ending as a result of the renewed dialogue between Quebec and Ottawa.

Nevertheless, the arrival of a new Quebec premier at the federal-provincial conference table took place in an atmosphere of considerable ambiguity. Was it Bourassa's youth—he was, after all, only thirty-seven at the time—or his lack of experience? Or was it Pierre Trudeau's stubborn determination to patriate the constitution? Or was it the profound differences between the Quebec leader's views and those of some of his fellow premiers? When he was expected to be conciliatory, he wavered. When they tried to accept him as a partner, he gummed up the works. With one setback after another, a deep distrust began to build towards Bourassa in English Canada, a distrust he still has to live with.

Although he had intended to put constitutional affairs on the back burner, he could hardly stop English Canada and the federal government from trying impatiently to wrap up the series of constitutional conferences that had been going on for the last three years. In those years English Canada had been forced to deal with three different Quebec leaders: Daniel Johnson in 1968, Jean-Jacques Bertrand in 1969, and Robert Bourassa in 1970. Each had been closely scrutinized for the least sign of a change in attitude, the slightest indication of a retreat.

Bourassa was in an awkward position. He was burdened by the legacy of two Union Nationale premiers and four constitutional conferences. After the confrontations over the "two nations" concept, Bourassa was left with a high hurdle to clear. There was nothing he could do but back off and stick to his "profitable federalism" stand. Either that or admit that René Lévesque was right in warning him against "the old defensive battle . . . the false consolations of verbal nationalism . . . "

Elected on April 29, 1970, he announced his cabinet on May 12 and convened the National Assembly on June 9. Before the summer was over, he was in Ottawa for his first constitutional conference. Already things were moving a little too quickly for a fledgling premier who had come to power without a clearly defined constitutional policy.

Bourassa is generally ill at ease at constitutional conferences, especially since they are conducted exclusively in English, a language he has not completely mastered. His statements were vague, and he appeared to be cautious. Actually, Bourassa was more confused than anything else.

Yet despite himself, he opened doors for the federal negotiators. When Ontario Premier John Robarts, enjoying his reputation as Confederation's "honest broker," proposed that "immediate priority" be given to drawing up a new amending formula for the Constitution, Bourassa kept silent. And the Quebec premier also supported a proposal for the adoption of a charter of rights and freedoms put forward by Ottawa. He was planning to endow Quebec with a similar act so he had no reason to oppose this federal initiative.

Although Bourassa himself opened three fronts—communications, immigration, and foreign relations—on which federal authorities were particularly sensitive, they were rather pleased with the new premier's first visit. It was as the old sages of the federal Liberal party, notably Jean-Louis Gagnon and Royce Frith, had said it would be. They had been right to reassure English Canada that this "youngster" wasn't hung up on "ideological questions that trouble public order." All was for the best. "The attitude of the new Quebec government represents an unequivocal endorsement of federalism, which is most desirable," concluded Trudeau after his first negotiating session with Bourassa.[6]

Since the summer of 1967, while the Quebec Liberals had been juggling labels like "special status" and "sovereignty-association," Pierre Trudeau had been hatching his own plan. It was very simple: a declaration of rights ("drafted so as to restrict the powers of all governments, federal as well as provincial"), an amending formula, and a reformed Supreme Court.[7]

Thus, when Bourassa endorsed the principle of a charter of rights and freedoms and did not protest too much against Robarts's proposal to patriate the constitution *before* renegotiating the division of powers, the new Quebec premier opened a door that would not be closed again until the famous night of November 5, 1981. And encouraged by this "yes-no-maybe" response from Bourassa, the federal experts threw themselves headlong into the process of constitutional reform.

Two weeks later, on Friday, October 2, 1970, Pierre Trudeau extended an olive branch to Quebec:

> Canada is not a trap or a betrayal or a swindle. It is a hope, it is a promise, it is an ambitious challenge we can meet if we believe in it, if we find within ourselves enough ardour, enough confidence, and enough energy to put an end to these quarrels and these secular animosities.[8]

The next Monday, at 6:30 in the morning, a man showed up at the Diamond Taxi stand at the corner of St. Denis Street and St. Joseph Boulevard in Montreal. The "events of October" had begun. For the next three months—until December 28, when the members of the Front de liberation du Québec's Chenier cell were arrested—the Bourassa government was paralysed by an unprecedented crisis.

Neither Trudeau nor his ministers had much confidence in Robert Bourassa. At the height of the crisis, Marc Lalonde would exclaim before witnesses: "That Bourassa, he has no balls!" During the following weeks, Trudeau and Bourassa communicated directly, several times a day. That may have reinforced Bourassa's image as a weakling, a leader incapable of protecting the Quebec people's sovereignty against Ottawa's strong-arm tactics. "Trudeau is a statesman, not a sentimentalist," Bourassa would say later.[9]

When British diplomat James Cross was kidnapped, on October 5, Bourassa and his ministers considered that this incident concerned the federal government. So much that Bourassa went ahead with a scheduled trip to New York: not going would only have served to dramatize the events back home.

Although Trudeau was not ready to give in to all demands by the kidnappers, he was considering releasing them to foreign countries, such as Cuba or Algeria. Bourassa appreciated the efforts the prime minister made to defuse the crisis. "He showed that he was ready to make quite humiliating concessions," he said.[10] Indeed, the federal government had accepted that the Manifesto put out by the kidnappers be read over the airwaves of Radio-Canada, and it referred to "Bourassa the Simard canary, Trudeau the faggot . . . "

On the other hand, said Bourassa, "there were things on which Trudeau did not want to negotiate, and I must say I agreed with him. He was particularly intransigent on the principle of not giving way on anything that went beyond the separation of powers, by which I mean taking measures that would affect the functioning of the justice system."

On the following Saturday, October 10, at 6:18 p.m., Pierre Laporte, the Quebec minister of immigration and manpower, was kidnapped while playing football on his front lawn with his son. The crisis took a whole new turn. Ten months earlier, Pierre Laporte had been a candidate in the leadership race against Bourassa. "Trudeau understood that my position was more difficult than his," Bourassa acknowledges.

The broadcasting of the FLQ Manifesto made quite an impact on the Quebec population. Opinion leaders, Claude Ryan, publisher of *Le Devoir* particularly, called for serious negotiations with the kidnappers. But he also felt that Bourassa was too weak to handle the negotiations and he feared the Quebec premier would let Ottawa take over. Ryan suggested, as a possibility, the formation of a provisional government made up of representatives from all parties and different elements of the Quebec society.

This idea of a "parallel" government raised concerns in Ottawa and Quebec City. Word from the negotiators indicated that the discussions with the kidnappers were going nowhere. And the Quebec police forces were getting exhausted by their extra duties. In the early afternoon of Thursday, October 15, the Quebec government officially asked for army support. A combat regiment based in Valcartier, near Quebec City, was moved to Montreal.

Meanwhile, the RCMP and the Sûreté du Québec had begun drawing up lists of suspects to be arrested. Bourassa and Trudeau went through them. "I remember that there were certain names that made me raise my eyebrows," he said. "And Trudeau was wondering about some of them too. We talked about it."[11]

To detain those 465 "suspects," the police forces needed special powers, and civil liberties had to be suspended. According to Marc Lalonde, Trudeau was not personally in favour of the imposition of the War Measures Act. "If that's what you want," he told Bourassa, "you'll have to ask me formally and say that you are faced with a state of potential insurrection."[12]

At 3:30 a.m., on Friday, October 16, Governor General Roland Michener signed the Proclamation of the War Measures Act. Thirty hours later, Pierre Laporte's body was found in the trunk of a green Chevrolet. James Cross was freed on December 3, and his kidnappers took refuge in Cuba. And on December 28, members of the FLQ cell who had jointly declared their responsibility for Pierre Laporte's death, were arrested.

Robert Bourassa's popularity did not immediately suffer as a result of the October Crisis. But he came away with the image, often unjustly invoked, of a weak leader. The Fifth Combat Group was barely back in its barracks at Valcartier on January 4, 1971, when, on the following February 8, Bourassa had to return to Ottawa for another constitutional conference. Despite the October Crisis, the federal bureaucrats hadn't let the grass grow under their feet. Nor had their counterparts in Quebec City been wasting their time. Social Affairs Minister Claude Castonguay had begun organizing some of his social programs; he realized that the basic questions of income security and family policy could not easily escape the constraints of national standards.

At the February 1971 conference, Quebec's minimum demand was for legislative priority and, in certain cases, exclusive jurisdiction in matters of social policy: income security, job training, social services, the administration of justice, health services, hospital and health insurance financing, housing, and recreational activities.

"The patriation of the constitution represents such a fundamental act for the balance of forces within Canada that it cannot be accomplished without major concessions," said Bourassa upon his arrival in Ottawa.

"Let's patriate, then we'll sit down to divide powers," replied Trudeau.

"My government doesn't believe in fairy godmothers," replied Bourassa. "We cannot allow the constitution to be patriated while waiting to see how sincere the federal government is about giving powers to the provinces."[13]

Some of Bourassa's fellow premiers, most notably Newfoundland's Joey Smallwood and Ross Thatcher of Saskatchewan, protested bitterly: "Bourassa wants to reduce the federal government to the role of tax collector, supplier of national defence, and commercial policy supervisor and nothing more."[14] (Exactly twenty years later, as part of the hysteria touched off by the Allaire report, Clyde Wells or Sharon Carstairs would echo these predecessors.)

The anglos pointed their fingers at some of the Quebec bureaucrats with whom they had crossed swords during the Union Nationale days, in particular Claude Morin. They thought they had seen the last of him after the April 29 election. An adviser to Lesage, Johnson, and Bertrand, he was a veteran of the great Ottawa-Quebec quarrels, and regarded as a troublemaker by the Trudeau entourage. "He wasn't the most popular person among the senior civil servants," Bourassa said, putting it mildly, "but I had confidence in his experience."[15]

Even so, the conference was not a complete disaster. Everyone went home feeling that, after forty years of talk, they were on the verge of settling the constitutional question. "After the pregnancy, the time comes to give birth, and that is as it should be," said Trudeau triumphantly.[16] The premiers had finally agreed on an amending formula that would, for all practical purposes, give Quebec a veto; most constitutional modifications would have to be approved by a majority of the provinces, including two from the Atlantic provinces and two from the West, along with Quebec and Ontario. This was the famous "Victoria formula" of which Trudeau was so proud—and justifiably so, since Quebec would never be offered anything better.

He even succeeded in convincing Alberta to open schools for its francophone minority, though the pill was coated in the sweet proviso: "in places where the language of instruction is chosen by a sufficiently large number of persons to justify the offer of the necessary facilities."

Trudeau seemed generally satisfied, and it was agreed that the first ministers should meet again in Victoria on June 14 to put their signatures on the whole package. Robert Bourassa seemed so complaisant that the prime minister interpreted his intentions in advance on Radio-Canada: "Allow me to remind you that the amending formula was accepted by Mr. Bourassa, and that [he] has been elected by a strong majority of the people of Quebec and [that his party] occupies the great majority of seats."[17] In other words: "It's time to deliver the goods, Robert!"

But it wasn't that simple. Bourassa couldn't help but remember the debate over the Fulton-Favreau formula that had finally forced Jean Lesage into retirement. His former colleague, René Lévesque, let himself go in the column he was writing at the time for the *Journal de Montréal*:

> Give me a big piece of social security and I'll swallow the amending formula. No citizen who is even remotely aware of Quebec's fundamental interests can condone such political weakness.[18]

Meanwhile, the October Crisis was barely over and the province was in a serious economic crisis. Unsure of himself, Bourassa wanted to sound out the mood of the National Assembly's standing committee on constitutional affairs, which strongly suggested that he should sign nothing at Victoria without a substantial transfer of powers—and the money that went with them.

When he arrived in British Columbia, the Quebec premier had no choice but to harden his tone. To their annoyance, his colleagues wound up spending most of their time talking about social policy. Bourassa refused to give way, steadfastly insisting on legislative priority over income security.

Between two meetings, probably to lighten up the atmosphere, the provincial leaders took time out for a cruise on Juan de Fuca Strait. On the deck of the ferry, the English-Canadian ministers and senior bureaucrats cast suspicious glances on the conspiratorial airs of the two Claudes: Castonguay and Morin. Jean Chrétien would later interpret the situation in the following terms:

> The social affairs minister let himself be convinced by Claude Morin that the distribution of powers in the social affairs field, such as family allowances, should be re-examined. Together they rattled Robert Bourassa so much, he rejected the accord.[19]

> "Bourassa is a leader who can't be taken at his word," Jean Chrétien told people. As for Claude Morin's supposed "dark plot," his master himself exonerated him.

> Morin himself felt at times that his presence could hamper the discussions. You could tell that he and Trudeau didn't exactly see eye to eye, and at times Morin abstained from participating so as to facilitate the discussions.[20]

On the morning of June 16, Bourassa asked for time to think things over. "Two months," he suggested. Trudeau, who was in a hurry, gave him an ultimatum: "Twelve days: take it or leave it." To those who later accused him of having been merely a puppet in the hands of the separatists, Bourassa explained:

> The fact that I asked for a delay showed that I hadn't made my decision in Victoria. I told them: I have to re-evaluate the situation. It was only six months after the October Crisis. There was still a certain nationalist feeling in Quebec, though it was dormant. I couldn't take the risk of setting off seven or eight years of political violence.[21]

There was agitation in any case. The Péquiste opposition, the intellectuals, the publisher of Le Devoir, Claude Ryan, and even Trudeau joined the fray. "You know, just about everywhere in Canada people are fed up with the constitutional question," said Trudeau. "These guys [the premiers] are going to find themselves around a negotiating table twenty or a hundred years from now."[22]

On June 22, half the Liberal caucus in Quebec and a good number of his ministers suggested that Bourassa should refuse Ottawa's offer. It was Marc Lalonde who took Bourassa's call at eleven o'clock that night. "Warn Trudeau," Bourassa said, "I'm going to meet the press, and the answer is no." After hanging up, Lalonde expressed his opinion of the Quebec premier in the colourful fashion that his intimates knew so well.

The next day, on the eve of the St. Jean Baptiste Day holiday, Bourassa was given a standing ovation by all sides in the National Assembly. Confronted by English Canada, Quebec had recovered its unanimity—just as it would do again on June 22, 1990.

Thus Canada would not get its "great charter": according to Trudeauite historians, Quebec was the guilty party once again (Jean Lesage had performed a similar about-face in 1965). "We could have continued the negotiations on social policy and tried to save the agreement," Bill Davis told Bourassa during the summer at a private meeting in Montreal.

Bourassa's distrust of Ontario and the federal bureaucracy was, in part, what led him to refuse Ottawa's offer. As he said later,

> It's obvious that there are strong links between politicians and civil servants. There was a common will on the part of the federal establishment and the people of Ontario to patriate the constitution.[23]

The Quebec government was not without support outside the province. Alberta and British Columbia in particular didn't see why the federal government was so determined to have a hand in social policy. But the more Bourassa insisted on gaining powers, the more he was accused of having given in to blackmail by Quebec nationalists, something he later confirmed:

> There was a lot of sympathy for Quebec's arguments. But I was isolated because we had to refuse patriation if we didn't immediately get the social changes we were asking for. The provinces offered their support, but they drew the line at refusing patriation on those grounds.[24]

But on June 23, the same day it became known that Quebec had said no to the agreement, there was a provincial election in

Saskatchewan: Allan Blakeney's New Democrats overthrew Ross
Thatcher's Liberal government. The new premier was very careful
not to pronounce on the Victoria accord. The premier of Ontario no
doubt had forgotten to drop in on him. Bourassa remembers feeling
as though he was caught in an iron collar:

> The Victoria conference was a lot worse than the October
> Crisis. I felt the vise closing in on Quebec. On the one hand we
> wanted to stay in the federal system; we wanted to profit from
> it. But on the other hand, we wanted to keep our pride, to
> assert ourselves, to have the maximum powers. The Quebec
> government is always caught between the two.[25]

Amid this constitutional conflict, he nevertheless managed to
launch "the project of the century." After a tour of Europe, and
France in particular (where he paid solitary homage to de Gaulle at
the late General's grave), the premier confided to *La Presse* correspondent Claude Masson that he would take advantage of the first
anniversary of his election to announce the development of the
James Bay hydroelectric project.

It was the era of great projects. Bourassa had the genius—or the
blind luck—to call another election before the effects of the 1973 oil
shock became widely felt. Construction cranes extended over the
streets of downtown Montreal; convoys of cement mixers rolled
toward James Bay, and mechanical shovels opened new highways.
The slogan "Bourassa builds" did a lot of damage to the PQ's
aspirations. On October 29, 1973, the province gave Bourassa an
overwhelming majority: 102 seats out of 110.

Now it was the Western provinces, rich with their oil and natural
gas resources, who were crossing swords with Trudeau. A veritable
black-gold fever swept the entire world. Peter Lougheed, who had
just come to power in Alberta, and Allan Blakeney in Saskatchewan
began to find that the "redistribution" of wealth from coast to coast
was costing them rather a lot. Pierre Trudeau, who had headed a
minority government since October 30, 1972, no longer had the
clout he once had.

*

In the spring of 1974, two events helped to seal the fate of Bourassa's career. First, on March 21, 1974, a mob of union goons belonging to the Quebec Federation of Labour's construction trades affiliate, which was led at the time by the raffishly colourful "Dédé" Desjardins, trashed the principal James Bay construction site. The outbreak brought into the spotlight two men who would have a decisive impact on the second phase of Bourassa's career: Brian Mulroney and Lucien Bouchard.

The sacking of the James Bay construction site provoked the government into establishing a commission of inquiry into the violence endemic in the province's construction industry. Brian Mulroney was one of the commission's members. Mulroney was best known at the time for his iron-fisted showdowns on behalf of management with the Montreal harbourfront unions and the newspaper locals at a number of dailies owned by Power Corp. financier Paul Desmarais. Mulroney was assisted by a young lawyer from Chicoutimi, Lucien Bouchard, who was named the commission's chief counsel; his partners had recently expelled him from his law firm (for making speeches in favour of local Parti Québécois kingpin Marc-André Bédard, it was said), and at the time he didn't have much of a public profile. "I came out of [the commission hearings] far better known than I was before," he admitted later. "I got to measure myself against all the big-time lawyers from Montreal, and I was on television every evening."[26] Both Mulroney and Bouchard went on, of course, to federal politics, and in 1985, they would be the ones to welcome Bourassa back from his sojourn in "the desert" where his November 1976 defeat had sent him.

Also in 1974, for the first time ever, the head of the Quebec government proclaimed French to be Quebec's official language, a stroke of impudence that Trudeau and English Montreal would never forgive. "If only he had called it the principal language, or the language of work, or the 'national language,' if he'd limited it to that, as in 'National' Assembly," grumbled Trudeau.[27] Bourassa insists he was surprised by the degree of resentment his language law evoked:

> I expected that the act of decreeing French as the official language would elicit a certain animosity or opposition among the English minority [in Quebec] and in the rest of Canada. But I was frankly astonished at its intensity."[28]

Bill 22, adopted on July 30, introduced linguistic aptitude tests for certain children whose parents wanted to enrol them in English schools. It set off the language powderkeg once more.

Now that French had become Quebec's official language, Quebec pilots demanded the right to speak French in the province's skies. The reaction of the Canadian Airline Pilots' Association (CALPA) bordered on hysteria. For good measure, incidents were deliberately provoked. Following a strike, an injunction, and an inquiry commission, the federal government finally bowed before CALPA. English would remain the language of the skies. "Trudeau is retreating before a bunch of English racists," charged René Lévesque.[29] The next day, Jean Marchand, the federal minister of environment, resigned from the cabinet. There was panic in the ranks of Liberal parliamentarians in Ottawa. Francis Fox, then a parliamentary secretary and chairman of the Quebec caucus, told Marchand:

> Whether you like it or not, your resignation is going to take on significant proportions. Gérard Pelletier is already gone. [He had been named ambassador to Paris.] Now you're going. Of the "Three Wise Men," only Pierre will be left. It's starting to look like a rout."[30]

Robert Bourassa interpreted Marchand's resignation somewhat differently. The French-in-the-skies affair had generated a fresh nationalist wind throughout the province, and the Parti Québécois was climbing in the polls; perhaps Trudeau himself had encouraged his former comrade-in-arms to resign in order to calm Quebec?

> They were old friends. I'm not sure Trudeau didn't tell him: "Listen, Marchand, resign over this to calm down Quebec." I can't prove it, but I'm sure they must have talked about it.

Marchand himself told me: "Look here, Robert, the situation is rough."[31]

Bill 22 was so rough, in fact, that the polls started showing that the provincial Liberals were in free fall. To register their indignation, the English community defected in great numbers to the Union Nationale. The Mouvement Quebec Français, a leading nationalist pressure group, cried treason for not imposing French in the skies, even though Bourassa had made French Quebec's official language.

Trudeau had not yet renounced his dream of a charter, cast in the concrete of a Canadian constitution, that proclaimed the supremacy of individual rights over collective rights, even those of a distinct society. In the spring of 1976, bolstered by the majority he had regained in the July 1974 federal election, he decided it was time to move. He was in a hurry. His marriage to Margaret had soured. He refused to contemplate a divorce, but leaving politics, he thought, might avoid a separation. "I felt strongly that the time remaining for him to achieve his *raison d'être* in politics was limited for family reasons," explained Bourassa, recalling the pressure Trudeau put on him to reopen the constitutional issue.[32]

March 3, 1976, is a date that Bourassa will probably never forget. A few days earlier he had innocently allowed himself to be photographed for the cover of *L'Actualité*, a French-language news magazine, just as he was about to take a hefty bite of a huge hot dog. It just so happened that the issue with the hot dog cover came out the week that Trudeau was scheduled to visit the provincial capital, and he happened to spot it on a rack as he passed through the airport after his plane landed. When he arrived at Bourassa's office, he was in no mood to elaborate on the "menu" for the meeting. "It seems he eats hot dogs," he said flippantly, brushing by the reporters who had waylaid him in the lobby. The media horde was in the mood for something sensational that day, and they seized on Trudeau's remark. From that moment on Bourassa became "the hot-dog eater," though Trudeau had never actually called him that. But it was what everybody wanted to hear.

The Ottawa bureaucrats were also in a hurry. They were convinced that it would be easier for a prime minister from Quebec to make Quebeckers accept the patriation of the constitution. But by 1976, Quebec was no longer the only holdout; the Western provinces had recently added the question of natural resources to the Victoria list of jurisdictional demands, and in the name of his fellow premiers, Alberta's Peter Lougheed was preparing for the prime minister a new and even longer list of powers sought by the provinces.

"It is not only possible, but perhaps preferable, to act unilaterally," an impatient Trudeau muttered in the House of Commons.

"My government will be held up to ridicule," Bourassa protested to Trudeau later.

"Too bad," replied Trudeau, "but for me this is fundamental, and I'm not about to sacrifice myself because history will judge you harshly."[33]

Bourassa, who does not normally indulge in games of chance, tried his hand at a bold tactic. He called an election. If he won, he would have the mandate he needed to stand up to Trudeau, by then worn down by eight years in power and mounting chaos in his cabinet (in the space of a few months, seven of his ministers had resigned).

And if the Parti Québécois were to be elected? They would block Trudeau too—or so Bourassa thought.[34]

Bourassa, who likes to take in the odd Expos game, chose a baseball metaphor to reassure those in his cabinet, most notably Jean-Paul L'Allier, who opposed a snap election less than three years after the last one: "In 1970 it was strike one. In 1973 it was strike two, and on November 15, 1976, it'll be strike out."[35] What happened instead is that the Parti Québécois hit a home run.

On November 15, 1976, a majority of Quebeckers voted for the "true" party of the Québécois, and René Levesque took over as premier. Bourassa would have to wait another ten years before Lévesque grudgingly gave him his due in his memoirs for his Official Language Act:

> When you consider the fact that the Liberals were "the party of the English," and that his government amply reflected that,

I consider that for once the premier was displaying a certain courage.[36]

Trudeau blamed Bourassa's defeat on the row over French in the skies. It was a pathetic excuse, if not outright hypocrisy on the part of one who had, more than anyone, weakened Bourassa's position.

Bourassa lost his election gamble, but Quebec did not retreat. Not yet, in any case. In 1990, Bourassa looked back on the consequences of his refusal to sign Trudeau's proposed Victoria charter:

> Here you have a fairly exceptional case of history repeating itself. He who said no in Victoria would find himself, twenty years later and in the same function, forced to bear the historic consequences. It's because I said no to Trudeau that the constitution was unilaterally patriated. And it was because he patriated it unilaterally that I tried to repair the damage with the five conditions negotiated at Meech Lake. The five conditions were rejected, and here I am, left with the consequences of what I did in Victoria, twenty years later.[37]

It was a sad turn of history for Bourassa, who had spent the five years of his first mandate holding out, without gaining anything whatsoever. It was a cold consolation for a leader of a state in the process of emancipation to be able to say that he had at least accepted no new servitudes.

In fact, Robert Bourassa had come back to the point at which René Lévesque had left him in 1967, in the basement of his house on Brittany Street: at square one.

CHAPTER FIVE

Crossing the Desert

*In terms of political strategy, when you hold a refer-
endum on the future of a people, you do it in such a
way that you can win.*

Robert Bourassa

After his election loss on November 15, 1976, Bourassa was not
content to leave it at that. After all, his record wasn't all that bad.
Work was advancing rapidly on the James Bay project, and despite
some regrettable misadventures, Quebec engineering firms had
finally been brought in as key players. Many of these firms, Lavalin
in particular, would soon go on to develop international reputations.
And it was the Bourassa government which, through its subway
expansion program in Montreal, had literally forced Bombardier to
go beyond snowmobiles and move into the public transit sector, the
firm's first step toward its transformation into an integrated trans-
portation equipment multinational.

In the area of social services, Robert Bourassa had also excelled.
His health and hospital insurance programs were more ambitious
than those of the other provinces, and as a bonus he had introduced
free dental care for children, free prescription drugs for the elderly,
and legal aid for those in need. His long-held dream of the farm
union movement came true when he instituted a crop insurance
system. Never had so many colleges been built, and the University
of Quebec was opening campuses in all corners of the province.

Even though the cost was exorbitant, the Olympic Games came off without a hitch. "Quebec's international reputation was saved," a relieved Bourassa told his protocol chief, Gilles Loiselle, after the 1976 Games.[1] The Americans had even started calling the province "The Texas of the North."[2] Five years after the October Crisis, three years after Bourassa had imprisoned the heads of the province's three largest union groups, twelve months after the James Bay rampage, people were praising Quebec for its political stability. Talk about a turnaround!

And it shouldn't be forgotten that it was Robert Bourassa who established French as Quebec's official language.

It was surely only a matter of time before history would recognize his accomplishments. But, as his old friend Jacques Godbout reminded him, history has a fickle memory. Godbout's uncle, Adélard Godbout, who had been premier of the province during World War II, had introduced great reforms—women's right to vote in 1940, compulsory education in 1942, the first electrical nationalization in 1944. But these achievements had been all but forgotten. What was remembered was that Godbout had caved in to conscription.

Thus it was that for a while all people recalled about Bourassa was the softness of his spine when Marc Lalonde, the federal disciplinarian, cracked his whip. That and the "corruption" of his administration. Beaten in his home riding of Mercier by poet Gérald Godin, whose imprisonment he had approved during the October Crisis roundup in 1970, Bourassa was seen as a pariah, the party's "black sheep"; he was "the most hated man in the province," said caucus members who owed him the blessings of six years in power.

The federal Liberals, refusing to admit that Pierre Trudeau had contributed to Bourassa's humiliating downfall, blamed the election loss on Bourassa's lukewarm attitude toward federalism. If only he had listened to Marc Lalonde instead of Claude Morin in Victoria in 1971. If only he had renounced his infamous Bill 22. Trudeau said, "By declaring his opposition to the federal bilingualism policy, [Bourassa] moved the debate to the only ground where the separatist party had an advantage over him."[3]

English Canada revived old demons by harping on the endemic corruption of Quebec's political regimes: the "Liquor Board affair," which *Le Devoir* publisher Claude Ryan happened to pluck from his files in mid-election campaign; the "good patronage" dispensed to right-thinking "highway contractors" and certain unions, as well as the James Bay construction firms; the commission of inquiry on organized crime . . . Robert Bourassa was held responsible for all these problems.

"It smells of Québécois garlic,"[4] railed one columnist at the *Gazette*, who was then immediately invited to repeat himself on CBC national radio.

There was one "affair" that touched Bourassa directly, or at least his in-laws. It concerned Paragon Inc., a company that produced business forms, which was owned in part by his wife Andrée and his brother-in-law, Claude Simard, who was also minister of tourism at the time. Paragon, which had a virtual monopoly in its field in the province, turned out to have obtained a number of substantial contracts from the Liberal government. But then it had also done a comparable volume of business with the previous Union Nationale government, just as it would go on to ring up huge sales to the Parti Québécois administration. "A man has to be unassailable when it comes to personal integrity, but you can't censure him because his wife has a personal fortune," Bourassa protested.[5]

Robert Bourassa corrupt? Imprudent rather, as he recognizes today.

On November 15, 1976, Bourassa felt hurt and humiliated, abandoned by everyone—but even then he lost graciously . . . "I would like to address myself, in the name of all Quebeckers, to those in the economic spheres, in particular business and labor, and to ask them to make a thoughtful response to tonight's events," he said from his party's headquarters on Montreal's Guilford Street.

René Lévesque said he found Bourassa's message "extremely appropriate and courageous."[6] Then, his voice breaking with emotion, the new head of the Quebec government intoned: "I have never been so proud to be Québécois! We are not a small people, we may be something like a great people." The people, who had come from all corners of the metropolis and beyond to the Centre Paul Sauvé to belt out the PQ campaign song, "*À partir d'aujourd'hui*" (From Today On), then took to the streets, marched on the West Island, symbol of the alienation from which they had finally freed themselves, and, on the way, broke a few windows.

A small group left the main body, walked toward Pine Avenue and proceeded, from the foot of Mount Royal, up Maplewood Avenue to Bourassa's residence. But the provincial police officers guarding the house, who still called him "Mr. Premier" (after all, he hadn't yet resigned), had advised Bourassa to spend the night elsewhere. Like an overthrown despot, Bourassa was in hiding.

Bourassa was ready to go even farther from his old home. His mind was made up: in ten days he would be gone—to Brussels, where he would study the workings of the European Economic Community and forms of "sovereignty-association," an idea that was the topic of much discussion at the time. "I'll be back in time for the referendum promised by the PQ," is all he told his wife. "One day we'll return to power," he told his close friend Ronald Poupart. "I'll be back someday."

The next day he advised the Liberal executive that his resignation as party leader would take effect on January 1, 1977. At the regular Wednesday morning cabinet meetings, several of his colleagues tried to dissuade him; Gérard D. Lévesque, in particular, who had seen Maurice Duplessis "buried" in October 1939, only to come back stronger than before in August 1944—and for fifteen years at that—tried to convince Bourassa to stay. But Bourassa cut them off.

> Beaten in my own riding, responsible for a snap election, a Parti Québécois majority government, and a campaign that depended on me personally: in these conditions one draws one's conclusions and withdraws.[7]

On the Thursday afternoon, when René Lévesque paid him a visit at his office in the Hydro-Quebec building, Bourassa described his plan to go to Brussels and the studies he intended to pursue. Lévesque later recalled:

I could only encourage him, but I doubted he'd be able to stay in exile. All his life had been devoted to political ambition. His career had been oriented toward that and that alone.[8]

Lévesque was right: whatever he said, Robert Bourassa hadn't really resigned himself to his defeat. But since the defeat had been his, so the rehabilitation had to be his alone.

For the next three years, Bourassa observed from afar as Quebec manoeuvred itself toward the referendum on sovereignty-association, and as Ottawa executed its greatest coup, the patriation of the constitution. With partisan fervour, Bourassa fought his new enemy—the Parti Québécois. In the little office at the Quebec delegation in Brussels, which Lévesque had put at his disposal, Bourassa spent as much time devouring the newspapers from home as he did poring over the chapters of the Treaty of Rome.

When he turned his attention to the contemporary European scene, what interested him was not so much the nuts and bolts of the emerging federal system there, as the evolution away from the goal toward which the Parti Québécois intended to take Quebec.

"The best way to learn is to teach courses,"[9] Bourassa would say later, with a hearty chuckle. In Brussels, in Fontainebleau, in Washington, in Los Angeles, in New Haven, in Quebec City, in Montreal, and even in Ottawa, Bourassa visited institutes and universities, as though rehearsing his speeches for his return to the stage during the referendum campaign. During the course of his teaching tour, he gained a knowledge of the European Economic Community that was unsurpassed by any other Quebec politician.

His sojourn in Brussels also marked a return to the source of his original inspiration, for he had been in London when the Treaty of Rome came into force on January 1, 1958. Then, as a young student of economics and political science at Oxford, he had had a front-row seat for the birth of Europe. There, Bourassa had acquired two convictions that would remain at the heart of all his "federalist" speeches: first, great economic unions contribute to the political stability and the economic prosperity of their member countries, and, second, such unions are part of a universal movement. Even today Bourassa remains critical of General de Gaulle for having failed to grasp what the new European arrangement represented for France. De Gaulle, difficult as ever, refused to have anything to do with the new institutions. Bourassa says:

> It was a mistake for him not to recognize European federalism. During the 1960s, de Gaulle was offered a federal Europe in which France would have played a predominant role. At the time, Germany couldn't assert itself politically because of the war.[10]

As a young student preparing for a political career in 1958, Bourassa had imagined great things for Quebec. Without taking himself for a de Gaulle, he was convinced that Quebec could still "play a leadership role" in a modernized Canadian federation. When he returned to Europe in 1976, the situation there simply confirmed the impressions he had formed in 1958. After a difficult start, the European community had grown to nine members, with the inclusion of the United Kingdom, Ireland, and Denmark in 1973. From a simple customs union, it had developed into an economic and monetary association of states, equipped with a common monetary unit (the ECU—European Currency Unit), and was already planning to elect a Parliament by universal suffrage.

Finding himself on sabbatical in Europe at the time of the sovereignty-association debate was a windfall for Robert Bourassa. Drawing on current events in Europe, he was able to counter, one by one, the arguments put forward in the PQ referendum manifesto, a government White Paper entitled "Quebec-Canada: A New Deal."

"All things considered," he declared during the heat of the referendum campaign, "it appears that a situation is being proposed in which Quebeckers would be less Canadian than the French are European."

In 1990, a few weeks after the Meech Lake collapse, before Bourassa had even worked out the mandate for the commission on Quebec's political and constitutional future, he was back perusing his lecture notes from the Institute of European Affairs in Brussels. As though he was already preparing for the debates of the Bélanger-Campeau Commission, he said:

Europe provides an appropriate comparison. I studied it with
a great deal of interest from 1977 to 1980 because I told myself,
"Maybe in Quebec one day we'll find ourselves in the same
situation."[11]

Robert Bourassa had promised to be back in Quebec for the referendum. As it turned out, after his stint at the European Institute of
Business Administration in Fontainebleau in 1977, and at the Johns
Hopkins School of Advanced International Studies in Washington
in 1978, a pair of providential contracts from Laval University and
the University of Montreal brought him back to Quebec in 1979.

The timing was perhaps a bit premature, for the humiliations
were not yet over. First, Bourassa had to watch helplessly as Raymond Garneau, his former finance minister, whom he had regarded
as something of an heir-apparent, was defeated by Claude Ryan in
the Liberal leadership race. Then he felt a sting of ingratitude as a
group of Liberal MNAs—including Raymond Mailloux, whom
Bourassa had named to the cabinet at Garneau's request—went to
Ryan on bended knee. Wasn't Ryan the one who had preferred the
PQ in 1976, Bourassa protested timidly when some of his former
organizers showed almost indecent haste to fall in with the new
leader. "We have no choice," one of them told him. "If he's
elected, we'll be stuck with him, but don't worry, Ryan will certainly never be premier."[12]

At the convention, there was a palpable resentment against
Bourassa, and Claude Ryan was pointedly frosty toward him. During the opening ceremonies, where it is standard practice to pay
homage to the outgoing leader, Bourassa was included, almost as an
afterthought, in a gala spectacle in honour of all the former party
leaders, from Georges-Émile Lapalme, to Gérard D. Lévesque
(then the interim leader), by way of Jean Lesage. The man who had
led the party to an unprecedented sweep five years before made his
reappearance on the political stage amid the general hubbub and
semi-darkness of a slide show. When the lights went back on, he
looked like a shadow that had escaped from a historical fresco.

Bourassa had hoped that the upcoming referendum campaign
would provide him with an opportunity to be of use again, and a

starting point for his re-entry into Quebec politics. But Claude Ryan told him coldly: "You'll have to wait another ten years."

In the fall of 1979 came yet another humiliation when Bourassa had to ask to be invited to the inaugural ceremonies of the La Grande complex of the James Bay hydro project. But the affront stung considerably less after the project workers gave him an enthusiastic ovation—more enthusiastic than the one they gave René Lévesque.

When the referendum campaign at last got under way, there seemed to be no role for Bourassa. But this time he didn't insist too much. "The hot-dog business wasn't that far in the past, and I didn't particularly want to be seen on the same stage as Trudeau," he said later.[13] (As it turned out, on May 7, 1980, in Quebec City, Bourassa made a discreet appearance alongside Trudeau, Claude Ryan, Jean Chrétien, and the other "No" camp headliners.)

Claude Ryan ran the "No" camp with an iron fist, and his incessant squabbles with Chrétien left little room for Bourassa. In any case, nobody quite knew what to do with Bourassa, and in the end he had to content himself with the odd jobs that nobody else wanted.

His series of debates with Pierre Bourgault before student audiences and his speeches to local Rotary clubs and chambers of commerce enabled him to give minor notables in the four corners of the province a discreet reminder that he was still around and available. But the television networks and the province's big newspapers concentrated on the large rallies, followed Ryan and Lévesque on their campaign rounds, and faithfully recorded every word of Trudeau's three speeches. Nobody noticed that Bourassa was resurfacing.

His speech, which he had prepared in Brussels and polished during exchanges with students, was essentially a highly technical thirty-one-page presentation.[14] One wonders how students and small businessmen could sit through the whole thing—particularly since Bourassa often shared the stage with Bourgault, who was known for his flights of oratory. As Bourgault recalled later:

> I've debated with everybody, with Pierre Elliott Trudeau, with Gérard Pelletier, with Jean-Luc Pépin, with everybody when

you get down to it ... I can beat these people pretty easily,
except for Robert Bourassa ... During the referendum campaign, we came to a common agreement that we should stop
doing it because it was turning into a freak show ... We each
knew too well what the other was going to say, his strengths,
his weaknesses ... We always ended up in a tie. He was
diabolical. That's something I'm not. I stop halfway. At one
point I said no, it's too much, my friends are going to laugh at
me. As for him ... whether his friends laugh at him or not,
he'll go all the way no matter what. That's how he wins. He's
diabolical![15]

The 1980 referendum campaign turned out to be a remake of the
1967 debate that led to Bourassa's rupture with René Lévesque. In
sum, a second round. This time, however, the European example
lent weight to Bourassa's arguments. Meanwhile, the Parti Québécois technocrats—Jacques Parizeau and Bernard Landry, in particular—had refined René Lévesque's somewhat muddled thesis.

Bourassa knew very well that the currency question had always
been the Achilles heel of the sovereignty thesis. And he didn't
hesitate for a moment to lay out, paragraph by paragraph, the
inherent contradictions of the Lévesque government's White
Paper.[16] "The government is painting itself into a neo-federalist
corner," Bourassa sneered, getting out his lecture notes.

In the same vein, to counter the idea of a Quebec currency,
Bourassa brandished the threat of instability, of devaluation, of
difficult exchange markets in front of Quebeckers who "were trav-
elling more and more to foreign countries."

"Ah, if only Quebec weren't situated in North America, and if its
trade sector weren't so important," sighed Bourassa, "then maybe
it could envisage creating a Quebec currency. But the reality is
something else entirely."

Since the fall of 1978, the Parti Québécois had given up the idea
of creating a Quebec currency, and had dropped its plan to entrust
its independence to the central bank: interest rates were soaring in
the spring of 1980 and the hapless governor of the Bank of Canada,
Gerald Bouey, was the object of such vehement attacks that the

RCMP considered offering him a bodyguard. René Lévesque was now proposing a hybrid formula that involved equal say in the administration of the Bank of Quebec-Canada, as well as a minority status for Quebec on less important matters.

Joint management, Bourassa explained, is not terribly practical for an institution that has to make its decisions on the spot when exchange rates drop, when a surge of speculation upsets the money markets, or simply when Quebec and Canada's interests diverge. For instance, Quebec might want to fight unemployment and plan to lower the value of the common "dollar" to favour its exports, while at the same time, Ontario might choose to fight inflation by increasing the value of the same "dollar" to reduce the cost of its imports. Bourassa concluded:

> Equal joint management is unrealistic because Quebec is asking for 50 percent of the votes with a quarter of the economic strength and demographic weight of the new union. This option will lead to an impasse every time the two countries have different points of view.

To counter the proposal that Quebec should accept a minority status in the institution that would manage monetary policy, Bourassa replied:

> The Parti Québécois cannot seriously accept such a constraining situation, which would not only doom Quebec to a minority status, but (what a paradox) to an institutionalized servitude in a key sector of economic activity.

When he could find no more bones to pick with the government's White Paper, he invented some. He even maintained—and Europe proved him right, so who could reproach him?—that it is impossible to separate fiscal policy from monetary policy:

> If one admits that a single authority must possess the tool of monetary policy and fiscal powers, one must also admit that this authority can only be answerable to the people's elected representatives . . . *No taxation without representation!*

This is precisely what had occurred to the Europeans who, by happy coincidence, had decided in June 1979, six months before the launch of the referendum campaign, to elect members to a European parliament by universal suffrage. Of course, this parliament had no real power. In fact, it was the European Council, the equivalent of the First Ministers' Conference, that made all the important decisions. But what interested Bourassa was the direction that Europe was taking at the end of the 1970s, and the way it showed that the sovereignist thesis was going against a great universal current.

Thus, from 1980 on, Bourassa heaped derision on the concept of a union of two entities, and eventually adopted Jean Chrétien's traditional argument that among ten it is enough to reach a general consensus, whereas between two the only options are unanimity or divorce.

As Bourassa's referendum speech shows, the level of debate he maintained was far more elevated than that of most of his colleagues in the "No" camp. He stood in sharp contrast—perhaps this is why he attracted so little attention—to the overblown protestations of groups such as the "Yvettes" (homemakers who supported federalism in the name of traditional family values). Nor did his comments have much in common with Marc Lalonde's thinly veiled but closely calculated threats, as when he announced that Quebec would have a $16 billion energy deficit, or Monique Bégin's alarmist statements on pensions. The "No" camp was typified by statements of the sort heard by René Lévesque while visiting a senior citizens' home: "Be careful, if the separatists win, we'll never see oranges in Quebec again."

The PQ took Bourassa's lecture notes seriously enough to have them reviewed by an old European ally, Michel Rocard, an influential member of the French Socialist party, and a future prime minister of France under François Mitterand. Claude Morin called Rocard's reply "an extremely useful analysis. Rocard contradicted some of Bourassa's oversimplifications, where he had either misunderstood Europe's evolution, or simply decided to translate its meaning in his own way."[17]

Rocard's critique subsequently found its way into the hands of *La Presse* in the midst of the referendum debate, and it elicited cries of "foreign interference" from a scandalized "No" camp. Morin suspected Bourassa himself of being the author of the leak, which is not impossible: the university professor in him could well appreciate debates about ideas, but that made him no less a partisan politician.

In 1990, Bourassa still held to the ideas contained in his speech. While negotiating the composition of the Bélanger-Campeau Commission with Jacques Parizeau, he spoke once again of the possibility of translating the European community model into Canadian terms.

> There are things which are interesting, and which I've studied: the whole question of the links between economic integration and political integration. In Europe they are talking about a common currency, common social security, common defence, and a common foreign policy. These people, who are our ancestors, the French, the British, the Germans, the Italians, these people are deciding to put more and more in common, under a common political structure. I look at that and it seems inevitable to me that it all starts with a relatively integrated political base.[18]

The "superstructure" administration evoked by Bourassa was to be elected by universal suffrage, just like the EEC's Strasbourg parliament. Observers even began wondering if Bourassa's interest indicated that he was taking a sovereignist turn. He had already let Claude Morin know in 1979 that he would not necessarily respond negatively to the Parti Québécois question if he found their proposition to his liking. In March 1979, he had even told one of his students at Laval University, Jacques Noël, how he would have worded the question:

> Do you wish to replace the existing constitutional order by two sovereign states associated in an economic union, a union which would be responsible to a parliament elected by universal suffrage?[19]

One begins to understand why Claude Ryan had advised Bourassa to lie low for ten years. If Claude Morin and his Parti Québécois colleagues had stumbled on that question, the "No" camp might have been in for a few awkward moments.

Thus, it wasn't so much the question itself that interested Bourassa. The politician in him was more interested in the number of votes he would get. He had his "Gaullian" side after all. As he said later,

> The mistake was to hold a referendum that they weren't sure of winning. In terms of political strategy, when you hold a referendum on the future of a people, you do it in such a way that you can win.[20]

That should have been obvious. Bourassa would not have held a referendum that guaranteed him anything less than a 75 percent "Yes" vote. "With that you can make some real progress," he said. This ambition he shared with René Lévesque, who also expected to win a clear majority among French-speaking Quebeckers, "something like 75 percent."[21]

On May 20, 1980, the "No" carried the day with 59.6 percent of the votes cast, while the "Yes" side came away with 40.4 percent. The vote was going to set Quebec back by 113 years.

The day after the referendum, Pierre Trudeau dispatched Jean Chrétien to sound out the provinces on a constitutional plan of Trudeau's own devising. Three weeks later, the heads of government would find themselves at the prime minister's official residence in Ottawa.

The great federal helmsman now knew which way to turn the rudder; he had decided on his navigational course in 1967, and was taking no detours. Ottawa moved quickly to separate the claims of the provinces—a "shopping list" to which the Quebec government was forever adding items—from the aspirations of the citizenry—the "people's package"—which evidently included the federal Charter of Rights and Freedoms and the Victoria amending formula.

Meanwhile, with a provincial election looming in Quebec, Robert Bourassa was anxious to get involved in the debate. "After all, I'd won my stripes back during the referendum campaign."[22] But once more, Claude Ryan slammed the door in his face. "I'd rather lose without you than win with you," he declared.[23] Though at the time he didn't know how right he was.

The story of the patriation exercise, right up to the night of November 4 to 5, 1981, would end unhappily for Quebec.[24] In seeking to match wits with Trudeau, René Lévesque and his ministers would traffic with the "enemy," Saskatchewan and Manitoba in particular, who would drop them at the first opportunity.

The cabinet secretary for federal-provincial relations, Michael Kirby (today a senator, the federal Liberal party's official pollster, and an organizer for Jean Chrétien), clearly articulated, the day after the referendum, the dilemma in which the Lévesque government found itself: the Parti Québécois had to think about preparing for the next election while remaining loyal to its sovereignist ideal; it also had to prove it could be a good negotiator, particularly in the face of a federal authority that was more determined than ever. The cynicism of Kirby's memorandum, which outlined various constitutional options and strategies for the benefit of the federal ministers, so shocked a senior bureaucrat in the External Affairs Department that he had a copy dropped off in Claude Morin's mailbox. The impact of such a leak during a constitutional conference in September 1980 assured its failure, and the Lévesque government felt more justified than ever in resisting such a strategy.

Pierre Trudeau then tried to push through his patriation project, supported by only the governments of Ontario and New Brunswick. The other provinces, including Quebec, responded with a legal guerrilla campaign which they risked losing. As René Lévesque remarked, "The Supreme Court, like the tower of Pisa, always leans in the same direction."

On the political level, Quebec, being a good negotiator—as Kirby had foreseen—along with Saskatchewan, constituted the nucleus of a group of eight dissidents. "The Gang of Eight," as they were called in Ottawa, were prepared to talk about constitutional reform, but on their own terms.

On April 16, 1981 (it was undoubtedly no coincidence that the Lévesque government waited until the day after its re-election to sign and make public the accord between "the eight"), the Quebec government went back to its position in 1964, before Daniel Johnson sounded the alarm. The agreement stipulated that the provinces would abandon their court fight and that they would commit themselves to a program of constitutional reform for the next three years, and proposed a new amending formula that the Western provinces, most notably Alberta, had been dreaming of for a long time. The official communiqué announced:

> Most of the constitutional modifications would require the approval of the legislative assemblies of two-thirds (seven) of the provinces representing at least 50 percent of the population of the ten provinces. This formula confers judicial equality on all provinces.

The only progress, in relation to the Fulton-Favreau formula (which Lévesque himself had defended while in the Lesage government), was the promise of "satisfactory compensation" if one province opted out of an amendment proposed by two-thirds of the provinces.

At the time, Bourassa was living in Los Angeles, sharing with his students at the University of Southern California his reflections on "the needs of a parliament elected by direct universal suffrage in an advanced system of economic integration."

"I didn't say too much, because I was somewhat retired from politics," he says. "But I was flabbergasted when I saw the Parti Québécois accept this 7/50 formula, which put Quebec in a very vulnerable position."[25]

Actually, Quebec was already vulnerable. The Supreme Court ordered Pierre Trudeau back to the negotiating table with the provinces, stating that the support of only two provinces was insufficient to patriate the Constitution. But at the same time it did not insist on unanimity. Implicit in the decision was the understanding that the approval of Quebec—which had always believed it possessed a right of veto, readily invoked by Bourassa in 1971—was no longer indispensable.

On the other hand, having ratified the principle of the "judicial equality of the provinces," Quebec could hardly protest a patriation that had obtained the assent of "two-thirds (seven) of the provinces representing at least 50 percent of the population of the ten provinces," as the communiqué had said.

It was not so much the fact of having gambled with its veto right that was dangerous for the Quebec government as the fact that it had signed an interprovincial agreement in which Quebec was recognized as a province "like the others." René Lévesque was wasting his time claiming, as he did in a letter to Pierre Trudeau dated November 25, 1981, that his government had never really renounced its veto right.

We all know the rest . . .

The amending formula adopted by Quebec and its allies in the Gang of Eight on April 16, 1981, subsequently had its "opting-out" clause amputated, having been denounced by Trudeau as "a bonus for separation." The accord reached on November 5 finally gave Trudeau the famous Canadian Charter of Rights and Freedoms he had been dreaming of since 1967. The only compromise he would accept was a "notwithstanding" clause, which allowed governments to override the Charter of Rights and "whose malignancy," he later said, "would finally become apparent at the end of December 1988, when Premier Bourassa would invoke it to validate Bill 178 [Quebec's sign law forbidding outside English commercial signs]."[26] Finally, the 1981 accord made no provision for further negotiations on the division of powers, an objective pursued by every Quebec government since 1967. On the other hand, the native peoples were promised three constitutional conferences on the issues that interested them.

For Quebec: nothing! Not even a consolation prize for Claude Ryan, leader of the "No" camp in May 1980, that glorious episode everyone seemed to have already forgotten; all anyone—especially those in English Canada—remembered was the fact that he had supported the election of the Parti Québécois in 1976.

The year 1981 thus ended in a disaster from which the Lévesque government never recovered. It could no longer even use the "good negotiator" argument to save its skin. And, as Pierre Trudeau had predicted, the populace hadn't exactly taken to the streets with pitchforks over his new constitution.

While René Lévesque was flying the Quebec flags at half mast, the professors at the University of Montreal went out on strike.

"But over a salary matter," scoffed Bourassa. The educated classes, intellectually drained by the referendum debate no doubt, raised little protest. "The sky hasn't fallen on us, far from it," Gilles Rémillard, then teaching constitutional law at Laval, told *L'Actualité*.[27] Rémillard, whom Bourassa would appoint a few years later as his constitutional point man and his chief Meech Lake Accord negotiator, saw at the time "the possibility of a special status" in the 1981 constitution. "Ottawa should call a constitutional conference within a year," he added. "Certainly the sharing of legislative powers and the reform of federal institutions will be on the agenda."

Bourassa, however, never hid the fears that the 1981 patriation inspired in him. He was particularly concerned that the Charter of Rights and Freedoms, which encompassed all the laws of the National Assembly, would act as a straitjacket. At least Saskatchewan's Allan Blakeney had had the good sense to insist that certain of the charter's articles be subject to a notwithstanding clause. To avoid having the courts interpret terms like "within reasonable limits" or "within the framework of a free and democratic society," which were vague to begin with, Saskatchewan and later the four Western governments claimed the explicit right to suspend some of the charter's civil liberties and judicial guarantees. Even so, no doubts were cast on the intentions of the provincial premiers who pushed so hard for the notwithstanding clause. After all, they were seeking to protect social democracy. As Trudeau later said:

> For Blakeney, the insertion of the clause was necessary to protect certain union rights, acquired through long hard struggle, from being declared unconstitutional by the courts. Others feared, for example, that the charter's freedom of expression guarantees would render the laws against child pornography unconstitutional.[28]

A lot has been made of the 1981 "notwithstanding" clause, even though it had been part of the Canadian tradition for a quarter century. Had not John Diefenbaker inserted it into his Canadian declaration of rights in 1960? And didn't Pierre Trudeau's government invoke it to justify his indefinite application of the War Measures Act in 1970?

All the premiers who had had similar charters adopted—Peter Lougheed in 1972 and Robert Bourassa in 1975—had furnished them with a notwithstanding clause. It seemed like such a normal thing to do that even Pierre Trudeau did not protest too much in 1981. Indeed, at the time, he said:

> I have to say frankly that I'm not really afraid of the notwithstanding clause. Like anything, it can be abused. But you only have to look back to the declaration of rights adopted by Diefenbaker in 1960: it had a notwithstanding clause that didn't cause any great scandal.[29]

One can understand that after eleven years the prime minister might have forgotten Quebec's reaction to his invocation of the War Measures Act. But it is surprising to note the contrast between the serenity of Trudeau's tone in 1981 and the hatred he showed in his 1990 memoirs.

> I have to say right away that to my way of thinking this clause stands in flagrant contradiction to the essence and existence of the Charter . . . I accepted this clause with doom in my heart, exhorting everyone who would listen to put pressure on the provinces so that we could rid ourselves of it in future negotiations.[30]

What happened between November 1981 and March of 1990 to make him change his tune? The insufferable Robert Bourassa had rammed through a law that allowed only French on exterior commercial signs in Quebec, while allowing signs in other languages inside the same business's premises. What a "malignant" law! What tyranny! Some West End Montrealers in quest of a carton of milk might wind up in a shoe store . . .

Bourassa finally got used to the idea of living with the federal Charter of Rights. After he was returned to power, he discontinued the PQ practice, established immediately after the proclamation of the charter in 1982, of systematically invoking the notwithstanding clause for every piece of provincial government legislation. Neither Pierre Trudeau, nor English Canada had raised a stink about the PQ practice, which tends to confirm that they are harder on "federal-ists" than "sovereignists."

Bourassa was worried, and with good reason, about the "Cana-dian" amending formula. The Charter of Rights and Freedoms placed a constraint on Quebec for as long as it remained part of Canada. But what about the amending formula: would it prevent Quebec from leaving the federation, other than by a political show of force? As Bourassa said:

> Suppose there were a referendum with a positive result. The government could, in theory, accept it, and ask the British government to pass a law as a result of that referendum. But if the constitution is patriated, with its new amending formula, it would be necessary to have the approval of a number of other provinces, because it represents a radical constitutional change. If one of these provinces were to oppose the accept-ance of the referendum verdict, it would mean that the federal government would be constitutionally obliged to take all means at its disposal to preserve the country's territorial integ-rity.[31]

After threatening the PQ government with cutting the gas and oil pipelines from Alberta, would the armed forces then be deployed throughout the province to protect the bridges, the Seaway, the airports, the train stations, federal office buildings, and federally chartered banks—in short, everything that came under Ottawa's jurisdiction?

"This time we'll go underground," said Lucien Bouchard in all seriousness.[32]

It wasn't surprising to hear Bourassa use such language about a referendum. He quoted, if not the letter, at least the spirit of a memorandum drafted by Senator Maurice Lamontagne for the federal cabinet.[33] A copy had come into Bourassa's hands in March 1971, three months before he travelled to Victoria. According to the old constitution, it was up to the British parliament to accept the result of a referendum approving the separation of a province. All that was required was a simple recommendation from the Canadian parliament. Ottawa didn't even have to consult the other provinces. Because, explained Lamontagne, "the procedure for leaving Confederation should logically be the same as the procedure for entering." Not all that long ago (in 1949, in fact), Ottawa and London approved Newfoundland's entry into Confederation without consulting the other provinces.

In 1971, Maurice Lamontagne affirmed that "the constitutional framework makes Quebec's separation difficult, but legally possible." Unfortunately—and this was the object of his memorandum—the amending formula proposed in Victoria (the 1981 formula would have the same effect) removed the federal government's prerogative. As Lamontagne said:

> Separation shall require not only the approval of parliament, but also of at least six other provincial legislatures. This new [amending] formula contains a time bomb that will inevitably explode if one day a majority of Quebec voters declare themselves in favour of independence. The federal government would be under the constitutional obligation to fight it by all available means.

One might ask, in retrospect, if it would have been possible for Quebec to throw off the double straitjacket of the federal Charter of Rights and Freedoms and the 1981 amending formula. Robert Bourassa thinks not:

> Never in the federal government's history has it made such a gesture to reduce the powers of a province without its consent. The 1981 patriation constitutes the first example of an amendment that imposes a reduction of powers on a province without its consent . . . And Ottawa couldn't even resort to the pretext that it was dealing with a separatist government: Mr. Ryan didn't go to the party in Ottawa either.[34]

One wonders whether, if Robert Bourassa had been in the National Assembly in 1981, he would have got involved in the debate. What would have happened if the veteran of Victoria, the apostle of "profitable federalism," had protested publicly? To a certain point, his silence made him an accomplice to Ottawa's power play. And that satisfied everyone, Trudeau as much as Ryan.

But the federal Liberals' opposition to his comeback, as well as Claude Ryan's hostility, finally worked in Bourassa's favour: no longer could it be said that he was Trudeau's puppet. On the contrary, his rehabilitation in the ranks of his party membership was, in a way, the warning shot that heralded the barrage that would sweep away John Turner's candidates in the federal election two years later. When Claude Ryan resigned as leader on August 10, 1982, abandoned by the party's grass roots and detested by its organizers, whom he had generally treated like dirt, he did not even have enough clout to influence the choice of his succession, much less to crown his heir.

By then, a wind of panic had begun to blow through the federal capital. Bourassa was still feared in Ottawa, so much so that he was even offered a federal job in order to keep him from making a comeback on the provincial scene. "Marc Lalonde called me," confirmed Bourassa. "He told me, 'Listen, if you're interested in an appointment, we can talk.' I appreciated the gesture, but I declined."[35]

When they found they couldn't buy him, the federal Liberals tried to neutralize him. They considered parachuting someone in from Ottawa, but they knew that might result in a crash landing in hostile territory. "After what happened in 1981 ... " they were repeatedly told in a threatening tone. Ottawa therefore pinned all its hopes on Raymond Garneau, who was judged to be the only contender capable of beating Bourassa. Pierre Trudeau even went to the trouble of inviting the former finance minister and his wife to Sussex Drive in an attempt to convince him to run against his former boss. "I found Mr. Trudeau's zeal, to the point of summoning a candidate and his wife, somewhat unusual," Bourassa would say later. "I concluded they were really determined to block me."[36]

So what were the federal Liberals afraid of? Bourassa later speculated:

> They knew my hands were totally free, that I didn't owe them a thing. They knew very well that there could be a Meech Lake Accord. In fact, they knew there would be a price to pay for

Quebec's adherence to their 1981 constitution. It was a price they didn't like.[37]

When Bourassa was finally elected to the leadership of the Liberal party on October 15, 1983, Pierre Bourgault spoke for many when he deplored Bourassa's return as an example of Quebec's inability to renew its political establishment: "Trudeau, Lévesque, Bourassa: it's been going on for thirteen years."

Less than a year later, the shakeup Bourgault had been so hoping for finally happened. Brian Mulroney replaced Pierre Trudeau; then Robert Bourassa took René Lévesque's place. The interregnum of John Turner's prime ministership in Ottawa and Pierre-Marc Johnson's stint as premier in Quebec, lasted only a brief time. The time it took to turn a page.

When Bourassa slipped back into his political harness, he found a Quebec that was shut in with a double lock on the door. But he had a hankering for revenge. As he later said,

Be it in one year, in three years, or in fifteen years, Quebec could not placidly accept having its negotiating strength nullified, wasted, set aside, without reacting.[38]

CHAPTER SIX

The Marriage of Convenience

*What I wanted was a constitutional peace [the
Meech Lake Accord] that would allow us to reach the
year 2000, perhaps, in a climate of relative stability.*
                                    Robert Bourassa

Robert Bourassa had a lot on his plate: he had to finish his "project of the century," the second phase of James Bay construction; he hoped to use the free trade agreement with the United States as a springboard to launch Quebec's "rising guard" of businessmen into worldwide conquests; he wanted to restore order to the province's finances; and above all, he intended to establish linguistic and constitutional peace, without which there could be no political stability in Quebec.

But the constitutional train had left the station on June 11, 1983, when Brian Mulroney had been elected leader of the Progressive Conservative party of Canada. He wanted Quebec to sign the 1982 Canada Bill "with pride and dignity." Convinced that his province was not dealing from a position of strength, Bourassa decided to reduce his demands to a minimum. Even so, they were still too much for English Canada which, in a few hours, would give birth to a stillborn constitutional accord . . .

Bourassa II, as he was now being called, was in 1985 still only fifty-two years old. At that age René Lévesque had not even become a member of the National Assembly, whereas Bourassa had already headed a government for close to seven years. His years in the desert, the slow reconquest of power, and the second takeover of his own party, had matured him more than aged him; he was still the same person, though perhaps a bit more pragmatic. A few years later he remarked:

> You get elected, you're surrounded, flattered, and sought after. You get defeated, and it's like you've died. I had the chance to know power, to lose it, and to take it back again, and that gave me a little lesson in philosophy . . . I didn't turn into a misanthrope but I learned that there is a lot of calculation in politics, a lot of opportunism. I don't harbour any grudges against anyone. I don't know, but all things considered, you sleep better if you don't carry grudges.[1]

No grudges, but a touch of cynicism all the same. When he named Claude Ryan to the prestigious but sensitive education portfolio, his friends protested. "If he succeeds," he reassured them, "my government will benefit. If he fails, I'll be rid of him, but people will say I tried all the same."[2]

In English Canada, Bourassa's election was greeted with sighs of relief. "Separatism may not be dead, but it has been banned from the province for a while," concluded the *Vancouver Sun*. Ontario was the first to salute the resurrection of the man they were already calling the "Lazarus of Quebec politics." Ontario Premier David Peterson was already rubbing his hands: "Geography has made us neighbours, economics has made us partners, and history has made us friends." On December 6, he was in Montreal for a tête-à-tête with Bourassa; they discussed the sale of electricity and rights of way for Hydro-Quebec lines across Ontario.

Everyone hoped that the province would finally revert to the golden age of business as usual. Anglo-Quebeckers, the political refugees from Bill 22, took to Highway 401, in the opposite direction this time. On the billboard welcoming visitors at the Ontario-Quebec border, someone had scrawled in by hand: "Under new management!"

The new Bourassa didn't owe anything to anyone. Having taken the full blame for the defeat of 1976, he alone patiently undertook his rehabilitation. His self-confidence was unshakable. When the federal Liberals twisted Raymond Garneau's arm in an effort to get him to run against Bourassa, Bourassa told his former finance minister:

> Prove to me that I'm hurting the party. I like politics, I'm free, I have experience, I've been premier for seven years, and I can be premier again. Don't ask me to back off. If you can prove that you would be more useful to the party than me, I won't stay around another five minutes.[3]

In the end it was Raymond Garneau who backed off. And the manoeuvring by Pierre Trudeau and Marc Lalonde wound up being of indirect help to Bourassa's comeback. "Nobody can say he's a puppet any more," admitted Pierre Bourgault. "The man has achieved his own independence."[4]

Miraculously restored to power, the uncontested master of his party, the premier was going to govern alone, for better or for worse. He knew that after nine years of constitutional battles, Quebeckers wanted to hear about the economy instead. "People were saying, 'With Bourassa we were well off, the economy was working, we had jobs,'" said Bourassa a few years later.[5]

In fact, his comeback occurred at just the right time. The economy was beginning a growth cycle that would last for several years. The federal government had recently begun free trade negotiations with the United States. "If we lose this opportunity, we'll be an underdeveloped nation by the end of the century," Bourassa told himself.[6]

Bourassa promised to run a businesslike administration with himself in the role of chief executive, using the latest in modern management methods. His plan called for technological innovation, trimming the fat from the bureaucracy, the privatization of lame-duck crown corporations, fiscal reform, and the negotiation of a pan-Canadian common market for farm products, similar to the European arrangement. Whereas before he had left himself open to charges that his concept of public morality was somewhat elastic, he now moved swiftly to rid himself of ministers who blotted their copybooks with dubious behaviour. At the first hint that his solicitor-general, Gérard Latulippe, was involved in a conflict of interest in 1987, Bourassa sent him packing.

Having suspected since 1983 that Pierre Trudeau would not be in the political arena for much longer, Bourassa had allowed himself to believe that constitutional peace wasn't far around the corner. "Between now and 1986 I'll come to a constitutional agreement with Ottawa, and in an atmosphere of calm," he assured his troops the day after his return as party leader.

And since his anglophone electorate still associated him with the affront of Bill 22, he even allowed himself to go so far as to promise a relaxation of its Péquiste successor, Bill 101. "We have to return to common sense," he said. "On signs, French could be obligatory and all other languages optional."

He was ready. He knew what he wanted. It was generally expected that Bourassa's first "hundred days" would produce an avalanche of important decisions. Such predictions, however, did not take into account Bourassa's chronic tendency to vacillate once he was ensconced in power, particularly now that he was running a one-man show. How could a man so steadfast in the face of real adversity show himself to be so indecisive in power? It remains a mystery even to his closest friends.

On December 2, 1985, Bourassa had to take a back seat at his own political comeback. After winning 80 percent of the seats in the National Assembly, he was ready to move back into his bunker on Grande Allée to plan his takeover of the government on December 12. But since he had been beaten in his home riding of Bertrand on Montreal's South Shore, where he had won a by-election earlier that year, Bourassa had to sit in the visitors' gallery to listen to his first throne speech. He was able to take his seat in the Assembly only after he had won another by-election on January 20, 1986, this time in St. Laurent, a riding in dangerous proximity to the anglo West Island, which had rejected his party's language policy in 1976.

His personal defeat on election day in one of suburban Montreal's nationalist bastions was a cruel reminder that not all Quebeckers were prepared to trust him. During the campaign leading up to the January 20, 1986, by-election, Bourassa met with a group of influential businessmen to discuss his government's priorities. His colleagues were all part of the new generation of Québécois entrepreneurs and had come of age during the febrile climate of the great language battles—over the Union Nationale's Bill 63, the drive to make McGill a French-language institution, and Bourassa's own Bill 22. "Never mind the English," one of them told him. "All that counts is social peace."[7]

Bourassa's fears of unleashing another battle over language was exacerbated by the polls that showed a hardening of nationalist attitudes. While René Lévesque and his team were still in power, francophone Quebeckers had indicated a willingness to loosen the strictures of Bill 101. But without Lévesque's reassuring presence, their generosity towards the English-speaking minority evaporated. Now that Bourassa was back in power, they became more vigilant than ever.

Brian Mulroney suggested to Bourassa that he could settle the signs question and reassure francophones with a few spectacular programs aimed at promoting the use of French in areas like science and technology. The first summit meeting of French-speaking countries to be held in Paris that year would provide the perfect occasion to announce them. But the Supreme Court gave Bourassa the excuse he needed to put off making a decision. Bourassa II had barely begun his fresh mandate, and already he had slid a time bomb under his own premier's chair.

Once again, Bourassa, the straight-A student, the fiscal expert, the specialist in great economic unions, the man with whom Quebeckers believed that they were economically well off, who had promised to reach a "calm" accommodation with Ottawa "before 1986," allowed himself to be dragged back into the treacherously shifting sands of the constitutional question and the language issue.

During a discreet lunch in a St. Denis Street restaurant in Montreal, Trudeau advised him against reopening the constitutional "can of worms": "If you don't want any trouble, Robert, concentrate on the economy."[8] Even Lucien Bouchard, who had been part of the PQ government legal team that fought the 1981 patriation of the constitution before the Supreme Court, advised him not to be in too much of a hurry. Shortly before he left to take up his post as Canadian ambassador to Paris at the end of the summer of 1985,

Bouchard unburdened himself in an interview with *Le Devoir* publisher Jean-Louis Roy, who would join him in Paris in 1986 as Quebec's delegate-general:

> The absence of [Quebec's] signature at the bottom of the constitution is an explosive element. Maybe that's why there should be no rush [to resume constitutional negotiations]. With time, the signature will grow in weight and importance, so perhaps it shouldn't be given too quickly. It might be best to let them want it for a while. There is still a glowing log, a live ember under the ashes.[9]

The office of the new prime minister was distinctly unhappy with this statement, and the new ambassador told to abstain from any public declarations about Canada's internal affairs.[10] Having already set in motion the machinery that would result in the Meech Lake Accord, Brian Mulroney was particularly anxious that no one should do anything to knock it off course.

When he was elected federal Conservative leader on June 11, 1983, after ten hours of suspense and four interminable ballots, Brian Mulroney's mandate had been very clear: to "deliver Quebec," by ending the Liberals' quasi-monopoly on the province (in the 1980 election they had won seventy-four of the province's seventy-five federal seats). Everyone expected that Pierre Trudeau would soon leave politics, and that his replacement, according to the tradition of alternation, would be an English Canadian.

The Conservatives were sure they had finally hit on the winning combination. But for many Quebeckers, Brian Mulroney wasn't necessarily the answer to their prayers. In 1981 he had lined up with Pierre Trudeau and supported the patriation of the constitution. During the leadership campaign he had openly criticized Joe Clark's overtures to Quebec. "Before I ask Canada to give René Lévesque a plugged nickel," he declared during a televised debate in Toronto, "I'm going to ask him what he's prepared to do for Canada."

When Trudeau's successor, then Prime Minister John Turner, called the federal election in 1984, there was panic at Conservative headquarters: the party had no French-language platform. At the time, Lucien Bouchard was in Chicoutimi nursing his black mood.

He had known Brian Mulroney since they studied law together at Laval University, and had worked for "the little guy from Baie Comeau" during his first run at the Tory leadership in 1976. After the 1980 referendum, relations between the two became more distant. Bouchard appeared to be suffering from post-referendum depression, whereas Mulroney had espoused Pierre Trudeau's ideas so enthusiastically that Trudeau had offered him a place in his cabinet. "We weren't on the same wavelength, but since we didn't want to quarrel, we just talked to each other a lot less, that's all," recalled Bouchard.[11]

The 1984 election campaign brought things to a head and facilitated a reconciliation between the two. The Conservatives' chief organizer in Quebec, Bernard Roy—another pal from Laval law school days—recruited Bouchard for the duration of the campaign. Because his previous Péquiste affiliations made some of the senior Quebec Tories, most notably Jean Bazin, distinctly nervous, Bouchard was discreetly installed in a hotel suite, and worked out of a small office reserved for the leader of the Opposition on Wellington Street in Ottawa.

To help him prepare a Conservative electoral platform, Marcel Masse gave Bouchard a pile of working papers prepared by Quebec members of the party in recent years. Among them Bouchard found the report of an internal party committee on the constitution prepared by Senator Arthur Tremblay at Joe Clark's request. "I found it to be quite good," recalled Bouchard. (It is worth remembering that Arthur Tremblay had been Paul Gérin-Lajoie's deputy minister in the Quebec education department during the 1960s, as well as under Robert Bourassa during the 1970s. Thus the Quebec connection finally reached into the office of the prime minister of Canada. Robert Bourassa could no longer escape his destiny.)

Near the middle of the federal election campaign, Brian Mulroney was once again scheduled to visit his home riding of Manicouagan, and Bernard Roy asked Bouchard to prepare a speech on the economy for the occasion. "I don't think it's terribly bright to go and make a speech on the economy in Sept-Îles," grumbled Bouchard, who had never been truly at ease with the subject in the first place. Furthermore, the Conservative party's ideas on the economy did not readily lend themselves to grand rhetorical flourishes. When Bouchard sought assistance from several well-known Montreal economists, none wanted to work for the Conservatives. Discouraged, he went back to Senator Tremblay's paper on the constitution.

"What would you think if I did a speech on the constitution?" he asked Mulroney. "I think it would be a good thing to do in Sept-Îles." The suggestion raised eyebrows in the senior Tory ranks, for polls had showed that Canadians didn't want to hear another word about the constitution. Now that Trudeau was gone, they wanted to relax a little.

Meanwhile, Raymond Garneau had returned to the Quebec political scene with a bang. Even though Jean Chrétien was still around—and deputy prime minister at that—Garneau passed himself off as John Turner's Quebec lieutenant, and promised nothing less than to "go to Ottawa and regain Quebec's right of veto."[12] "Garneau's arrival on the scene made a lot of people nervous in Ottawa, and that helped me,"[13] recalled Bouchard.

Mulroney finally decided to deal with the issue of national reconciliation in Sept-Îles on August 6, a month before the vote. In preparation, Bouchard shut himself up in his Chicoutimi law office with a copy of the Tremblay committee's report. He took advantage of a visit by Mulroney to nearby Roberval to show him a draft of the speech; the Conservative leader found it to his liking, as he liked all of Bouchard's speeches.

Although he wrote well in English, Mulroney was ill at ease writing in French. Lucien Bouchard rectified this by giving his speech a passionate style that brought out the best of Mulroney's Québécois side.

"The speech made a lot of people nervous in Ottawa, says Bouchard. "They worked on it. They played with it, and diluted it somewhat. But the idea of redress was there. And it stayed." Thus it was in the municipal arena in Sept-Îles that the future prime minister would make an offer to the government of Quebec to draw up a list of amendments to the 1982 constitution that would bring Quebec into its fold:

If you elect our Quebec candidates and give me a majority in Parliament in Ottawa, we will give Quebec back its rightful

place in Confederation. We will amend the constitution in
such a way that Quebec can sign—with pride and dignity—the
document it rejected in 1982.

It should be noted that he said "Quebec," and not "René Lévesque." Mulroney was enough of a realist to understand that English
Canada did not want to return to the constitutional bargaining table
with the Parti Québécois government.

As for Robert Bourassa, he came through with such a show of
benevolent neutrality that people spoke openly of a "rainbow coalition" dominated by the red of the provincial Liberals. Raymond
Garneau's overtures to Quebec made no difference. Trudeau might
be gone, but Quebeckers still had a score to settle with the Liberal
Party of Canada, and in particular the two who had crowded in close
to the Queen for the official photograph on April 17, 1982, and
whose signatures appeared on the bottom of the constitutional
document: André Ouellet and Jean Chrétien. When Garneau
promised to go to the wall for Quebec's veto right, Gil Rémillard,
speaking for many of Quebec's intellectuals, said in a scathing tone:
"A waste of time and energy."

The Conservatives' arrival in power increased the likelihood of
national reconciliation. Although it had no interest in reopening
constitutional negotiations with René Lévesque, the new Conservative government was nevertheless anxious to prove that something
had changed in Ottawa. Within a few months, therefore, Mulroney
and Lévesque settled a dispute that had been dragging on for a
quarter of a century over Quebec's participation in a summit of
French-speaking countries. This idea of a commonwealth of francophone countries had been tossed around in several African countries, Léopold Senghor's Senegal in particular, since the end of the
1950s. Gaullist France regarded Quebec's participation as essential, but Canada had insisted on a seat for itself alone. In March
1970, in Niamey, Nigeria, Quebec slipped a foot in the door of the
new international agency for technical and cultural cooperation
between francophone countries. As a "participating" member,
Quebec had been granted a sort of stool next to Canada's full
member's chair.

But the summit of francophone countries, like that of the British

Commonwealth, required the participation of heads of sovereign countries, who dealt exclusively with international issues. For sixteen years, Trudeau had resisted pressure from a succession of French presidents; in less than nine months, René Lévesque and Brian Mulroney settled the details of Quebec's participation in the first francophone summit in Paris. The message to the federal bureaucracy and the Ottawa diplomatic corps couldn't have been clearer. The agreement convinced the political establishment that Brian Mulroney was serious. During a meeting with René Lévesque on June 25, 1985, Mulroney opened the constitutional dossier and announced that in the fall the two governments would begin formal discussions "aimed at guaranteeing Quebec's adherence to the 1982 constitution." Much as Robert Bourassa might have wanted to let "the live ember under the ashes" smoulder for a while, as Bouchard had advised him, he could no longer do so.

A few weeks before he announced his retirement, René Lévesque asked the Parti Québécois to enumerate its "conditions for Quebec's adherence to the Canadian constitution": a somewhat ambitious list, which reiterated in detail the twenty-one demands of 1981, and also, in its general thrust, all the demands Quebec governments had made since 1960. The first condition required that "the existence of a Quebec people be explicitly recognized by the Canadian constitution."

Robert Bourassa was more modest in his demands—he contented himself with five conditions—but he chose his words with greater care. In June 1985, the Quebec Liberal party's political platform demanded "the inclusion in the preamble of the new Constitution of a statement explicitly recognizing Quebec as the homeland of a distinct society and the cornerstone of the francophone element of the Canadian duality."

At the very time that the Liberal party was honing its strategy, Gil Rémillard, Bourassa's future minister of intergovernmental affairs and chief negotiator for the Meech Lake Accord, was putting the final touches on volume two of his study of Canadian federalism. It did not go unnoticed in Ottawa, for Mulroney invited himself to the book launch at the National Press Building.

Rémillard was squarely opposed to the concept of Quebeckers as a "people," a term he felt should be applied to all French Canadians, "linked by socio-political affinities, but without a specific territory or government":

> One can speak of a Quebec nation, in that Quebeckers live on a given territory and have a government. However, the term "nation" can lead to controversy, whereas the term "society," while being correct, would also be more acceptable to the whole of the Canadian community.[14]

"People," "nation," "society." What mattered above all was to find a word that wouldn't raise too many hackles in English Canada. It was a measure of Robert Bourassa's wisdom that he did not hide his preoccupation with appearing modest, while avoiding getting bogged down in semantic questions.

> When I became leader again, I drew up a program that took into account both the referendum defeat and the unilateral patriation. While I couldn't ask for everything in every sphere, I summed up everything that I regarded as essential. But "special status," "associated states," and "distinct society" are concepts that work together in a certain way.[15]

The Liberal party had been playing with the concept of a distinct society for twenty years. Had not Paul Gérin-Lajoie's report in 1967 said, "Quebec can no longer accept the 1867 constitutional framework if it is to remain a distinct society"? But Bourassa, caught between Trudeau and Lévesque, had put the report aside at the time. On January 9, 1980, with the referendum campaign in full swing, the Liberal party's constitutional committee, under Claude Ryan, had formulated the same concept:

> Quebec forms, within the Canadian federation, a distinct society in terms of language, culture, institutions, and lifestyle. There is in Quebec an important anglophone community and numerous ethnic communities, concentrated primarily in the Montreal region. These communities and their institutions are an essential dimension of Quebec life. But in a general manner, Quebec perceives and expresses itself as a society that is

French in language and spirit. Within the Canadian family, Quebec society possesses all the attributes of a distinct national community.[16]

But this "Beige Paper" by Claude Ryan gathered dust on the shelves of the federal justice department, where the minister at the time was Jean Chrétien; Pierre Trudeau did not even bother to give it a quick scan.

Nevertheless, the distinct society concept had won its letters patent even in the federal capital. In 1979, the Task Force on Canadian Unity, headed by Jean-Luc Pépin and John Robarts, expressed its strong conviction that "Quebec is different and should have the necessary powers for the preservation and development of its distinct character within a viable Canada."[17] The commission laid out two alternatives. One would have accorded Quebec special jurisdiction "in matters related to culture, language, immigration, social policy, communications, and certain aspects of international relations." The other, which was "far preferable" to the task force, would have given all provinces the same powers as Quebec to preserve their special culture and heritage, and they would have been free to use them or not as they chose. It was to this second avenue—which, on the whole, didn't attract many admirers—that Bourassa would finally resign himself at Meech Lake on April 30, 1987.

The Royal Commission on Canada's Economic Union and Development Prospects—which Pierre Elliott Trudeau had created and to which he had appointed his spiritual heir, Donald Macdonald, as head—devoted five pages of its voluminous report to "Quebec as a distinct society." In it one can read, among other things:

An unexpected chance has come up to seal a new agreement between Quebec and the rest of Canada. What is required, in terms of principles first of all, is a declaration in the constitutional preamble which could read as follows:

Recognizing the distinct character of Quebec society, the principal but not exclusive homeland of francophones in Canada, and accepting the dual character of the Canadian federation as an essential factor ...

During the 1980 constitutional negotiations, intense discussions on this question nearly resulted in a consensus. We believe that in 1985, such a consensus could be reached fairly quickly on the basis of a text such as the one proposed herein.[18]

Thus, no one was greatly surprised when Robert Bourassa relaunched the idea of recognizing the distinct character of Quebec society. It had, after all, been discussed for twenty years and endorsed by high-level federal commissions. In fact, the question left the Quebec public largely indifferent. For its part, the Parti Québécois interpreted Bourassa's position as a retreat. Only when the distinct-character status was rejected by English Canada did it become an untouchable symbol in Quebec.

What surprised English Canada, and even Pierre Trudeau, though he thought Bourassa "a very poor negotiator," was how few conditions the Quebec premier put forward. Bourassa says:

> I wanted to settle. But I couldn't turn the page without coming to an agreement on something significant. The five conditions were Quebec's traditional demands, whose number and terms had varied over the course of thirty years. We could have tripled them, but we would have had no chance of succeeding. All the same, you have to remember that Quebec was not in a position of strength at the time, not in a position to demand the maximum. It was in a position to demand the minimum, or at least to be reasonable, and to make moderate proposals.[19]

In May 1986, at Bourassa's request, his minister of intergovernmental affairs, Gil Rémillard, attended a symposium at Mont-Gabriel whose theme was, "Quebec and its Partners in Confederation: A Renewed Collaboration." It was a subject guaranteed to elicit yawns of boredom from the general public, which paid very little attention to the conference. Nevertheless, a number of bureaucrats from the federal government and from the English provinces were present and took notes.

English Canada was all the more attentive in that Robert Bourassa's "federalist" government had begun giving assurances that things had changed in Quebec. Two months earlier, Bourassa had officially discontinued the practice of applying the constitutional "notwithstanding" clause to every piece of government legislation and had recognized the primacy of the Canadian Charter of Rights and Freedoms. As Gil Rémillard said:

> After four years of interpretation by our courts, we felt that the charter was, on the whole, a document of which we could be proud as Quebeckers and as Canadians. We wanted the fundamental rights of Quebeckers to be as well protected as those of other Canadians.[20]

Gil Rémillard's tone was by and large conciliatory: "The 1982 Constitution Act applies to Quebec, even though [the province] did not agree with it." The Quebec government thus no longer objected to the fact that Canada had taken over full jurisdiction for its constitution from London. Rémillard went on:

> What we object to is that patriation served as a pretext for a substantial modification of the Canadian Constitution without taking Quebec's historic rights into consideration. Therefore Quebec is hoping to resume constitutional negotiations.

There were, however, certain conditions. The former university professor spiritedly explained how Quebec's five conditions were interdependent and indissociable. The first condition, he said, was the "explicit recognition of Quebec as a distinct society." This was the prerequisite to any resumption of negotiations and any adherence by Quebec to the 1982 constitution.

The second condition was control of immigration:

> From the recognition of Quebec's special status flows the necessity of obtaining real guarantees to protect our culture. This means in particular that Quebec must have complete power to plan its immigration so as to maintain its francophone character by creating a counterweight to, or even reversing, the demographic tendencies which might lead to a diminution of its relative importance in Canada.

The third condition was "a limitation to federal spending powers" so that Quebec could act exclusively in its fields of jurisdiction. Quebec and other provinces had always complained about a spending power that allowed Ottawa to launch new programs, particularly social programs, with no guarantee that it would keep financing them forever. After a certain number of years, the federal government would leave the provinces to foot the bill. This is exactly what was happening at the time under Mulroney's Conservative government.

Fourth, Quebec wanted to recuperate the veto right it claimed to have lost in 1982. It turned out that Quebec had never had such a veto, but the new formula adopted in 1982 made sure that only seven provinces acting together could amend the Constitution.

Finally, since constitutional changes were not always effected through the amending process, but also through ordinary Supreme Court judgments, Quebec demanded "participation in the nomination of the judges."

In the comfortable leather seats of the first-class section of a Boeing 747 flying over the Atlantic between Montreal and Paris, Lucien Bouchard commented on the Mont-Gabriel speech to Jean-Louis Roy: "It's ... far too weak. Bourassa is squandering the small advantage we still have for peanuts, for trifles."[21]

Quebec's new delegate general couldn't wait to report on the conversation to his minister, Gil Rémillard, who relayed the information to Ottawa. From that moment on, it was decided to leave Lucien Bouchard "out of the loop." Along with him, all the most nationalist parliamentarians, like ministers Benoît Bouchard and Monique Vézina, who had voted "Yes" in the May 1980 referendum on sovereignty-association, were cut off from all information about the progress of the negotiations between Quebec and Ottawa. The only ministers who were kept abreast of the operation were Marcel Masse and Jean Charest, whose federalist faith had been left unshaken even by the referendum campaign and the unilateral patriation of 1982.

After his Mont-Gabriel speech, Rémillard embarked on a tour of the English provinces accompanied by a handful of advisers, including Bourassa's right-hand man in the premier's office, Jean-Claude Rivest. While Bourassa was wandering in the desert, Rivest had taken advantage of Raymond Garneau's resignation to move into his Jean Talon seat in the National Assembly for seven years, all the better to see to his master's interests during his absence. Rémillard also took along a discreet and austere professor from the University of Montreal, André Tremblay, and a civil servant named Diane Wilhelmy, perhaps the most ardent federalist in the group, whom the anglos would affectionately nickname "Madame Meech."

As Bourassa prepared for the twenty-seventh annual premier's conference in Edmonton, his envoys reported to him that it would be difficult to limit the discussion to Quebec's claims. Newfoundland's premier, Brian Peckford, wanted to discuss jurisdiction over fisheries along the Atlantic coast. In Ontario, where a number of political advisers inherited from Pierre Trudeau were still influential, David Peterson wanted to re-open the debate over the notwithstanding clause, perhaps by linking it to the recognition of Quebec society's distinct character. Manitoba's New Democratic premier, Howard Pawley, who had just been ordered by the Supreme Court to restore all the rights of his francophone minority, didn't want to hear any more talk about the Constitution. Alberta's Don Getty, who would chair the premier's conference in August, was holding out for Senate reform. Finally, Social Crediter William Vander Zalm of British Columbia insisted, as the Pépin-Robarts report had suggested, that all the conditions Quebec was seeking, notably increased powers over immigration, should be offered to the other provinces as well.

It was a troublesome start, but from the beginning, and for the duration of the Meech Lake saga, Robert Bourassa's reassuring charm would make the difference. Among other things, he enjoyed the prestige that came with being the dean of the conference of premiers; he had attended his first constitutional conference in September 1970. Apart from Richard Hatfield, elected premier of New Brunswick in 1970, who had attended the Victoria conference in 1971, the eight other premiers Bourassa joined in Edmonton on August 11, 1986, were, for the most part, making their first forays into the constitutional arena. They therefore watched Bourassa with great interest. As Grant Devine commented:

Since Mulroney's election, the climate around the table had changed. There were no more of the confrontations we'd known with Trudeau and Lougheed. Brian was the sort to say:

"You mean you scrapped and you fought over this stuff? Can't you just get together, put your partisan stuff aside, and go do good for once?[22]

Around the premiers' table, the password was now: "Let's fix it!" Devine went on:

It was such a contrast between Lévesque and Bourassa! Bourassa seemed like a breath of fresh air compared to the more strident and sort of hard position of René Lévesque. Bourassa was more reasonable. And he presented his views like he had done his homework on what would be the most reasonable way to present his case to a Saskatchewan rancher, or farmer, or oilman. Robert was also very comfortable talking on economics. So are we in the West and that made us more comfortable with him.

The Quebec premier could count on a number of allies in the room: Richard Hatfield, who felt obliged to help out his colleague from the Trudeau years; Don Getty, to whom Bourassa had promised that Quebec's signature on the Constitution would open the door to a series of conferences on Senate reform; and David Peterson, who, on the theme of "Robert, Brian, and me," let on that these old friendships could help reconstitute Confederation's golden triangle: Toronto-Quebec-Ottawa.

The "Edmonton Statement," as some people would pompously refer to the short, two-paragraph item in the conference communiqué signed on August 12, represented at once a victory and a retreat for Quebec. A victory because the provincial premiers started talking about a "Quebec round" of constitutional talks; Bourassa could go back home and give the impression that he had them all in his pocket. But it was also a retreat because the premiers had succeeded in appending other topics (like Senate reform, the fisheries question, and property rights) to Quebec's five conditions, and because they had not specified exactly when—the communiqué concluded with a dangerously vague "et cetera"—these other subjects would be brought up. Four years in advance, the first paragraphs of the Charest Report and its "shopping list" were starting to take shape.

What the communiqué didn't say is that the Western provinces were already balking at giving Quebec a right of veto. "If one is gonna have a veto, we'll all have a veto," declared Grant Devine of Saskatchewan. "Whether in law Quebec has it or not, particularly over the Senate reform, is not what's important. If the right of veto is good for one, it's good for all."[23]

That fall, Gil Rémillard and his small team repeated their tour of the provinces. This time they were followed by a parallel group: the federal government's special envoys. Rémillard's opposite number in Ottawa, Lowell Murray, the minister of federal-provincial relations, was a veteran of constitutional conferences. Named to the Senate by Joe Clark, he had led the fight against the unilateral constitutional patriation in 1980 and 1981. He had even voted against the project, thereby gaining a measure of credibility in Gil Rémillard's eyes.

Also in the federal group were Murray's deputy minister, Norman Spector (a former cabinet secretary for the premier of British Columbia during the 1981 patriation), and the deputy minister of justice, Frank Iacobucci. They, however, would not be the ones to bring Quebec's point of view in line with that of the other provinces. Rather it would be Jean Chrétien's former deputy minister of justice, Roger Tassé, and Senator Arthur Tremblay who would wind up bridging the gap between Mulroney and Trudeau on the one hand, and between Mulroney and Bourassa on the other. In fact, through their contacts with Diane Wilhelmy, it was the efforts of Tassé and Tremblay, more than the many phone calls between Mulroney and Bourassa, or between Bernard Roy and Gil Rémillard, that got Ottawa and Quebec marching to the same drummer and in the same direction.

In November, the premiers met with Mulroney in Vancouver for a conference on the economy. There, for the first time, the head of the federal government could formally add his name to the bottom of the "Edmonton Statement" and officially launch the "Quebec round." But was it really Quebec's turn?

During the course of numerous discussions between Quebec and the other provinces, between Quebec and Ottawa, between the English provinces and the federal government, the list of misunderstandings grew at an alarming rate. For example, as Gil Rémillard had said at Mont-Gabriel a few months earlier, one might think that

Quebec's will to control its own immigration was nothing more than basic common sense. But Ontario understood to what extent this claim clashed with a fundamental element of the Trudeau vision. If Canada's survival depended on assuring French Canadians that they could feel at home in the whole of the country, then English Canadians, in turn, should be able to "circulate" freely and without constraint from one end of the country to the other, including Quebec. Hence the clause in the Canadian Charter of Rights and Freedoms that guaranteed the freedom of circulation and of establishment. Quebec, however, was not content to control merely its proportional share of immigration; it was claiming 5 percent more. Quebec would therefore be assured of choosing and approving 30 percent—close to one-third—of all immigrant and refugee applications. "And what about the others?" asked Ontario's attorney general, Ian Scott. "Would an immigrant who chooses to establish himself first in Toronto have the right to 'circulate' freely and to 'establish' himself in Quebec if he so wishes?" The question embarrassed the Quebec negotiators, and Ontario found unexpected allies in the other provinces.

National reconciliation or no national reconciliation, the leaders of the provincial governments threatened to live up to Pierre Trudeau's characterization of them as a "power-hungry" bunch, each jealous of the slightest gain made by one of their colleagues. For this reason, no doubt, Mulroney discreetly forced their hand: three weeks before their meeting at Meech Lake, he sent them a six-page letter in which he took it for granted that "there is now an agreement in principle on the constitutional recognition of Quebec as a distinct society and the existence of two major linguistic groups in Canada."[24] The letter's generally optimistic tone contrasted with the cautious, sometimes alarmist leaks in the English-Canadian media from his own minister, Lowell Murray, and from the federal bureaucracy. But Mulroney's letter closed with an ambiguous challenge, to which the response would soon be forthcoming.

> The problem now facing us is to find the best compromise between the principle of equality of all the provinces and the needs of Canada and Quebec—the only province with a francophone majority and a distinct legal system protected by the

constitution—in order to preserve the special aspect that Quebec brings to Canada.

When Mulroney greeted his colleagues at Willson House at Meech Lake shortly after noon on April 30, 1987, he immediately imposed his own negotiating style. During Trudeau's time, the first ministers were accompanied by their senior advisers, and the conferences quickly turned into debates among experts around a table strewn with technical documents and legal opinions.

At Meech Lake, Mulroney literally "locked up" his ten colleagues. The only two civil servants in the room with them— Norman Spector and his Alberta counterpart, Oryssia Lennie, a deputy minister who had worked with Peter Lougheed on constitutional affairs ever since the Victoria failure—were there to take notes, not to participate.

Willson House was well suited for the tactical isolation of the government leaders. Mulroney kept them on the second floor, where there was only a large meeting room and a small kitchen to prepare meals and coffee, as well as the booths for the translators. The first ministers' advisers were confined to the ground floor, in a large room that opens out on an immense staircase guarded by RCMP officers. No contact was possible between the premiers and their advisers. And since cellular phones had not yet become the rage they are today—Quebec would equip itself with them in June 1987—the provincial leaders had access to only one telephone line, operated by employees of the Prime Minister's Office. At Meech Lake, the first ministers could not communicate with their advisers until the tea break, after five hours of discussion. (It was during this break, while drinking a cup of coffee after intense negotiations about enshrining the Supreme Court in the Canadian constitution, that Bill Vander Zalm leaned toward one of the two advisers who had accompanied him to Ottawa, to ask: "Just what exactly does 'enshrining' mean, anyway?"[25])

Under these conditions, Robert Bourassa didn't even bother launching a major plea in favour of Quebec's special nature and its historic right to be different. Instead it was Mulroney who did all the work: he negotiated the reform of the Senate, much as he had negotiated, in another life, the overtime allowance factor accorded for legal holidays in a labour contract. Bit by bit, clause by clause, give a little here, take a little there.

The first of Quebec's five conditions to be discussed was the fifth one and the one that normally would have raised the fewest number of questions: the enshrining of the Supreme Court and of its composition, with three Quebec judges. But what was there to discuss, since a good many constitutional experts had maintained that the 1982 Constitution already met Quebec's needs? In effect, two articles of the Canada Bill dealt indirectly with the Supreme Court as we know it today: nine members, of whom three must practise civil law, which means they must be registered with the Quebec bar, which means, in all probability, that they are Quebeckers. But if this is not the case, Gil Rémillard had said at Mont-Gabriel in May 1986, "the federal government remains the sole master of our Supreme Court ... something which is utterly unacceptable." No one had thus far raised any objection to what seemed to constitute a clarification of the situation, rather than an amendment.

But the very fact of bringing up the fundamental characteristics of a federal institution touched a raw nerve with the smaller provinces. For it went without saying that if three judges were to come from Quebec, then three would have to come from Ontario, leaving the other eight provinces to share the remaining three seats. Prince Edward Island and Alberta were particularly insistent that they be guaranteed representation.

Unexpectedly, the discussion turned to the role of the provinces in nominating members of major federal institutions. To cut short a discussion that had been going on for close to three hours, Brian Mulroney guaranteed all provinces the same privileges. Thus, the principle whereby every gain realized by Quebec would be offered to the other provinces was subtly established. The Quebec round had just become the "round of the provinces." And so it was quickly forgotten that this meeting was supposed to be about redressing the unjust treatment that Quebec—and Quebec alone—had suffered during the night of November 4 and the early morning of November 5, 1981.

In their eagerness to put all the provinces on an equal footing, the premiers even failed to realize how ridiculous some of their agreements were. In the field of immigration, for instance, not only Quebec, but all the provinces were assured a proportion of the immigrants accepted into Canada, based on their percentage of the total population plus 5 percent. The upshot was that the ten provinces together were to be given the right to receive up to 150 percent of all immigrants accepted into Canada.

The only one of Quebec's conditions that the other provinces did not claim for themselves was the recognition of their distinct character. Devine explained to Vander Zalm: "What does Quebec want? A clause recognizing its distinct character? Well, frankly, most of the French-speaking people live in Quebec and most of the English-speaking people live outside Quebec. They have a 'distinct' language, culture, legal system. What other word could describe what it is?"

"Oh, well, if that's all that meant, that's fine," Vander Zalm replied.[26]

The only issue that encountered serious stumbling blocks was Senate reform. Don Getty was taking his role as that year's premiers' conference chairman very seriously, and he arrived on the eve of the meeting with a voluminous report that he hoped would be discussed immediately. He was no longer content, as he had been in Edmonton nine months earlier, with a vague commitment to deal with the question in a second round of constitutional negotiations. "We have to establish here and now how we're going to reform the Senate, in what time frame, and, most important, what exactly we intend to change," Don Getty insisted.

Among the English provinces, there was about as much consensus on Senate reform as on the sex of angels. Bourassa, for his part, would have preferred to avoid the question altogether for fear of having to come right out and say that he was against any form of elected Senate with equal representation from the provinces. One thing led to another, the discussion ground on about the Senate, and doubts began to arise about the amending formula. On this point, Bourassa was intractable: the 1981 formula put Quebec at the mercy of a majority of the English provinces. Senate reform could be imposed on Quebec immediately if Ontario were to side with the West.

Brian Peckford had a particular talent for cutting short discussions that had become mired in their own complications: he ventured a proposal that Senate reform be put on the agenda of the annual constitutional conferences henceforth, and that in the meantime, the provinces would have input into Senate nominations, as they did with Supreme Court judges. It was an offer they couldn't refuse. What premier could resist the temptation to get a hand in on the most glorious of all forms of political patronage?

Upstairs at Willson House, everyone was in a hurry to get this thing over with, Robert Bourassa more than the rest: back home in Quebec City, the National Assembly correspondent for Montreal's CTV affiliate, CFCF, had got his hands on a copy of the budget that Finance Minister Gérard D. Lévesque was scheduled to present the next day, and had spelled out its salient features on the six o'clock news. Had it not been for Bourassa's legendary cool—he immediately advised his finance minister to go directly to the National Assembly and release the budget officially—the Meech Lake conference could have ground to an abrupt halt then and there. God knows when it would have been resumed.

By eight o'clock that evening, it was all wrapped up. All that was left was to notify the bureaucrats, whose task it would be to translate the deal into legislative legalese. By 10:45 the premiers were congratulating each other and exchanging autographed copies of the "Accord," and applauding Mulroney who, seated alone at the centre of a long table, described its basic details on national television.

The moment was so "historic" that Gil Rémillard hastily engaged a personal photographer to record him shaking the hand of the Prime Minister of Canada.

But was there truly cause to celebrate? Quebec had come to Ottawa to obtain recognition of its own special position in Confederation. But this was now diluted in a splintered Canada in which Prince Edward Island would exercise the same powers as Quebec. As for the recognition of Quebec society's distinct character, nothing could have been more ambiguous. "Quebec has come out a winner," Bourassa trumpeted back in Quebec.

"The recognition of the distinct character of Quebec society does not imply any change in the division of powers, and it doesn't give Quebec any powers it doesn't already have," said Senator Lowell Murray on CTV's "Question Period."

Once again the federal bureaucracy was talking out one side of its mouth or the other, depending on whether it was addressing Quebec or the rest of Canada. Lowell Murray's declaration, two days after the historic agreement, provoked a crisis in Quebec. A furious Bourassa phoned Brian Mulroney at eight o'clock the next morning to complain bitterly about his minister's blunders.

In fact, in the same televised interview, Lowell Murray perfectly summed up the main reason that English Canada, the federal government, and perhaps Robert Bourassa himself supported the Meech Lake Accord: "The only sure thing is that the Meech Lake Accord will be a severe blow to separatism and give federalism a tremendous hand in the province of Quebec." Bourassa himself later said:

> I wanted constitutional peace. I told myself that we can't do everything. Amends were made for the injustice of 1981; we were getting constitutional recognition that we are a distinct society; we got key powers over immigration that would allow us to confront the demographic problem; we had a veto right on institutions that could affect us; we had the right to opt out. We were going to see how it went. Why couldn't Quebec get those things? It would allow us to reach the year 2000 perhaps, in a climate of relative stability.[27]

What Bourassa wanted, in sum, was ten years of constitutional peace, "perhaps"! In retrospect, this marriage of convenience, based on too many ambiguities and wrapped up in an afternoon, had little chance of enduring. The ink was barely dry before the Quebec federalists clashed over its implications. *Le Devoir* reported that Donald Johnston, MP for St. Henri-Westmount, had denounced the accord as being "inspired by the two nations theory," and "nurturing the seeds of separatism by assuring the emergence of a unilingually French Quebec within English Canada."[28]

"It's the Westmount Rhodesian mentality," protested his colleague André Ouellet, Trudeau's chief Quebec organizer and lately converted to the virtues of national reconciliation.

"It's the perception of an Eaton's saleslady ten years ago," scoffed Jean Lapierre, then still a Liberal young Turk who was about to join the Bloc Québécois in 1990.

"Donald Johnston talks like Lord Durham and the English minority at the turn of the century," jeered Raymond Garneau.

But the accord was not getting a much warmer reception among the Conservatives and the New Democrats. Some premiers were already agitating for amendments, even though the accord had not yet been drawn up in legal form and was still a mere political statement of intent. Some of the crusty dinosaurs in the Tory caucus deplored the absence of a public debate. Brian Mulroney had told them in effect, "Take it or leave it."

As so often happens when there is discord in a household, a small incident that no one could have foreseen turned out to be the last straw and unleashed the real battle of Meech Lake. One Friday afternoon, two weeks after the Meech Lake meeting, Jean-Luc Pépin arrived at *Le Devoir's* office in Ottawa. The former federal minister and co-chairman of the Task Force on Canadian Unity was one of the finest teachers that Quebec's political science faculties have ever produced. He proposed nothing less than to demonstrate that the accord was "a text of Trudeauite inspiration."[29]

> What [the accord] says about immigration is a continuation of the 1979 agreement between Quebec and Ottawa. What it says about the Supreme Court is a continuation of 1971 when the Victoria Charter proposed something identical. What it says about spending powers represents another 1971 proposal to define a suitable mechanism for spending powers. What it says about opting out is an extension of the 1982 formula.

As for the famous clause about Quebec society's distinct character, Pépin drew from his pocket an article from *Le Devoir*, dated July 15, 1980, under Pierre Elliott Trudeau's byline. At the time the former prime minister had remarked on

> the existence of the country's two principal linguistic and cultural groups, of which the French [group] has its principal home and its centre of gravity in Quebec, though it extends throughout Canada. This constitutes a social and political fact that must be most explicitly recognized.

Pépin's actions were more than Pierre Trudeau could tolerate. Already his faithful disciples—Donald Johnston, David Berger,

Michael Pitfield, Marc Lalonde, and a few others—were after him to do something. When he saw his former minister ascribing to him paternity of the Meech Lake Accord, he sent his old friend Gérard Pelletier to meet with the editor-in-chief of *La Presse*. "Trudeau and I are concerned about this Meech Lake Accord," Pelletier told Michel Roy. "We can't let it pass. We want to launch a debate, and to do it we want to start with a big bang."[30]

Talk about a bang! The first ministers were scheduled to meet again on May 29 for the formal signing of the constitutional agreement. On May 27, headlines in *La Presse* and the *Toronto Star* trumpeted Trudeau's anti-Meech blast: "April 30, 1987, was a black day for Canada. It is hard to imagine a more colossal blunder ... "

The honeymoon had lasted exactly twenty-seven days. For the next three years, Robert Bourassa would see Quebec's allies fall by the wayside one by one.

"With dignity and pride," Mulroney had promised. Despite Robert Bourassa's best intentions, what awaited Quebeckers was now more like insult and humiliation.

CHAPTER SEVEN

The Fall Guy

*I came back in spite of Trudeau. Therefore, I don't
see any need to ask him for favours.*

Robert Bourassa

The relationship between Robert Bourassa and Pierre Trudeau constitutes one of the most disgraceful episodes in contemporary Canadian politics. A consenting victim at times, the designated fall guy, the scapegoat, Bourassa took it all on the chin—knowing that through him the whole of Quebec was absorbing the blows.

It was without much enthusiasm that he agreed to a suggestion by his chief of staff, Rémy Bujold, to have lunch with Trudeau in 1986 to see how the land lay. There was no talk of a Meech Lake Accord yet, but "the Old Man," as he had become known among Quebec Liberals, knew enough about Bourassa's five points to let Bourassa know he disagreed.

Should Bourassa try to convince him anyway? That wasn't Bourassa's style. "The less he asks of me, the more I want to remain independent," he said.[1] In any case, as far as he was concerned, Trudeau was, literally, history. He had been replaced by John Turner, and his party had come out almost unanimously in favour of Quebec's five conditions. The loyal Raymond Garneau, who had dislodged Jean Chrétien as the federal Liberal Quebec lieutenant, was taking care of business in Ottawa.

The only person Bourassa really needed on his side was Mulroney. Bourassa hoped that together he and the prime minister could update the old Confederation pact, which, after all, was a deal cut 120 years before by two groups of white, male, Christian politicians whose only difference was the language they spoke at home, since at constitutional conferences they spoke only English to each other.

The Meech Lake meeting of 1987 was eerily reminiscent of the conference in Charlottetown in 1864. The eleven heads of government were also all white males and all were Christians. Four were Catholic (Mulroney, Devine, Bourassa, and Vander Zalm), four belonged to the United Church (Peterson, Peckford, Getty, and Buchanan), Pawley was a Unitarian, Ghiz an Anglican, and Hatfield a non-practising Protestant. And it was only during the brief asides between "Brian" and "Robert" that a few words of French were spoken.

But this wasn't how Pierre Trudeau saw his country. In 1980, he said:

> We are no longer in the era of Upper and Lower Canada. The Anglo-Saxon conquerors, as we like to imagine them in Quebec, have become a minority in the country as a whole. This is obvious in the Western provinces, but one has only to look at cities like Toronto or Vancouver to see that the "ethnics," as they are called there, pose a serious cultural integration problem for Canadians of old stock.[2]

It was true that English Canada had changed considerably since Charlottetown. Religious practices had become more diversified, and more languages were spoken. A succession of constitutional conferences had allowed Canada's native peoples to realize where they stood politically. Women were no longer prepared to allow major political decisions to be made without them.

In 1987, ethnic groups, the native peoples, and women's groups feared the worst from Meech Lake, not because of what it said, but because they had been excluded from the negotiations.

Trudeau's opposition to the accord was more fundamental. For him, the Meech Lake Accord represented a concept of Canada that contradicted his very deepest beliefs. Not only did the agreement allow the "nationalist crew" he thought he had vanquished in 1980 to rear their heads again, it was now embraced with enthusiasm by federalists whose credentials he doubted, people like Robert Bourassa, as well as others whom he had thought true to the faith— Brian Mulroney, David Peterson, and Richard Hatfield.

No doubt Jean-Luc Pépin was exaggerating somewhat when he tried to portray the Meech Lake Accord as "a text of Trudeauite inspiration." In the field of immigration, for example, the Trudeau government had concluded an administrative agreement with René Lévesque. So why would Bourassa insist on constitutional guarantees? "You can't put your faith in a government that is responsible to another culture," Bourassa explained. "You can't be that naive."[3]

Bourassa's chronic suspicion of federal power, even when it was wielded by Quebeckers, was taken as an insult by Pierre Trudeau. But even that would have been a minor annoyance had there not been, to top it off, this insistence on the recognition of Quebec society's distinct character, which explicitly challenged the integrity of "his" Charter of Rights and Freedoms.

It was during the night of June 2, 1987, at the Langevin Block in Ottawa, as a result of strong pressure from Ontario, that article 16 was added to the April 30 agreement. This article specifically protected multicultural groups and native people from any use, or abuse, of the clause recognizing Quebec's distinct character. "*Inclusio unius, exclusio alterius* [the fact of including one excludes all the others]," responded Trudeau. "Why not simply say that the charter takes precedence?"[4]

Trudeau had good reason to be worried. Pressed by Quebec Opposition Leader Pierre-Marc Johnson, Bourassa ended up acknowledging that his intention had indeed been to exclude his government, in language matters at least, from the federal Charter of Rights and Freedoms. As he said:

> We must acknowledge that in the distinct society we are getting a major gain that is not limited to the purely symbolic, since the country's entire Constitution must henceforth be interpreted to conform with this recognition ... It must be underlined that the entire Constitution, including the Charter of Rights, will be interpreted and applied in the light of the

article on the distinct society. This directly involves the exercise of legislative powers, and will allow us to consolidate our gains and make even greater advances.[5]

Between the April 30 meeting at Meech Lake and the meeting at the Langevin Block on June 2, Robert Bourassa fought against an initiative by Manitoba and Ontario to limit the implications of the recognition of Quebec's distinct character:

> There was a floor [of powers] they couldn't take away from us. But there was no ceiling. We fought to keep it that way, with no ceiling, because there were those who wanted to put the ceiling at the level of the floor.[6]

Bourassa had no reason to be smug. Whether because of jealousy or bad faith, English Canada could never swallow the idea of Quebec's getting the least extra scrap of power. And the Meech Lake Accord could very well have made Quebec into a province "truly unlike the others," since a good number of jurisdictions created after 1867 fell into the vague area of "residual" powers, that is, powers which were not specifically identified in the 1867 British North America Act. There was no talk, then, of airports, or cable television, or telephone. Once, Trudeau said that "the Fathers of Confederation had not read their Jules Verne." The fur began to fly. Former Senator Eugene Forsey, a Newfoundland native, was clearly alarmed:

> If the Quebec legislature should decide to exploit fully the distinct society clause, it could legislate in areas like marriage, divorce, broadcasting, copyrights, patents, telephone service, railroads, road transport, or atomic energy.

The prize for collective paranoia went to those Manitoba feminists, very active in the Women's Legal Action and Education Fund, who feared that the distinct society clause would be invoked to justify laws aimed at restricting child custody, or women's access to professional training, or abortion, if it could be shown that such a law was related to language and culture.

★

In the face of so much hostility, Robert Bourassa committed a strategic error. At Brian Mulroney's behest, he left it up to the federal government to defend the Meech Lake Accord in English Canada. The federal politicians and a few provincial premiers then had the nerve to say that the recognition of Quebec's distinct character was purely symbolic. "Robert Bourassa and his advisers must be either mischief-makers or imbeciles to think that this provision will give Quebec significant gains," concluded Michael Bliss of the University of Toronto, "unless the distinct society clause effectively represents an important transfer of responsibilities [as Bourassa insisted], in which case, special status is being conferred on a province."[7]

On the whole, the debate on the distinct society clause, as it was carried on by Mulroney and Bourassa, involved more than a simple misunderstanding; it veered dangerously close to false representation. That the two would think they could get away with two different explanations, each on his own side of the language divide—and without the rest of the country, particularly Pierre Trudeau, catching on—suggests a certain naiveté, if not cynicism.

Determined to go one better than his sovereignist opposition in the National Assembly, Robert Bourassa boasted that among other things he had got back Quebec's right to self-determination:

> There is in this free and voluntary process of Quebec's adherence to the 1982 Constitution Act, a particular expression of the Quebec people's right to decide their future, as we did in a more explicit manner in 1980 by choosing the Canadian option.[8]

Pierre Trudeau couldn't believe his ears:

> [Bourassa] has just got the Meech Lake Accord, the Langevin Block accord, the whole shooting match, and now he's saying: "We still have the right to be independent. We've signed a marriage contract, but article 1 says we can get a divorce at any time."[9]

In 1982 Bourassa was convinced that Quebec had lost that right with the patriation of the constitution. He even went so far as to say that the federal government would be "constitutionally required to use all means necessary to enforce respect of [Canada's] territorial integrity." Thus, how could the simple recognition of Quebec's distinct character re-establish the province's right to self-determination?

During confidential conversations in 1980 with his colleagues from Saskatchewan and Ontario, Allan Blakeney and William Davis, Pierre Trudeau maintained that the recognition of Quebec as a distinct society would allow the province to ask the United Nations to recognize its right to self-determination.[10] This explains his systematic refusal to include the concept of a "distinct nation" or a "distinct people" in the Canada Bill.

The United Nations has long recognized "the right of peoples to decide their own future, that is to say to freely determine their political, economic, social, and cultural status." And for more than ten years now, English Canada has resigned itself to the idea that Quebeckers constitute a "people." Trudeau would not let himself be taken in by such a subterfuge.

For twenty years at least, the international arena had been the scene of a succession of skirmishes between Quebec and Ottawa. And to the amazement of the nationalists, Bourassa remained faithful to the tradition of asserting Quebec's international personality, sometimes very loudly. Gilles Loiselle, today a federal cabinet minister, experienced several changes of government while he was at the Quebec delegation in Paris. "Quebec is stronger than any electoral vicissitudes," he told the French after Daniel Johnson's death and Robert Bourassa's victory. "If you think we're going to go back to being quiet little Quebec, you'll be disappointed."[11] (Loiselle also witnessed a unique event in the history of Quebec diplomacy. It occurred during the 1976 Olympic Games. Bourassa was, in effect, the only premier of Quebec to have presided over a state dinner for the Queen of England at the Ritz Carleton Hotel in Montreal. At the head table were Bourassa and Queen Elizabeth. Andrée Simard was paired with Prince Philip. "And Trudeau, at the end of the table with some Japanese princess, was stewing the whole evening," Loiselle still sneers.[12])

Beyond these skirmishes of protocol, and despite Claude Morin's complaints that Bourassa put too much importance on the economic dimension of his international visits, Bourassa deliberately created precedents he regarded as important. But, as always, and to the despair of Quebec's specialists in high-profile diplomacy, he did so without much ostentation.

Since the agreement on Quebec's participation at the summit of francophone countries, Bourassa had been making his presence felt. At the first meeting in Paris in 1986, he spoke up about the crisis in Lebanon and proposed a reconstruction program without bothering to warn the federal delegation. As he said later:

> It was intentional. It is the only international summit where we have a distinct role, where we have a distinct place, and where Quebec therefore has to assert itself . . . The precedent is now established: at every francophone summit, Quebec can now participate in keeping with its policies and make its own proposals.[13]

That's what really got to Pierre Trudeau. As he explained to his senatorial coterie:

> As prime minister, I represented Canada at international conferences, be it the Big Seven summit, Commonwealth or NATO conferences. But when it comes to French-language conferences, even though my name is Trudeau and I come from Quebec, I couldn't go by myself. I would have to be accompanied by the premier, because we have given the province special status in international affairs.[14]

What an affront, in effect. But "the Paris incident" would go no further. To be sure, Brian Mulroney threw a fine Irish tantrum, but he quickly made up with Robert Bourassa. Unlike the federal diplomats who snubbed the Quebec delegation for several days thereafter, Mulroney was content to have a "virile" exchange with Bourassa, as René Lévesque would have said, and to turn the page.

The incident's low-key consequences illustrated the informal relationship that had developed between Mulroney and Bourassa. And that relationship didn't sit well with the federal bureaucracy. For half a century they had been used to functioning in a system consisting of "levels" of government. The Ottawa mandarins behaved as though they were from a higher order of government. Weren't people always referring to the federal government as the "senior government"? And didn't Trudeau make a habit of calling the provincial premiers his "parish wardens"?

When there is such a wrenching change in government as there was after the 1984 election of Brian Mulroney's Conservatives, it is normally followed by an equally sweeping turnover in the senior ranks of the federal civil service. At least that's what Mulroney's organizers had promised. A transition committee, headed by Peter White—an associate of financier Conrad Black and a former crony of the prime minister from his Laval days—drew up a hit list of "Trudeaucrats" to be eliminated, as well as a list of perceived Tory sympathizers to be promoted to high places in key departments. Outright dismissals, a rare thing in the upper bureaucracy, would have to be provoked by personal differences between ministers and their deputy ministers. Such were the fates of De Montigny Marchand, who rubbed Marcel Masse the wrong way in both communications and energy, and Robert Rabinovitch, whom Benoît Bouchard could not tolerate as undersecretary of state.

But there was no wholesale housecleaning, mostly because the federal civil service generally impressed the new Conservative ministers with its professionalism. Deputy minister Paul Tellier, in particular, surprised his new masters. During the 1984 election campaign, well before the outcome was foreseeable, he ordered his underlings at the Department of Energy, Mines and Resources to draft an implementation plan for a proposal forwarded by Conservative energy critic Pat Carney. Carney's program represented a 180-degree turn from the National Energy Program of Marc Lalonde and Jean Chrétien, under whom Tellier had previously served. But as he himself said: "Deputy ministers aren't there to influence or make decisions. They're there to help decisions get made."

The speed with which Tellier adapted himself to his new political masters so impressed Brian Mulroney that he held him up as an example to his colleagues, and in August 1985, he promoted him to the top job in the federal mandarinate—clerk of the Privy Council. From that vantage point he was able to protect many of his long-time colleagues and therefore to avert the wholesale bloodbath the

Conservatives had promised. Tellier won so many battles against Peter White, who had by this time become the prime minister's special adviser for appointments of all sorts, including senior civil service postings, that White packed up and went back to the private sector.

A year after he had promoted Tellier, Mulroney reached into the premier's office in British Columbia for his new cabinet secretary for federal-provincial relations, Norman Spector. Spector had been involved in the 1981 constitutional negotiations on the side of the provinces, and his nomination was regarded as another sign of goodwill.

Spector replaced Gérard Veilleux, who had been Jean Chrétien's associate deputy minister of finance at the end of the 1970s. Veilleux had been a key player in the 1981 negotiations, though he stayed very much in the shadows behind Pierre Trudeau and Michael Kirby. He was also the architect of an economic union plan that was supposed to reinforce Ottawa's powers in the areas of manpower and industrial development, a plan that Saskatchewan's minister of intergovernmental affairs, Roy Romanow, and Claude Morin fought against tooth and nail.

For Robert Bourassa, these nominations were especially promising. From 1970 to 1972, Tellier had worked with him as assistant to Julien Chouinard in the provincial privy council office. There he had come to know first hand "how the provincial guys feel toward the feds."[15] Nor was Norman Spector an unknown quantity in Quebec. As Premier William Bennett's deputy minister in British Columbia, he had participated in the organization of the provincial common front that opposed Trudeau's patriation initiative in 1981. But according to Claude Morin,[16] he was also in cahoots with Saskatchewan's Roy Romanow, who had been one of the first, along with Ontario's Roy McMurtry, to plot the sabotage of the same provincial common front and Quebec's isolation.

Bourassa, for his part, would shortly bolster his team of advisers with Louis Bernard, who was the former deputy minister of intergovernmental affairs, senior adviser to the Parti Québécois administration, and chief of staff for the PQ National Assembly caucus between 1970 and 1976. In a way these appointments suggested a remake of the constitutional conferences of the past twenty years.

Paul Tellier and Jean-Claude Rivest on the one hand, Norman Spector and Louis Bernard on the other were former comrades in arms. But in their earlier battles, the Quebeckers had always wound up in the losing camp, while the feds were always in the group that was cracking the champagne.

Brian Mulroney thus gradually surrounded himself with a powerful federal bureaucracy, inherited from the Trudeau era and trained by the two Michaels, Pitfield and Kirby. Another sign that this "Trudeaucracy" was taking over again was the rehabilitation of De Montigny Marchand, whom Marcel Masse had twice tried to torpedo. Another Trudeau era hold-over who had been shuffled sideways and slightly down in 1985 was Bob Rabinovitch, whose comeback was marked by his contribution to the Charest Report in the Meech Lake endgame.

Once Brian Mulroney had the same advisers as Pierre Trudeau had had, he reverted to the latter's methods in federal-provincial relations management. The appointment in 1990 of Gérard Veilleux as president of the CBC was probably not as fortuitous as it appeared at first sight. Not long after their arrival at corporate headquarters, Veilleux and the new chairman, Patrick Watson, summoned the heads of the CBC's news and public affairs departments in Toronto. The message was direct: the corporation had to cooperate with the last-ditch effort to save the Meech Lake Accord.

A few weeks later, as though by pure coincidence, Daniel Gagnier, the Ontario premier's chief of staff, circulated a strategy paper that suggested that Newsworld, the CBC's twenty-four-hour-a-day television news channel, should be used in the Meech Lake rescue effort. The document also suggested that the three recalcitrant premiers would be depicted as instable, unpredictable, and unreliable.[17] The strategy was curiously reminiscent of the one used against the Parti Québécois government during the years leading up to the referendum. But that was hardly surprising: at the time Daniel Gagnier was working for Paul Tellier, whom he would later succeed as head of the Canadian Unity Information Office.

David Peterson, predictably, dissociated himself from the document when it was leaked into the public domain, even though it had been prepared by his own office. But the manipulation of public opinion, aided and abetted by CBC Newsworld, did indeed come into play.

Throughout the marathon seven-day conference held in Ottawa from June 2 to 9, 1990, the same scenario was played out day after day. The premiers, thrown together behind closed doors, had little contact with their delegations, and few leaks got as far as the 600 media types camped outside. Every evening, shortly before ten o'clock, Norman Spector would give a private briefing on his version of the day's events to the CBC and Radio-Canada anchors, Peter Mansbridge and Daniel Lessard. That way the CBC and Radio-Canada could get their headline items about the conference onto the air before the premiers had a chance to give their own version.

Then Newsworld came into play. By coincidence, only Newsworld's Ottawa bureau chief, Don Newman, had a direct feed from the sound system furnished by the federal government. Therefore, Newsworld became a sort of electronic pool from which the other networks had to take their sound clips. At least two premiers complained to Mulroney that Don Newman was always asking "the most embarrassing questions, as though they'd been suggested to him."[18]

These daily manoeuvres, aimed at influencing the coverage of the premiers when they emerged from the negotiations, were a success unprecedented in the annals of federal-provincial conferences. At that time of the evening, most radio and television stations were on the air, and they usually wound up broadcasting unedited the message that the federal strategists were trying to put across that day via Newsworld. As for the newspaper journalists, most of whose deadlines fell only an hour later, they too got most of their information from the same source.

It was important for the government to transmit one single message to the Canadian public, because every night that week it polled strategic areas of the country—Manitoba, Newfoundland, and Quebec. One night, for example, after the news flashed out about "a breakthrough in Ottawa," support for sovereignty in Quebec plunged from 63 percent to 53 percent. The results were then invoked to twist the arms of the holdout premiers.

A jubilant Bourassa waves to the crowd with his wife, Andrée,
after being elected premier in 1970. At thirty-six, he was
the youngest premier in the province's history.

Bourassa chats with Pierre Trudeau at his first federal-provincial conference in Ottawa in 1970. "Already things were moving a little too quickly for a fledgling premier who had come to power without a clearly defined constitutional policy."

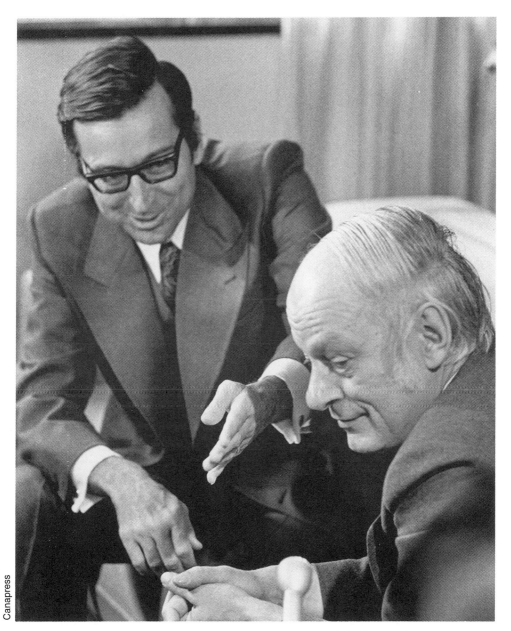

Nine years after René Lévesque stormed out of the Liberal party, Bourassa met with his former political ally in 1976 to discuss handing over the reins of government to the Parti Québécois.

Casting a long shadow: Bourassa lecturing at Laval in 1979,
his first job in the province of Quebec since his defeat in 1976.

On the campaign trail again: Bourassa's son François,
a jazz pianist, gives his father a quick lesson before a rally
in Boucherville in 1985.

Eleven would-be fathers of Confederation in 1989. Standing, left to right:
Clyde Wells, Grant Devine, Bill Vander Zalm, Gary Filmon, Joe Ghiz,
and Don Getty. Seated: John Buchanan, David Peterson, Brian Mulroney,
Robert Bourassa, and Frank McKenna.

An exhausted-looking Bourassa is applauded by members of Quebec's
National Assembly after giving his reactions to the failure of the
Meech Lake Accord in June 1990: "No matter what anyone says or does, Quebec
has always been, is now, and will always be a distinct society,
free and capable of taking responsibility for its destiny and development."

Up on the roof: Bourassa at work in his favourite spot
on the roof of ''The Bunker,'' high above Quebec City's Grande Allée.

Robert Bourassa and New Brunswick Premier Frank McKenna confirmed that Mulroney and the federal bureaucracy put enormous pressure on their colleagues, brandishing the threat of dire economic consequences in the event of a constitutional impasse. As McKenna said later:

> Certain people, particularly in the federal government, were being very alarmist. Bourassa could have done something about it, but I was sitting next to him and I knew he was thinking that this isn't at all what he wanted to do.[19]

Bourassa confirmed McKenna's comments: "I don't like to make threats. But there were others who were ready to do it for me, and in a very crude manner at times."[20] With Meech Lake dead and the country facing an unprecedented crisis, Brian Mulroney would have no choice but to turn to a team of professional advisers who had fought another major battle against the Parti Québécois, some years earlier. Bourassa would now have to watch himself.

Many Quebec Conservatives and a few provincial premiers raised their eyebrows when, instead of firing the federal government's chief constitutional strategist after the failure of the Meech Lake negotiations, Mulroney named Spector as his new chief of staff. By refusing to take seriously the reservations expressed by the opponents of Meech Lake, Spector had displayed an arrogance that would have impressed some of his predecessors in the prime minister's office: Marc Lalonde, Jim Coutts, and Tom Axworthy. As principal political adviser to the prime minister, he now seemed likely to convert the Conservative party, traditionally receptive to regional demands, into the champion of reinforced "central" authority.

The choice of Spector's replacement to head the office of federal-provincial relations, was even more surprising. In the fall of 1990, Paul Tellier tapped Gordon Smith, who was in Brussels at the time, and largely an unknown quantity to the Conservative ministers. A Michael Pitfield recruit, Smith had been regarded as his likely successor, and would probably have risen to the top job had the Liberals not lost power. A brilliant graduate of McGill University and the Massachusetts Institute of Technology, he was assigned by Pitfield to evaluate the performance of senior bureaucrats. To a considerable extent, half of Mulroney's deputy ministers owed him their career paths.

Tellier, Spector, and Smith, three Quebeckers recruited by Michael Pitfield to serve a particularly centralist vision of Canadian federalism, had twice as many years of service under Pierre Trudeau as under Brian Mulroney. As for Daniel Gagnier, he too had been brought back to Ottawa by Paul Tellier after the Liberal government was defeated in Ontario. Promoted to the rank of Privy Council undersecretary for communications, the author of the memo on how to manipulate public opinion during the Meech Lake conference in 1990 was now in command of the federal government's entire information strategy, including the Citizens' Forum headed by Keith Spicer.

This resurgence of the Trudeaucrats is no doubt what aroused the suspicion of one of the commission members, Robert Normand. Publisher of the Quebec City daily *Le Soleil*, he decided to give up one of the paper's senior columnists, Michel Roy, a well-respected Quebec political commentator who had no known enemies. Discreetly, and with the complicity of Gilles Loiselle, who was by now in the federal cabinet, he put the suggestion in Brian Mulroney's ear that he should take on Michel Roy as his senior constitutional adviser, an act that would at least restore some credibility in his constitutional team among the Quebec nationalists in his parliamentary caucus.

But it was a gigantic task for Michel Roy: others before him—Gil Rémillard and Arthur Tremblay in particular—had been offered the same prestigious title but had been unable to reroute the march of the powerful federal bureaucracy. For one thing, Tellier and Smith had quietly camouflaged a new "Canadian unity task force" in the organizational chart of the Secretary of State's department, which was more than a little reminiscent of the old Trudeau era Canadian Unity Information Office.

Some thirty professionals were assembled and comfortably installed with an $8-million annual budget to interpret the Quebec Liberal party's Allaire Report (which recommended a substantial dismantling of Confederation) and the report of the Bélanger-

Campeau commission. They provided special advice on constitutional matters to the federal bureaucracy in general, and charted future publicity campaigns. The 125th anniversary of Canada would give them many events to organize in 1992. The group's coordinator was a certain Richard Dicerni, who had been officially assigned to Claude Ryan's referendum "No" group in March 1980 by Jean Chrétien. With Dicerni came a button that would soon become the main federalist slogan: "Non, merci!" (No thank you).

It wouldn't take much more for English Canada to exclaim: "Deep down, Mulroney is Pierre Trudeau," an association that gained a certain credibility when his back-room workers wrote him speeches attacking the sovereignist "dream merchants."

Before long, the situation would come full circle: someone would discover that "Deep down, Bourassa is Bourassa." If Quebec once again enters into conflict with the federal machine, it will at least have the advantage of knowing its enemies.

CHAPTER EIGHT

The Jealous Big Brother

*If you think you can build Montreal at Toronto's
expense, you're making a serious mistake . . .*

David Peterson

Maurice Duplessis and George Drew in 1947; Jean Lesage and
Leslie Frost in 1960; Daniel Johnson and John Robarts in 1966.
Every time Quebec and Ontario teamed up to play axis politics,
Ottawa lost face—and a few tax points into the bargain.

But Bill Davis preferred Pierre Elliott Trudeau to Bourassa I.
And Bourassa II liked Brian Mulroney better than he liked David
Peterson. The magic of the Toronto-Quebec axis was dispelled first
by cultural misunderstandings, then by economic rivalries. The
two Ontario premiers Bourassa had known had protested too
eagerly and too often that there was no anti-Quebec undercurrent in
their province not to arouse suspicions.

When Bourassa called to congratulate Bill Davis on his victory at
the Ontario Conservative party leadership convention in February
1971, Davis quickly proposed a courtesy visit to Montreal. At the
time Quebec was barely over the shock of the October Crisis.
"There's no backlash from the kidnappings last fall," the new
master of Queen's Park told the journalists waiting at the door of the
Beaver Club in Montreal. "The people of Ontario feel very close to
Quebeckers." But in private he complained about certain Quebec

bureaucrats who were making waves in Ontario's francophone community. At the time, Quebec was providing more funding to the
Association Canadienne Française de l'Ontario than the Ontario
government itself. How embarrassing!

In July 1972, Bourassa and Davis once again found themselves
raising a glass together, this time at the Hélène-de-Champlain restaurant near the old Expo '67 site in Montreal. Both explained the
champagne was to celebrate the "*entente cordiale*" that was to domi-
nate relations between the two. Later that same year, after Trudeau
had managed to avoid being defeated by Robert Stanfield's Conservatives by the skin of his teeth, thanks largely to the fifty-six Liberals who had been elected in Quebec, Bill Davis had to rein in the
Toronto resentment: "The vote pattern in Ontario [where the Liberals had lost twenty-four seats] was not, and I emphasize was not,
dictated by any backlash or anti-Quebec feeling, and I want to make
that categorical," he said.

But during the 1981 election campaign, Davis was still holding
out against official bilingualism for Ontario, even though it was
supported by both the Liberals and the New Democrats. Seated in
the back of his campaign bus between his wife, Kathleen, and his
adviser Hugh Segal, somewhere between ultra-Orangist Orillia and
Toronto, Davis remarked: "You can't provoke this province. Official bilingualism is political suicide. It was because of his official
language policy that Trudeau almost lost the 1972 election."[1]
Under his easy-going exterior, the man they called Mr. Ontario
resented his neighbouring province's nationalist initiatives, which
in turn upset his own electorate. Less of a diplomat than his boss,
Hugh Segal (who became a senior adviser to Brian Mulroney in
1991) revealed Davis's deepest feelings about Quebec and Robert
Bourassa when he said:

> Bill always resented in a little way the razzmatazz Robarts got
> for doing not very much [for the Franco-Ontarians]. Yet he
> became the great saviour of Confederation. Billy had to deal
> with all the Quebec nationalism, with guys like Bourassa and
> Lévesque who said language rights outside Quebec didn't
> matter a shit . . .[2]

And when Davis quietly favoured Robert Bourassa's comeback

in 1983, saying he thought Bourassa had "matured," was he not implying that he had found him a little green when they had crossed paths at first ministers' conferences?

Bourassa never worried about his popularity in English Canada. But he also underestimated the lack of respect, at times even the scorn, that some of his colleagues felt towards him. He thought the other premiers were his and Quebec's allies. But with him, they made only tactical agreements, on which they would renege at the first opportunity. "René Lévesque forced English Canada to take a good look at itself, and to change," said Bill Davis, the day after Lévesque's death. But six years earlier, the same Davis had been the first to support Trudeau's constitutional strategy, ultimately leading to Quebec's isolation.

As for David Peterson, he had never been comfortable with nationalism, not only the Quebec variety, but also the Canadian version. During the long night in the Langevin Block, he had tried until the wee hours of the morning to preserve the predominance of individual rights over the collective will of Quebec's francophone majority. In an interview a few weeks later, he gave a hint of the debate that had raged behind the closed doors before he finally rallied to the concept of Quebec society's distinct character:

> There's nothing remarkable about recognizing that Quebec
> is different. What's hard is to reconcile that with the diversity
> of the Canadian federation. You can go pretty far with nation-
> alism: it's emotional, not rational, and there are a lot of peo-
> ple who have killed in the name of nationalism. Indeed
> nationalism tends to regard all individuals as being the same.
> But people aren't all the same.[3]

One can understand why Peterson felt that way. After inheriting a political party that for years stood no chance of getting off the opposition benches while it remained a prisoner of its rural and traditional electorate, he was the first to realize that Ontario, and particularly its urban face, had changed. The small mining towns in the North had become as Italian or Polish as they were English. Some of the rural communities were so predominately German or Dutch that it was a struggle to keep English schools open. Mean-while, the heart of Toronto teemed with Italians, Portuguese, and

Chinese. The 425,000 Franco-Ontarians, scattered throughout the four corners of the province, were lost in the sea of greater Toronto, where bilingualism (on things like street signs) was more likely to favour the Chinese, who were four times more numerous.[4]

Not only was there no attempt to integrate this mosaic of languages and cultures, but the province's rich diversity was systematically cultivated. As Peterson said in 1987, "Since 1867 we've learned to recognize differences, special schools, language and cultural rights . . . All things considered, we've behaved in a fairly civilized fashion."[5] It was true that Ontario no longer officially celebrated July 12, the anniversary of William of Orange's victory and the establishment of a Protestant dynasty on the British throne. The old slogan: "One school, one flag, one language: the same rights for all and no privileges for anyone," had become meaningless since the last official Orangeman premier of the province, Bill Davis—sometimes nicknamed "King Billy," like the victor of the Battle of the Boyne—restored government funding to the province's Catholic separate schools, renounced the Union Jack along with everyone else, and timidly opened the door to bilingualism.

The arrival of a million and a half immigrants—Italian, Spanish, Portuguese, German, Dutch, Polish, and Ukrainian, and particularly the "visible" newcomers, Chinese, Koreans, Vietnamese, and East Indians—pushed the last of the old-order Ontario bigots to the rural fringe of the province's "Orange belt." But deep down, traditional Ontario had always been hostile towards Catholic French Canadians and towards their resistance—passive at first, then agitated, and now aggressive—to being swept into the melting pot of a country in which people spoke only one language, practised one religion, and raised a single flag, all of them derived from Great Britain.

Bilingualism and its notorious complement, multiculturalism, were beginning to undermine the primacy of the English. Over the past two decades, four Catholic prime ministers—Trudeau, Clark, Turner, and Mulroney—had succeeded each other at 24 Sussex Drive, and imbued the laws of the land and the constitution with pluralism and religious freedom. The political clout wielded by French Canadians was now such that it was they who determined the fate of governments, and there was even talk of "French power" in federal institutions.

For its own protection, therefore, and since it wasn't quite able to be distinctly "Ontarian," the province invented for itself a "Canadian" identity. As Peterson said:

Ontario is the only province without a regional identity. You never hear people calling themselves Ontarians, unlike Quebeckers, Westerners, Maritimers, or Islanders. The word is practically never used.[6]

In a way Ontario is Canada. By going back one or two generations—Peterson, for example, is the grandson of Norwegian immigrants—Statistics Canada could say that 40 percent of all Canadians are immigrants, and thus justify a policy whereby every square inch of terrain reconquered by the francophone minority was immediately challenged by half a dozen other "ethnic" groups.

This was the heritage of twenty years of "multiculturalism," a policy of appeasement invented by the Royal Commission on Bilingualism and Biculturalism after the untimely death of its Quebec co-chairman, André Laurendeau. In presenting his new policy in 1971, Pierre Trudeau explained: "This kind of policy should help diminish the discrimination and jealousy [so *that*'s what it's for!] engendered by cultural differences."[7]

David Peterson's political genius was to realize to what extent Trudeau's federal policies had changed Ontario society. Bill Davis's efforts to perpetuate the old Orangist dream of a solidly anglo-Protestant Ontario worried the ethnic minorities as much as it drove the province's francophone minority to despair. The brief interlude during which Frank Miller (the little motel operator from Muskoka who never gave up his hideous plaid jackets) was premier of Ontario was merely an accident of history. Six months before Quebec turned back to Robert Bourassa, Ontario embarked on the Liberal adventure with relish.

The Peterson family originally came to Ontario from Saskatchewan. The "great crisis" of 1930 compelled David's father, Clarence, to sign the Regina Manifesto, the charter of Canadian socialism. When

David was born in 1943, the family had moved to London, Ontario, where they lived in comfortable circumstances. There was even enough money to send young David to study in France.

Peterson's first contacts with Quebec went back to 1963, when he was his university's delegate to the Congress on Canadian Affairs at Laval University. There he spent a few long nights sipping beer with one Robert Lemieux. Peterson later lost sight of Lemieux until the day he popped up on TV screens during the October Crisis as lawyer for the FLQ. One night in 1969 Peterson had even made the acquaintance of Brian Mulroney at a McGill student party at a bachelor apartment in Westmount.

In 1970, David Peterson, the young Osgoode Hall graduate, went into the family business. He had the smarts to buy a small electronics import house and to negotiate a Canada-wide monopoly on Sharp products with the Japanese firm. At the age of thirty he had already made his first million. Shortly after that, he took up with a young actress named Shelley Matthews, the daughter of one of London's richest families. They made a strange couple: she, worldly, elegant and at home in artistic circles; he, always badly dressed in nerdy short-sleeved shirts and tortoiseshell glasses.

One night, in June 1984, two very similar men, both of whom looked like credit union managers more than anything else, were seated at a corner table in Cibo's restaurant in Toronto: Bourassa and Peterson were meeting for the first time. Both were leaders of the opposition, and at the time neither looked like a sure bet for a promising future.

But from that summer on, the young Ontario millionaire began a metamorphosis. And as time went by, he would distance himself more and more from his Quebec counterpart, physically and ideologically.

While Shelley Peterson was on tour with her theatre troupe, David Peterson would take charge of the couple's three children, one of whom was still in diapers, which meant one drawer of his desk in the opposition leader's office at Queen's Park was stuffed with Pampers. One of these times, a friend happened to photograph him on the beach, playing with his children—with his glasses off. The result was so arresting that Peterson no longer feared handing himself over to the image doctors.

Three years later, at Meech Lake, Bourassa's slightly stooped silhouette hadn't changed a bit; he still looked like a credit union manager. David Peterson, on the other hand, now looked for all the world like a Bay Street baron. The two were so different that it was hard to imagine that they could develop any intimacy. Peterson delighted in good scotch, smoked like a chimney, showed off his wife and children at all manner of political events, and carried on with his advisers like the leader of a merry band of good old boys for whom politics was a game. Bourassa, on the other hand, was austere, without vices, jealously protective of his privacy and not given to gossiping with his underlings in the corridors of the National Assembly.

But much more than style separated the two. David Peterson had surrounded himself with a small clan of advisers who represented the new Ontario: Hershel Ezrin, Vince Borg, Daphne Rutherford, Mordecai Ben-Dat, Anitha Johns-Noddle, Tom Zygis—Jews, Italians, Maltese, Asiatics, very few WASPs, and no French Canadians. Unlike Bourassa, who was leery of great social debates, Peterson eagerly waded into public frays, as he did in 1989 when he took on the mob of bigots who had trampled the Quebec flag. "I detest hypocrisy, the anti-everythings who manipulate people's emotions and flee without leaving any footprints," he said one day, putting up his dukes in a fighter's reflex that recalled his college boxing days.[8]

This political yuppie wanted to make Ontario a modern state, open to everyone, in the image of Japan, which he had visited numerous times as head of Import House Canada, his electronics firm. When he opposed free trade, it was not because he feared the United States, but because he felt Ontario could manage without it.

One day Peterson said of Bill Davis: "He was a small-town politician concerned with his political survival . . . As far as Quebec is concerned, Ontario lost its credibility as a partner and its reputation as a sympathetic neighbour."[9] Today there are many in Ontario, including Peterson himself perhaps, who would reverse the names of the provinces and apply the phrase to Robert Bourassa.

When he came to power, at roughly the same time as Bourassa regained his, David Peterson thought for a while that Ontario had found an ideal partner in Quebec. "Today when you sit down with a group of Quebeckers, you talk about business and international markets instead of the old cultural and linguistic problems," he said, no doubt recalling his long ago tavern conversations with Robert Lemieux.[10] Alas, he would soon discover that his sessions with Bourassa would drag him back to the constitutional barricades and the linguistic battlefield. But most important, Peterson wanted Ontario to treat Quebec like a major client. Above all, no waves—hadn't Peter Ustinov compared Toronto to a New York run by the Swiss?—and no futile quarrels.

> In 1989, our exports to Quebec brought in more than $16 billion, and generated more than a 100,000 manufacturing jobs in the province. And commerce is a two-way street: Ontario imported more than $13 billion worth of goods from Quebec, creating as many jobs in the province as in the sectors of agriculture, forestry, and mining combined.[11]

On the theme of "Brian, Robert, and I," David Peterson let on that with his accession to power, and Bourassa's election six months later, Confederation would reorganize around the golden triangle formed by three capitals—Ottawa, Quebec, and Toronto. The honeymoon, however, was short-lived. David Peterson openly disliked Brian Mulroney, whose political opportunism, sense of public morality, and cynical attitude toward the electorate he found repugnant. Commenting on the way in which the federal government tried to buy New Brunswick's support for free trade with a contract for six new naval frigates to be built at the Saint John shipyards, Peterson denounced "the mentality of people in Ottawa who think they can get away with appealing to people's lowest instincts. Their mentality makes them believe they can buy off their adversaries . . . Which says a lot about what they think of themselves."[12]

Relations between Peterson and Mulroney were such that the dream of a three-way coalition dissipated in no time—or in about as much time as it took for Peterson to reassemble in Toronto the old gang of Trudeau advisers, all of whom had a score to settle with the Conservatives.

★

Instead of the three-way coalition, Peterson and Bourassa eventually attempted to establish an Ontario-Quebec axis. During the
night of June 2 to 3, 1987, when he finally rallied half-heartedly to
the Meech Lake Accord, Peterson gave in to a kind of blackmail.
"Do you want to wind up totally isolated, like Lévesque in 1981?"
he was told, in effect.

Peterson's political base was Metro Toronto, home to half of the
hundred largest enterprises in the country, which were doing $19
billion worth of business; where the stock exchange registered
three-quarters of the share transactions in the country, and where
four-fifths of the foreign banks were established. Peterson's Liberals were in a minority. That meant that another electoral deadline
was approaching. No one wanted to make any waves. Economic
stability was well worth a timid signature at the bottom of the Meech
Lake Accord.

But despite all the solemn declarations of friendship, the intimate
dinners, carefully announced to the TV networks well in advance,
and the little personal touches, like the bottle of milk in an ice
bucket that awaited Bourassa in his suite every time he arrived in
Toronto, relations between the two men grew ever more distant.
Peterson was no doubt somewhat jealous of the special relationship
that Bourassa had with Mulroney. During the free trade debate and
the November 1988 federal election, he was sincerely shocked by
Bourassa's overt display of political opportunism. A few weeks
later, the rupture was complete. David Peterson was stuck with a
Meech Lake Accord that was increasingly unpopular in Toronto and
within his own party. When Robert Bourassa told him that he
planned to invoke the notwithstanding clause to limit English on
public signs, it was the last straw. "You're mixing the language
question up with the Meech Lake Accord. You'll never get away
with it,"[13] Peterson shouted over the phone.

In June 1990, it was David Peterson himself who tossed the
notwithstanding clause on the table at the last-chance conference in
Ottawa. None of the premiers wanted to let go of the clause; indeed,
several had found occasion to invoke it, though their actions didn't
cause as much of a stink as Quebec's Bill 178. Robert Bourassa
patiently explained to them that the very existence of the clause
rendered the recognition of Quebec's distinct character largely

symbolic. "We have more with the notwithstanding clause," he told them, "and we've shown we're prepared to use it."

But when Bourassa refused to participate in any discussion on the distinct society clause on Thursday, June 7, it was evident where Peterson and the others were headed: they were out to dilute Quebec's distinct character in a Canada that owed its existence also to its native peoples and to various cultural communities. Along with the recognition of Quebec's distinctiveness, a "Canada clause" would have recognized the fundamental rights of native peoples and the contribution of various ethnic groups. "When the discussion split on that Canada clause," explained Bourassa, "I tell you, I was in a tough position, because if we were to stay in Canada, how could we oppose the Canada clause? Even some of my ministers, including Claude Ryan, were in favour of it."

The relationship between the two provincial governments had been strained for the past four years. The rupture was predictable. The fact that the break was over money matters made it even more serious. Quebec might well be a "credible partner and a sympathetic neighbour," as Peterson had said, but it was first and foremost one of Ontario's competitors. When it came to economic issues, David Peterson behaved like a middle brother in a family who was forever jealous of the shameless favours bestowed on the baby in the family by the big federal brother. "If you think you can build Montreal at Toronto's expense, you're making a big mistake,"[14] he had said, protesting a proposal to establish Montreal as an international banking centre. What really irked the Ontario premier was the ostentation with which the Mulroney government conferred its favours on Quebec—and the fawning way Bourassa would express his thanks.

The empty shell that is the Canadian Space Agency should not have constituted much grounds for jealousy on the part of wealthy Ontario, which was already home to two-thirds of the country's advanced electronics industry. But the way in which Mulroney and some of his Quebec ministers carried on the debate provoked an anti-Quebec backlash that complicated David Peterson's life. And in the final analysis, the Meech Lake Accord itself was perceived as a special favour for Quebec. An Ontario premier could do business with Quebec, but he wasn't supposed to give things away. In 1990 the electorate would remember Peterson's signature on the accord. The ethnic groups that Peterson had seduced so smoothly in 1985 and 1987 would return to the NDP, a party to which they had long been attracted because it reminded them, albeit mistakenly, of the old European socialist parties.

Peterson knew he was beaten. Freed from the constraints that the premiership had imposed on him, and no longer obliged to defend the Meech Lake Accord, he gave vent to his true feelings. The man who for five years had called himself "Robert's friend" and Quebec's ally was the first in August 1990 to alert English Canada to the complicity of the two Quebeckers—Bourassa and Mulroney—who were trying to remake the country according to their convenience.[15]

Addressing Jacques Parizeau, he declared:

> Let me remind any province that thinks it can act alone and use the free trade agreement as an argument in favour of separation, let me remind that province that this agreement was signed between the United States and Canada, and not by any province and the United States.

And to the former friend who had dared to give birth to a "monster," Bill 178, he said:

> The charter of rights is a minimum guarantee. The obstacles to respecting the rights of individuals must disappear. I'm one of those who believe we should start with the notwithstanding clause.

And to the Quebec government, the "credible partner," which was now refusing to sit down with the other nine provinces and was insisting on dealing directly with the federal government on an equal footing:

> Changes in one part of the country affect all its parts. This is why the recent discussions involving bilateral negotiations dealing with the division of powers are particularly disturbing.

Robert Bourassa is now on his third Ontario "colleague" and his third party. Will the New Democrat, Bob Rae, be so very different from Bill Davis, the Conservative, or David Peterson the Liberal?

When the two met on a beach in Florida in December 1990, Rae let Bourassa know he was not without attachments to Quebec: his brother John is a vice-president of Power Corporation and Jean Chrétien's chief organizer. Which means he has useful contacts with the federal Liberals. The two "Bobs" got along so famously that Bourassa suggested to his Ontario counterpart that he should "visit Quebec more often."

But in Ontario business is business: a few weeks after the agreement between Quebec and Ottawa on the selection and reception of immigrants, Bob Rae sent his envoys to Ottawa to ask for the same deal, and a little more money while they were at it. After all, Ontario had taken in 54 percent of all immigrants to Canada in 1990. And it cost a lot of money to teach them English.

CHAPTER NINE

The Esteem of the Western Yuppies

The other premiers had more of a tendency to follow the party line, but Robert and I put the interests of our provinces before everything else.
William Vander Zalm

Robert Bourassa did not often venture out on the great Western plains. At best he would make a hasty stopover on his way back from some official mission to California, or make a quick trip for some intergovernmental conference. But that didn't stop him from having long, passionate conversations about agriculture with Grant Devine, or about the British Columbia-United States lumber trade with Bill Vander Zalm. In fact, after 1985, Robert Bourassa enjoyed a remarkable level of esteem and sympathy with Western premiers: a potential he was unable to exploit, and which he wound up squandering in the end.

Of the seven premiers he had known from the four Western provinces between 1970 and 1976, only one, Ross Thatcher of Saskatchewan, came from the same political family as he. And after the Victoria constitutional conference of 1971, Bourassa was seen as a leader who was intimidated by intellectuals, and who was not decisive or true to his word.

Bourassa was confronted by three New Democratic premiers in the West: Ed Schreyer, who had been governing in Manitoba since 1969, Allan Blakeney, who had come to power in Saskatchewan the

very day Bourassa turned thumbs down on the V.
and Dave Barrett, who was elected premier of British
1972. Since Robert Bourassa's Liberal administration
the social democratic tradition established by the Quie
tion, there should have been a certain affinity between Que
the West. But starting in 1973, the world was battered b   .o
successive oil shocks. Quebec, even more than Ontario, aroused
feelings of envy in the Western provinces, who felt somewhat
robbed by Quebec, which benefited from oil prices that were
below international rates. Then Bourassa launched his own energy
megaproject, the James Bay development, whereby he would
profit from the worldwide energy crisis, because electricity prices
were not regulated by the federal government. The resentment of
this in the West was such that at the height of the energy crisis,
Albertans plastered the bumpers of their cars with stickers that
read: "Let 'em freeze."

Unlike the rest of English Canada, Westerners were little moved
by the protestations of Quebec's English minority concerning
Robert Bourassa's language policies. The Westerners never felt any
great affinity for anglophone Montrealers, whom they lumped in
with the central Canadians in Ontario who ran the big banks and
dictated national energy and economic development policies. The
living symbols of their oppression were two former federal energy
ministers, Donald Macdonald from Toronto and Marc Lalonde
from Montreal.

It was more the conviction that Quebec was riding on the West's
coat-tails that enraged the Western establishment in Calgary,
Vancouver, and Winnipeg, a bitterness that was exacerbated by all
manner of biased studies that allegedly demonstrated that Alberta
was "keeping" Quebec. In 1990, two University of Calgary economists calculated that between 1961 and 1988, Alberta had paid out
$146 billion more to Ottawa than it had received, whereas Quebec
had raked in $137 billion over the same period, and of that, $95
billion since 1980 alone.[1] Albertans must really have been scratch-
ing their heads over why Quebec would want to separate from such a
sweet arrangement. "Tax Hydro-Quebec, as they did our barrels of
oil, and we'd have $7 billion to distribute to Western farmers,"
declared Preston Manning,[2] son of the former Social Credit premier

of Alberta and leader of the Reform Party, which has been rousing public opinion in the West against Quebec since 1988.

When Bourassa returned to power in 1985, a lot of things had changed. The election of the Conservatives in Ottawa and Brian Mulroney's promise to bring peace to federal-provincial relations led the West to believe it was at the dawn of a new era. The National Energy Policy, the dirtiest three words in the Western vocabulary, had been abolished. The promise of free trade with the United States and of generous farm subsidies and serious efforts at industrial decentralization rang like sweet music in Western ears.

The political establishment in the West was different from that in the East: less doctrinaire and more pragmatic, it was prone to more subtle political calculations. The West, in effect, wanted a reform of federal institutions; however, according to the terms of the 1982 constitution, such changes could be made only with the support of seven provinces representing 50 percent of the Canadian population. The Western premiers worried that if Quebec did not want to sit at the negotiation table, Ontario would, for all practical purposes, have a veto, and they knew that Ontario wouldn't want to reinforce Western provincial power in federal institutions, particularly in the Senate. "We told ourselves: [the Meech Lake Accord] brings Quebec in so we can fix these other things. Oh, that would be good. It was a notch in your political gun, on the handle of your pistol," said Grant Devine, evoking his rancher roots.[3]

The same calculation was made by Don Getty in Alberta and Bill Vander Zalm in British Columbia. Not a very smart one, as it turned out, because Bourassa, like David Peterson, was opposed to an elected Senate in which the Western provinces would have as many seats as Quebec and Ontario, and which would be invested with greater powers. "We'll worry about that later," the Western premiers told themselves, knowing they were trapped in any case.

Meanwhile, Trudeau's opposition to the Meech Lake Accord did not have the same effect out West as it did back East. "Trudeau is very unpopular here, still is," confided Devine. "They said here: 'If Trudeau's against it, I'd better be for it.'"[4]

For Quebec, the "Battle of Meech Lake" began in the West.

When Prince Edward Island's Joe Ghiz reneged on his promise to be the first premier to ratify the accord during the summer of 1987, it was Grant Devine who stepped into the breach. After having been the first province to drop Quebec in November 1981, Saskatchewan became the first to make amends.

It was not, however, a risk-free proposition for Devine. He was trailing in the polls by thirty points, and the opposition leader, veteran New Democrat Allan Blakeney, couldn't resist the temptation to squeeze some political capital from the issue. Backed by Liberal leader Ralph Goodale, a former aide to Pierre Trudeau, he tried to force the government into holding public hearings. Grant Devine not only resisted, he also managed to get every one of his members to vote in favour of the constitutional agreement. Three New Democrats, including Métis member Keith Goulet, voted against the agreement and against their own leader. Blakeney's anointed heir, Roy Romanow, a veteran of the November 1981 showdown, slipped out of the legislature along with a handful of other members just before the vote.

Grant Devine didn't pat himself on the back for what some considered a fine lesson in political courage. As he later said:

> I saw it as prudent. Clearly, the best thing to do was to deal with it quickly. It's popular, do it, discuss it, pass it. In fact, people would rather you did not talk about it. Fix it! And then go down and talk about the price of wheat, interest rates, and so on.[5]

There was an additional explanation for Devine's behaviour: the premier of Saskatchewan did not share the prejudices against Quebec nationalism held by his colleague from Ontario. "In fifty years this country will live through extraordinary changes, but these are forces that can work in favour of the nation, from which we should profit," he said, even before signing the Meech Lake Accord.[6] That Quebec was seeking to protect its language and culture didn't bother him much, since he himself had no intention of being pushed around on his home turf by the partisans of bilingualism and multiculturalism. Not that he was a francophobe, as some suggested, or a *"mange-canayen"* as they were called in another time. On the contrary. Married to the granddaughter of French immigrants, he sent two of his daughters—all of whom bore French first names—to study at Laval University in Quebec City. He even went so far as to make a bold promise to his 20,725 Franco-Saskatchewaners: the province would be officially bilingual by the turn of the century.[7] The interested parties, however, found that a little too far in the future, and feared that galloping assimilation might wipe them out before then. Devine later said:

> Put yourself in my place. Put yourself in the place of the pre-mier of a province where 97 percent of the population speaks English, who's signed the Meech Lake Accord, who's starting to introduce French in the legislature and the courts, and who's promising to offer services in French when 97 percent of the people don't want them. It's tough, but I'm going to do it.[8]

Like Robert Bourassa, Grant Devine was interested in economics before everything else. He hadn't stayed long on the family farm near Estevan, in the southeast corner of the province. Instead he went off to the University of Ohio to complete a doctorate in agricul-tural economics, then became a professor at the University of Sas-katchewan before going into politics. Devine later said of his relationship with Bourassa:

> When we meet, we talk a little bit about Constitution, and then normally about the economy. Because we have similar views on interest rates, the level of the dollar, and economic activity in building diversification. He would enjoy talking about that and because of my training as an economist, it was good to talk to him. As opposed to, say, Lévesque, who I don't think liked the term economics and didn't want to deal with it.[9]

The favourite topic at Bourassa-Devine tête-à-têtes was agricul-tural policy. Bourassa had studied it thoroughly in Europe, and Devine had his doctorate and extensive practical experience in the field; since 1985 he had reserved the provincial agriculture portfolio for himself. As close-mouthed and secretive about his private life as Bourassa, Devine was a sort of Western yuppie, one of the new breed of farmers who managed their spreads with computers, sur-veyed their herds from helicopters, and, despite the shitkicker boots they liked to wear at all times, did not feel the least bit out of place in the corridors of a GATT conference in Geneva.

Robert Bourassa also hit it off with Don Getty: at the beginning of the 1970s, the two had been caught up in the series of quarrels that the Trudeau administration regularly carried on with the provinces. As Peter Lougheed's energy minister in 1974, Getty had fought against Ottawa's first attempt at a national energy policy. "Trudeau," he said, "is an autocrat, a dictator, a dilettante, an academic trained by Jesuits and a Marxist philosopher."

The two might have crossed paths in their early years, as Getty was born in Westmount only five weeks after Robert Bourassa. But Getty, the son of wealthy parents, was raised mostly in Toronto, and studied business administration at the University of Western Ontario; he settled in Alberta after he went there to play quarterback for the Edmonton Eskimos.

With his Clint Eastwood physique, it was not surprising that Peter Lougheed recruited Getty to play the role of Lougheed's designated fixer and enforcer in Alberta politics. Yet, despite his strapping six feet and imposing two hundred pounds, which seemed to impress Pierre Trudeau's ministers, Getty was regarded with a suspicious eye in Calgary. There was nothing of the typical Albertan about him. Baldonnel Oil and Gas, which had poured several million dollars into his bank account, never found a single barrel of oil. His hundred-hectare farm produced neither grain nor beef cattle, but racehorses. He made rather a lot of trips to his luxurious home in Palm Springs, California, to work on his tan. His wife was charming and vivacious, and his four sons were so good-looking they got jobs as models for Toronto couture houses.

In short, his profile suggested a playboy and a pragmatic politician easily bored by debates between experts. Exactly six months after he signed the Meech Lake Accord, Don Getty got it ratified by his legislature. Two down.

Bill Vander Zalm was no problem either. "Robert and I are on the same wavelength," he confided to a visitor at Fantasy Gardens, his

botanical-garden-come-religious-theme-park in suburban Vancouver. Vander Zalm later explained:

> What brought us together wasn't politics, but a common
> preoccupation with preserving our provincial jurisdictions.
> The other premiers had more of a tendency to follow the
> party line, but Robert and I put the interests of our province
> before everything else.[10]

Born in Holland in 1934, Bill Vander Zalm was fond of telling
how he and his family had to eat roots and tulip bulbs to fend off
starvation during World War II. Newly arrived in Canada in 1947,
his father set up a nursery that employed Dutch and German immigrants whom he sponsored to come to Canada. Bill Vander Zalm
himself made a fortune selling tulip and daffodil bulbs to the huge
southern Ontario nurseries.

In politics, Vander Zalm tended to reinforce the anti-Ottawa
prejudices that British Columbians hold—the "bitchers," as Trudeau used to call them. "Quebec and British Columbia have this in
common," said Vander Zalm. "At one point or another in their
history they've felt alienated within the federation."[11]

Bourassa wasn't terribly eager to be seen in the company of a right-
wing radical like Vander Zalm, who, as the province's social affairs
minister, had threatened to distribute shovels to welfare recipients
and have them dig ditches in Vancouver to cure them of their lazi-
ness. But by 1987 Bourassa's corporate approach to provincial
administration wasn't all that different from what the Social Credi-
ters were doing in British Columbia. The Quebec government also
supported British Columbia in its fight over lumber exports to the
United States, which claimed that provincially conferred cutting
rights constituted unfair subsidies. And most important, Bourassa
set himself up as the apostle of free trade in central Canada. "Robert
showed courage when he proposed that," acknowledged an appre-
ciative Vander Zalm. "Especially since he wasn't from the same
party as Mulroney. I'm sure the Liberals didn't like that."[12]

It wasn't only the Liberals who were furious with Bourassa. The
fourth Western premier, Howard Pawley, flatly threatened to "make

Bourassa pay'' for his support of the Canada-United States trade treaty. Thus it was from Manitoba that the first Western salvoes against the Meech Lake Accord were fired.

It must be recognized that the province itself had good reason to be wary of what Quebec and Mulroney were up to. Howard Pawley came to power three days after the constitutional agreement of November 1981. He knew very well that the subject didn't make any friends in his province. In 1983, he had narrowly avoided being swept out of office by the furious debate over a Supreme Court decision that re-established francophone rights in Manitoba. Furthermore, in 1986 Brian Mulroney and his Quebec ministers—notably Robert de Cotret and Monique Vézina—gave the lucrative maintenance contract for the Canadian Armed Forces' fleet of CF-18 fighter aircraft to Montreal's Canadair, even though a Winnipeg firm, Bristol Aerospace, had submitted what appeared to be a better bid.

But Howard Pawley was a man of principle: he refused to let personal problems get in the way of constitutional matters. Therefore, he joined his colleagues at Meech Lake, even though he was beset with considerable doubts. And when he signed the agreement in 1987, he had every intention of respecting his signature.

Then along came the free trade debate, which disturbed him a lot more than the distinct society question. On December 17, 1987, there was a particularly stormy meeting at the prime minister's official residence in Ottawa from which Pawley came away absolutely furious. Bourassa, forgetting that he, along with his colleagues, was in a vulnerable position on the constitutional front, sided with the federal negotiators. Simon Reisman had told him that the treaty with the Americans would open enormous new markets for electricity from phase two of the James Bay project.

The same evening, in his suite at the Chateau Laurier, Howard Pawley exploded, and for the first time he brandished his threat to go back on his promise of June 1987.

> Bourassa isn't making my job easy. The worries about the
> Meech Lake Accord have intensified because of the free trade
> proposal with the United States, and we're going to get an
> earful. Even though I don't necessarily agree, more and more

people think there's a link between the two: the Meech Lake
Accord is weakening the federal government at the very time
that it's abdicating other powers to Washington.[13]

Pawley and the other New Democrats wanted to settle the free
trade issue in the next federal election. The polls had given them
reason to believe that Brian Mulroney's Conservatives could be
defeated. In Manitoba, Howard Pawley's majority hung on a single
vote. Only Liberal leader Sharon Carstairs was ''making a big deal''
out of the constitutional question. Gary Filmon, leader of the Conservative opposition, still officially supported the accord. ''I still
don't see any reason for not supporting it,''[14] he said reassuringly.

In the spring of 1988, therefore, an alliance seemed possible
between the Manitoba Conservatives and the ruling New Democrats. But that failed to take into account the old animosities towards
Quebec in the Western ethnic communities. Years before, in 1964,
during his tour of the country on behalf of the Commission on
Bilingualism and Biculturalism, André Laurendeau had tasted the
venom in the submissions by some of the groups in the West.

> The ethnic groups seemed to have the curious idea that giv-
> ing anything to francophones means taking something away
> from their groups, or, in any case, perpetrating an injustice.
> They were prepared to accept losing their native language, so
> why shouldn't everyone else? This was particularly true of
> the Ukrainians.[15]

A quarter of a century later, the Quebec New Democrats would
come to the same conclusion as their Western colleagues: ''It was
the New Democratic West that killed Meech Lake,'' declared
Claude Rompré, a former adviser to two national NDP leaders,
before he walked out, slamming the door behind him.

The New Democratic Party was born in the Western cooperative
movement, and despite unflagging support from the big labour
unions in central Canada, its greatest triumphs were always in the
West. In the 1988 federal election the NDP won thirty-three of the
forty-three Commons seats it had held in the West, and at the time it
appeared that the NDP was destined to form the next government
in two Western provinces—Saskatchewan and British Columbia—

and the official opposition in the other two. The regional concentration of the NDP vote also made it the true representative of Canadians of ethnic origin, the majority of whom live in the West.

"The NDP is naturally and fundamentally opposed to the principle of Canadian duality," concluded Rompré, an adviser to both Ed Broadbent and Audrey McLaughlin. He also revealed that, at a meeting of the party's federal council in March 1989, it was four Western leaders—Michael Harcourt of British Columbia, Roy Romanow of Saskatchewan, Gary Doer of Manitoba, and the "King of the Yukon," Tony Penikett—who forced Ed Broadbent to retreat from the favourable attitude he had shown towards Quebec for the past two years. Broadbent finally gave in to avoid a split in his party.[16]

After 1987, the New Democrats did not constitute a decisive force in the West. In fact, since Pawley's defeat in Manitoba in spring 1988, the only government controlled by the NDP was in the Yukon, which had a seat but no say in discussions at the first ministers' table. Instead it was members of the native community who deployed the handful of members they had elected to provincial legislatures to deliver the final blow to the constitutional agreement. As Claude Rompré later said:

> By insisting on the recognition of aboriginal rights and northern residents, the NDP's only aim was to open the door to constitutional recognition of immigrants and their descendants who people the West, and to put them on the same footing as the descendants of the French and English.[17]

The long-standing animosity towards French Canadians among the ethnic groups, the jealousy aroused by an economic balance sheet that outrageously favoured Quebec (the CF-18 contract being the classic example), and the tensions caused by the free trade debate should have caused Bourassa to be extremely careful, if only to make things as uncomplicated as possible for his allies: Getty, Devine, and Vander Zalm. Instead, Bourassa wound up with the Liberals, the Reform Party, the francophone minorities, and, finally, the Conservatives themselves, on his back within a few months. It made for a heavy load after a while.

To rid themselves of Brian Mulroney and his free trade initiative,

the Western New Democrats counted as much on John Turner as on
their own federal leader, Ed Broadbent, in the 1988 federal election.
Within the NDP, the rule of party discipline holds that the provincial leaders align themselves with the federal leader's policies.
Therefore, Howard Pawley couldn't understand how Robert
Bourassa could take a different position on free trade from that of
his federal cousins. "Bourassa has a lot more confidence in Brian
Mulroney than in John Turner," huffed the Manitoba premier.[18] "I
don't like playing the fall guy," said Raymond Garneau, in turn. "I
grant [Bourassa] the right to settle scores with Mr. Trudeau, but not
at John Turner's expense."[19]

At the same time, the Western Liberal parties, some of which
were rising to the giddy heights of 30 percent in some polls, were
bent on reconquering an area which despite all their best efforts had
delivered them only two members of Parliament in the last election:
John Turner in Vancouver and Lloyd Axworthy in Winnipeg. They
too would soon have a score to settle with Robert Bourassa . . .

For some time Liberals had been forced to meet in church base-
ments to continue defending Pierre Trudeau's vision. But Bourassa
was soon going to humiliate them where they lived. After the
Supreme Court judgment reaffirming French-language rights in
Alberta and Saskatchewan, strong pressure was brought to bear on
Getty and Devine to re-establish the rights of their francophone
minorities. The Saskatchewan government offered its minority
some privileges in the provincial legislature and courts, but categorically refused to re-institute its rights. People were getting defensive all over the country. The head of the Reform Party, Preston
Manning, protested:

> When Bourassa imposes the supremacy of the French lan-
> guage in Quebec, people say he's a great nationalist. But
> when a premier in the West does the same thing for English,
> he's called a dinosaur, a radical, a redneck.[20]

Francophones outside Quebec wanted Bourassa to intervene on
their behalf. "We've always considered Quebec our ally," said the
president of the Franco-Saskatchewan association. "If Quebec's
not with us, what have we got left?"[21] "Robert Bourassa should

carry on the tradition of Quebec premiers who have always been very alert to defend the francophone minorities outside Quebec," declared Jean Chrétien as he arrived in Winnipeg to lend his ally Sharon Carstairs a hand in the Manitoba election campaign.[22]

But Bourassa, like Mulroney, refused to intervene. On the contrary, during a visit to the West at the time, the two men were being rather supportive of the premiers of Saskatchewan and Alberta. "Bourassa is a traitor," protested the Franco-Albertans, whose statements made headlines in the Toronto dailies. In Saskatoon, Mulroney was greeted with a Gilles Vigneault tune whose lyrics go: "You hardly hear me, you don't hear me at all."

Robert Bourassa's attitude, and that of his Western colleagues, reinforced the suspicions of the Liberal intellectuals that the Meech Lake Accord was a monstrous plot designed to substitute two unilingual countries for the bilingual Canada Pierre Trudeau had wanted to build. The minorities felt abandoned. "Quebeckers have a right to the lion's share," complained the president of the Franco-Manitoban association. "And the Franco-Saskatchewaners settle for the crumbs."

Incidents like that convinced Frank McKenna and New Brunswick's Acadian community to hold out until the last minute before compromising. Because Quebec had refused to come to the defence of the francophone minorities, it became essential for them to give the federal government the right to get involved.

Another gaffe provoked the opposition of the Reformists, and probably cooled Bill Vander Zalm's and Don Getty's enthusiasm for Robert Bourassa and his constitutional plans. During the aforementioned visit to Saskatchewan, Bourassa met privately with a dozen of the area's influential businessmen. The discussion focused on the post-Meech era. The Quebec premier did not hide his feelings about Senate reform. "I have very serious reservations about the necessity of adding another level of decision-making made up of elected members,"[23] Bourassa said flatly. Word of his remarks raced like wildfire across the prairies and over the Rockies. The West got the impression it was being had. Even Grant Devine found it hard to restore calm. "It's not up to me to second-guess Bourassa on what he might do," he murmured diplomatically. "But I wanted to hook him into the country in an honourable way. Lock him in and we all work for a new Senate.''

The last nail in the coffin that the West was building for the Meech Lake Accord was the election of a minority Conservative government in Manitoba in 1988. The relations between Mulroney and the new Manitoba premier, Gary Filmon, had never been cosy. "We're not what you'd call great friends," said Filmon.[24] But the Manitoba Conservatives and New Democrats would both have liked to rid themselves of a problem that Liberal Sharon Carstairs was exacerbating in the reactionary rural south of the province. For several months the "two Garys" (Filmon and Doer) waited for the federal government to come forth with a modest compromise—a clarification of the consequences of the distinct society clause, for example—so that they could adopt the Meech Lake Accord and clear the air before the next provincial election. "It's what I told my colleagues in the federal cabinet. But they wouldn't listen," said Jake Epp, Manitoba's leading representative in the federal cabinet.[25] "I cannot forget that private meeting of provincial premiers in Saskatoon in the summer of 1988," recalls Bourassa. "Filmon told us: we've got to move, otherwise it will never pass.''[26]

The introduction of Bill 178, the "inside-outside" sign law, in Quebec's National Assembly in December 1988 was going to be the beginning of the end for Gary Filmon. Two years before the official death of the Meech Lake Accord in June 1990, the West had already turned its back on it.

> I took it on the chin. People will say that they believe my motives were honourable in trying to knit the country together. But the vast majority of Saskatchewan people did not understand it, and did not support it. Our government has a majority of seats in rural Saskatchewan where Meech Lake is most unpopular. And the multicultural nature of our province, with a high percentage of Ukrainians, Germans, Indians, Métis—they just felt rejected, and left out, and it's like you've abandoned them.[27]

As Frank McKenna commented:

If there has to be a hero—and there weren't a lot of them in
the Meech Lake debate—the title should go to Devine: everybody had his own reasons for concluding that it wouldn't
wreck his political career to support Meech Lake. But
Devine did himself a lot of harm.[28]

In fact, the Saskatchewan premier may never get over it. He was
well aware that Roy Romanow, himself of Ukrainian extraction, was
exploiting the situation. "Romanow is astute enough to play what
he thinks will work," says Devine.[29] But then the Saskatchewan
NDP leader was not without experience in this kind of thing. One
only had to ask Claude Morin what he thinks of Romanow, the man
he once thought was Quebec's ally:

You [Romanow] yourself, with whom I had spent so many
hours over so many months discussing the constitutional
issue [in 1981], why did you not call me so I could participate
in that night's session [November 4, 1981], from which Quebec was excluded? After all, you knew where to find me . . .
A lot of people at home think we were deceived and abandoned.[30]

The "deceitful" Romanow was the man with whom Devine
found himself face to face on the morning of June 23, 1990, after the
failure of the Meech Lake Accord. Two weeks earlier, Robert
Bourassa had come close to telling Devine goodbye. "Robert isn't
the kind of guy who will go overboard and hug you," said Devine,
"But he would give you a genuine 'Thank you for your support.'"[31]
Devine didn't have to read the papers to measure the impact that
his and his colleagues' failure had had on Quebec society. His
daughters, Michelle and Monique, called regularly from Quebec
City: "The attitude on the Laval campus is just, just a little bit less
true for English-speaking people," the Devine daughters told their
father. "You can tell that people are less interested in us now. We
understand, but we feel just a little less comfortable."[32]
Devine begged them to stay. He still believed it was important for
his daughters to learn French, just as he believed that Robert

Bourassa would not let him down on Senate reform. "Let history write what it likes about me. I thought it was good at the time. I believe today it'd be good for the country. And if I lose because of that . . . c'est la vie," he said.

CHAPTER TEN

The Bad Boys
of Confederation

*I believe that independence can only come about in
Quebec if it is imposed on Quebeckers by the rest of
Canada.*[1]

Richard Hatfield

How was it that among his three Liberal colleagues in the Maritime
provinces Bourassa could make no allies for Quebec? Beyond the
personalities involved, two reasons can be suggested: first, Bourassa
didn't take much interest in his colleagues; second, he left it up to
Brian Mulroney to sell them on Meech Lake—and to twist their
arms if need be. Which, inevitably, ended in disaster.

Thus from Richard Hatfield, who found himself thrown off the
train even before the first stop, to Clyde Wells, who hopped aboard
and immediately pulled the communication cord, the Meech Lake
saga in the Maritime provinces was punctuated by all that is disgraceful in politics: cowardice, tactical blunders, misunderstandings, and cheap shots.

"Meech is dead. Long live Clyde Wells," cried Newfoundlanders on June 24, 1990.

"Meech is dead. Long live Quebec," responded the crowd in
Montreal.

But it wasn't in June 1990 that the Meech Lake Accord's death
certificate was issued; it had been torpedoed three years before that
by someone who would come out of the exercise singularly

unsmudged. Named to the Privy Council in 1982 by Pierre Trudeau for having isolated René Lévesque, Richard Hatfield could, thanks to Brian Mulroney, look forward to spending his last years on the Senate benches after having let Robert Bourassa down on Meech Lake. (However, the Honourable Richard Hatfield died of cancer in the spring of 1991.)

"Today we are proposing that Canadians recognize something that has worked and which can still work: a Quebec which is occupying its rightful place [in Confederation]," Hatfield said in the wee hours of June 3, 1987. But when he returned to Fredericton, the Conservative leader was dangerously close to the end of his fourth mandate. And in the end Bourassa would have a hand in his downfall.

Between two negotiating sessions on the constitutional agreement, Robert Bourassa found the time to receive his colleague, the Liberal leader from New Brunswick, at his home on Maplewood Avenue in Montreal. As McKenna explained:

> It was a matter of building lines of communication with the political machinery in the province. It was useful for our election campaign: our election team met his, and we spent a day examining the Liberal campaign in Quebec, visiting their advertising agencies and listening to some of their strategists.[2]

Bourassa and McKenna were not without affinities. The son of a modest farming family, Frank McKenna had also married a rich heiress. But it wasn't so much the money that Julie Friel brought with her that was important: above all she came from Moncton, the capital of Acadia, and had a summer house at Cap-Pelé. Thus the young unilingual lawyer, who had been raised by his grandmother in the heart of an old United Empire Loyalist community, began spending his summers on the peninsula and discovered the Acadians. "These people have an extraordinary *joie de vivre*," he said with genuine enthusiasm. "They like music, theatre. Acadians are not a minority. They are a people."[3]

"McKenna had the passion of a fresh convert," confirmed one of his close political advisers. Also like Bourassa, McKenna turned his back on a career in Ottawa. After a short stint in political science at Queen's University in Kingston, he became an intern in Allan MacEachen's office at about the time of the Victoria conference. But like his Quebec counterpart, he never took to the atmosphere of the federal capital, so far removed from the "real world" of his province.

> Everything seemed phony. I saw a lot of yes-men and brown-nosers fluttering around ministers like moths around a candle, wielding power for the sake of power, without giving a damn about ordinary people.[4]

A final point he had in common with Robert Bourassa: he too named a woman, Aldéa Landry, as his deputy premier, which was not without consequence. Her husband, Fernand Landry, later became McKenna's chief of staff. Women and Acadians were very influential in the New Brunswick government.

Robert Bourassa and his political organizers may have been the involuntary architects of Richard Hatfield's defeat, but the Quebec Liberals' contribution was the final blow to an already tottering regime. Since October 26, 1970, when "Disco Dick" ended Louis Robichaud's Liberal reign, Hatfield had been governing New Brunswick like a despot. Re-elected with the biggest majority of his career in 1982, he still had a sixteen-seat majority in the province's fifty-eight-seat legislature in 1987.

Frank McKenna was categoric: Hatfield could easily have had the Meech Lake Accord ratified by the legislature before calling an election. "When Hatfield came back from Ottawa, the house was still sitting, and we could have extended the session a week or two. Why didn't he do it? I have no idea, but I must say I was surprised."[5]

True, for the previous year the polls had been predicting Disco Dick's certain defeat. And Richard Hatfield had been put through a difficult test when the RCMP came across a small bag of marijuana during a routine check of the premier's luggage just before he was to board an Armed Forces plane—which was also carrying, of all people, the Queen. Not only was this a monumental embarrassment, but as a result, his penchant for New York discothèques and his semi-discreet roistering with local university students found their way into the headlines. Moreover the province once more found itself embroiled in a language debate. But the constitutional question didn't really interest a lot of people. During the election campaign that fall, and even during the televised debate between the party leaders, it wasn't raised even once. Still, several Conservative strategists, after having campaigned in 1982 on Hatfield's reputation as the "Father of Repatriation," were of the opinion that claiming paternity of the Meech Lake Accord wouldn't have hurt the premier's re-election chances. McKenna adds: "It would have been difficult for us to oppose it. I don't know what our attitude would have been at the time of the vote, but that's not important. Hatfield had a solid majority and his caucus would have followed him."[6]

Miscalculation? Lack of political courage? The truth is probably simpler: Hatfield has always been unpredictable. Trudeau, as much as Mulroney, was always wary of the former "potato-chip seller." (Before going into politics, Hatfield had managed his family's potato-chip business.) Certainly no one doubted that he was sincerely sympathetic towards the claims of a federalist Quebec. "He was always a strong ally of Quebec," his successor acknowledges. And he always followed the strategies dictated by the federal bureaucrats with exemplary docility. During the patriation operation in 1981, it was the federal deputy minister of justice, Roger Tassé, who wrote his speeches.

All Brian Mulroney's advisers, in particular Dalton Camp, the former party president, a New Brunswick native and personal friend of the premier's, knew that Hatfield was finished. So why wasn't he pressured to settle the Meech issue before he took the plunge into an election he was destined to lose? McKenna swears to this day that his Liberals would not have rescinded New Brunswick's ratification of the Meech Lake Accord.

> When it came to free trade with the United States, we finally
> supported the federal government without getting anything
> in exchange, simply because when we thought about it, we
> realized we couldn't do anything else.[7]

In Ottawa it was assumed that New Brunswick wouldn't make any waves. But no one knew anything about Frank McKenna or his opinion of the Meech Lake Accord, something McKenna himself confirms:

> I never had any briefing from Hatfield or any contact with the federal government until I became premier. I got my information from newspapers. In fact, I got the impression that they simply weren't interested in my opinions.

Until the last minute—until the afternoon of June 22, 1990, to be more precise—neither Brian Mulroney nor any of his advisers would admit that one province would dare to continue its defiance to the bitter end. For generations the federal mandarins had taken the Maritimers for granted. After all, at Meech Lake on April 30, 1987, the fiercest opposition to the accord had come from Ontario and Manitoba. Maritimers had always been fairly accommodating.

John Buchanan, like Richard Hatfield, was not a major participant in the debates. Head of the Nova Scotia government since 1978, the debonair and worldly sexagenarian usually kept a low profile at federal-provincial conferences. He finally attained a certain level of notoriety in the federal capital, partly because of his surprise resignation and his subsequent appointment to the Senate in 1990.

Joe Ghiz was a far more serious matter. Traditionally, the speeches of the premiers of Prince Edward Island at constitutional conferences have been the signal for observers and experts to go for coffee and doughnuts. But with Ghiz, all that would change. Not only was his political situation unusual and intriguing—of Lebanese origin, he rose to become premier of the most thoroughly WASP province in the country and was the first Liberal to be elected to head a government in Atlantic Canada since Trudeau's departure—he also came to Ottawa with a solid reputation as a constitutional expert.

In 1978 he had, along with a certain Clyde Wells, been a member of the Canadian Bar Association's committee on the constitution. In 1980, he had written his master's thesis for Harvard University on control over natural resources in Canada. In fact, of all the premiers present at Meech Lake, Ghiz, along with Robert Bourassa, was probably the best versed in constitutional matters.

He knew that changes to the amending formula and reform of the Senate would affect his province's political clout. The old constitution effectively guaranteed Prince Edward Island's 128,000 residents four Senate seats, or one seat for every 32,000 Islanders, as opposed to an average of one for every 250,000 Canadians in the country as a whole. This situation was regarded with a particularly jaundiced eye in British Columbia, which had one senator for every 500,000 inhabitants.[8]

Robert Bourassa and Gil Rémillard went to Meech Lake to demand a "regional" veto; Ghiz lined up with his Western colleagues, who defended the principle of provincial equality. A former minister responsible for the status of women, Ghiz would also be the first, albeit in secret, to ask for changes in the Meech Lake Accord several days after he had signed it. Disgruntled by Ottawa's refusal, he sulked for a year before getting the accord ratified in his legislature, even though he had personally promised Robert Bourassa that he would be the first to do so.[9]

As for Brian Peckford, he had good reason to sympathize with Bourassa, since he also hadn't got everything he wanted from the 1982 patriation. It was Brian Mulroney, in 1985, who gave him control of the Hibernia oilfield and other oil resources that were believed to lie off the Newfoundland and Labrador coastline. Before Frank McKenna and before Clyde Wells, he too had been nicknamed the *enfant terrible*, the bad boy of Confederation. After all, wasn't he the one who made Jean Chrétien want to "throw up" when he said he preferred René Lévesque's vision of Canada to Pierre Trudeau's? Peckford belonged to the generation of Newfoundlanders for whom the notion of a distinct society held no terrors: they felt about as close to the mentality of mainlanders as Quebeckers feel to the inhabitants of Victoria.

But like his colleagues in English Canada, Peckford couldn't come back from Ottawa with his hands completely empty. Therefore, for form's sake, he decided to put up a fight about provincial control over fisheries. The Meech Lake Accord did not commit itself to much in that regard, save that it stipulated that the question would be on the agenda of "future" constitutional conferences, whenever they might be.

Nevertheless, it was this vague promise made to Newfoundland, more than the notion of a distinct society, that ignited the gunpowder of New Brunswick. The Acadians were opposed from the start to any agreement that left them at the mercy of a government whose majority depended on the Loyalist ridings in the south of the province. The Acadian villages along New Brunswick's French coast were also fishing villages: the inhabitants worried less about the threat to their cultural identity—which, after all, had survived the deportation and a century of isolation—than about the prospect of the big Newfoundland trawlers dragging in the Gulf of St. Lawrence, their only economic resource.

Perhaps this concern explains the Liberals' unprecedented triumph in the election that fall. If ever there was a "landslide victory," it was in that New Brunswick election on October 13, 1987, when Frank McKenna scooped up all fifty-eight seats in the Fredericton legislature.

The consequences of Frank McKenna's victory could have been foreseen as early as August 1987. While he was still opposition leader, he gave a presentation one Thursday morning in the federal Parliament's storied Railway Committee Room. Not a single federal bureaucrat showed up to hear what he had to say. Yet the objections he raised then to the Meech Lake Accord became the backbone of the parallel accord he would propose to Brian Mulroney three years later, and which would be hastily endorsed by the Charest Report.

A few months later, after McKenna had become premier, an imposing federal delegation was sent to Fredericton. It was doubly imposing in that the federal government sought to nail down the new Liberal government's support for both its constitutional proposal and its free trade initiative. "They insulted us," said one of the provincial advisers present at the meeting. "It didn't go very well," McKenna himself confirmed, somewhat more diplomatically.[10]

Lowell Murray, Norman Spector, and their batteries of experts weren't terribly interested in hearing what Frank McKenna or Aldéa Landry had to say, even though the New Brunswick ministers and senior bureaucrats had taken the time to study every comma in the accord, and were as well versed in the complexities of the constitutional question as the federal honchos. Frank McKenna adroitly chose to criticize the accord on legal rather than political grounds, and he stated his objections to one clause after another. McKenna later said, "They tried to explain to us what each of the clauses could mean, but they couldn't offer any legal guarantees. I thought at the time that we were going to clarify these points, but nobody really took us seriously."[11]

"You don't have three years to ratify this accord, you've got six months," threatened Lowell Murray.

"I'm in no hurry," McKenna replied calmly.[12]

A few weeks later, the new premier of New Brunswick attended his first federal-provincial conference. Like all rookies at these gatherings, McKenna was expected to keep his lip buttoned while he learned the rules of this ultra-select club. Instead, he leapt right into the fray, asking for clarifications of the accord, without necessarily insisting on changes. "I've prepared a text I'll be sending along later," he promised his colleagues.

Strangely enough, he thought he perceived a "remarkable lack of solidarity for the Meech Lake Accord" around the table.[13] But he was encouraged by the initial reaction to his proposal. For starters, Robert Bourassa said he was ready to sit down with him to discuss the rights of the Acadians.

During the months that followed, no one showed any interest in talking about the constitution with Frank McKenna. Free trade was the number-one priority now, and New Brunswick quickly came to support it. In the corridors of the intergovernmental conferences, the senior federal bureaucrats and Brian Mulroney's political henchmen began putting around the word that once again, as in the days of Richard Hatfield and Louis Robichaud, New Brunswick could be bought off. The bait was a $5-billion contract that the federal government was preparing to allocate to build six new frigates for the Canadian navy. Quebec and New Brunswick were the leading contenders.

David Peterson, who got wind of what was going on, quickly alerted McKenna. McKenna recalled later:

I was getting a little tired of these stories suggesting that you could "buy" the government of New Brunswick. I know very well that Maritime governments have long had a reputation for not sticking to their guns, for being "pragmatic." But I decided to change that. When we made our decision to support free trade—and it wasn't easy, because we had all the Liberals on our backs—the decision on the frigates hadn't been made. I wanted to make the federal government understand that it didn't have to buy us. I think Brian Mulroney got the message.[14]

The federal bureaucracy was not alone in dealing ineptly with New Brunswick. The Quebec bureaucrats, particularly those from the Canadian intergovernmental relations department, didn't exactly go out of their way to make friends.

There was a long-standing rivalry between Acadian bureaucrats and Quebec bureaucrats: the latter always had difficulty accepting their New Brunswick colleagues as equals, especially at the francophone summits. (For the Quebec mandarins, the downside of the agreement to give Quebec a seat at the francophone summits was that New Brunswick, being the only officially bilingual province in the country, was admitted with the same status.) As Richard Hatfield used to say:

It's generally accepted by Quebec leaders, by the Quebec bureaucracy, by the Quebec media, that only Quebec can speak for the French reality in Canada. I can't accept that.[15]

Any complicity between the federal and Quebec bureaucracies aroused the greatest suspicion among the Fredericton civil servants. And history would prove them to be right, McKenna says.

The compromise in the Meech Lake Accord on which the New Brunswick premier was most insistent dealt with the definition of the role of the Quebec government on the one hand, and the federal government on the other, in the "protection" or "promotion" of Canadian duality. In Quebec, McKenna's insistence on compromise was interpreted simply as a calculated political move by a premier who had recently won heavy support from the Acadian communities in the northern part of the province. But as in the free trade negotiations, McKenna was motivated more by principle than by political opportunism:

> I know too much about the effects of assimilation not to real-
> ize the importance of institutional protection [for minorities]
> in universities, hospitals, and school boards.[16]

To protect the Acadian minority from a reversal of the prevailing provincial policy of bilingualism, McKenna wanted the federal government to have the constitutional power to assure the promotion of Canada's fundamental character, "the existence of French-speaking Canadians, concentrated in Quebec, but present in the rest of the country, and English-speaking Canadians, concentrated in the rest of the country, but also present in Quebec."

In Quebec, this was considered an outrage. The idea of allowing Ottawa to advance the interests of the Royal Victoria Hospital, the Montreal Children's Hospital, McGill University, or the Protestant School Board sounded like sheer provocation. Bourassa and Rémillard, trying to defuse the situation, journeyed one after the other to New Brunswick to explain that the issue "could be easily settled in the second round" of constitutional negotiations. McKenna was being told, in effect: "Sign first and we'll haggle over the details later." Bourassa was sincere, McKenna thinks. But Gil Rémillard was a different kettle of fish . . .

In the fall of 1989, when the first ministers were merging the text of the Meech Lake Accord and the "clarifications" demanded by the other provinces, the question of the promotion of Canadian duality was revived. At the time, Quebec stubbornly opposed it. Then, when McKenna finally agreed to abandon Quebec's English-speaking community by concluding a bilateral agreement to limit the federal government's power in this respect to his province alone, the Quebec bureaucrats put their cards on the table. "Rémillard and the Quebec delegation fought against that too, and it was only Bourassa's personal intervention that allowed it to pass . . . We were right to insist," McKenna now says.[17]

In all, Quebec and Ottawa wasted more than a year ignoring Frank McKenna, who, after all, wasn't asking for very much; a few "clarifications" that would not really have altered Quebec's five conditions. In retrospect, the New Brunswick premier is bitter about the cavalier treatment he got:

> They never asked me for a written document or for an opinion. It was only after the Bill 178 debate that Ottawa started talking about a "parallel" accord, and Quebec about a political accord.

At the time no one expected there would be an election in Newfoundland, and there seemed to be ample time to negotiate an honourable compromise. All the more since Gary Filmon and Gary Doer were anxious to be rid of the constitutional can of worms that Sharon Carstairs had gleefully opened.

Frank McKenna's sense of fair play would once again delay the resumption of real negotiations for another nine months. "I had committed myself to holding public hearings," he explains, "but I didn't want to publish the committee report before the Quebec election [of 1989], so as not to hurt Bourassa politically."[18] The decision was one he would later regret. But "who would have predicted the election of a premier who was so doctrinaire that he would refuse any concession?" he sighs, referring to his colleague from Newfoundland.

For neither Ottawa nor Quebec, nor anyone in the rest of the country, was paying attention to what was happening in Newfoundland. Everybody thought Newfoundland was in the bag, ever since the House of Assembly, as the Newfoundland provincial legislature is called, had ratified the Meech Lake Accord on July 7, 1988.

Even so, it's not as if there had been no warning signs. The proponents of the Meech Lake Accord should have known that Pierre Trudeau and his followers would not give up so easily. The day after the accord was ratified by the federal Parliament, this group let it be known that henceforth the battle would be fought in the provincial legislatures. Immediately after Clyde Wells was elected as the head of Newfoundland's government, Marc Lalonde expressed his conviction that "he, at least, will have the nerve to go all the way."[19]

The Trudeauites knew what they were talking about. On March

18, 1988, Clyde Wells, then the new leader of the official opposition in Newfoundland, had rejected one by one the five clauses of the accord, adding, "When I become premier, I intend to rescind the province's ratification." Nor was Wells an unknown quantity in Ottawa. Like Joe Ghiz, he had been a member of the Canadian Bar Association's constitutional committee, and had registered a dissenting opinion in the final report because the committee had retained Claude Ryan's suggestion to turn the Senate into the "House of the Provinces."

Orthodox to the tips of his fingers, he had been chosen by the Trudeau government in 1980 to defend the federal government's case against Newfoundland itself, which was challenging the unilateral patriation project. "Newfoundland is a province like any other," he argued before his own province's Supreme Court.

The veterans of the constitutional wars in the Quebec bureaucracy had good reason to be suspicious of Wells. Every time a Liberal was elected to head the Newfoundland government, he had violently opposed any form of special status for Quebec. It was as though the province's Liberals were trying to make Quebec pay for the dubious deal they had struck in 1949 when they brought Newfoundland into the Canadian federation. Hadn't Joey Smallwood, Newfoundland's Father of Confederation, told Pierre Trudeau in 1967: "For Quebec, nothing, nothing, nothing. I don't mean almost nothing. I mean nothing whatsoever. Quebec should have nothing that Prince Edward Island or Newfoundland doesn't have."[20]

Clyde Wells therefore had an established political lineage, and he was dangerously well versed in constitutional matters. In the middle of his election campaign, to demonstrate how serious he was in his opposition to the Meech Lake Accord, Wells publicly renounced Brian Peckford's claim on fisheries jurisdiction. Then, when Wells met Robert Bourassa and his colleagues from the other provinces at the annual premiers' conference during the summer of 1989, Frank McKenna immediately alerted Brian Mulroney. "He's going to be an enormous obstacle," he told the prime minister. "You have to start taking him seriously right away."[21]

Despite these warning signs, the federal government did not try to get in touch with Clyde Wells, or to find out his opinion of Meech

Lake, for another six months. As with Frank McKenna two years earlier (or in the manner of the Trudeau-Peckford relationship nine years earlier), the federal strategists preferred to resort to scorn, insult, and even slander to deal with this other bad boy, Confederation's new *enfant terrible*.

During the 1980 constitutional conference, the federal functionaries had put out the word that Brian Peckford drank too much and received late-night visitors in his suite at the Ottawa Four Seasons Hotel. It would have been difficult to try the same technique with Clyde Wells, who was a paragon of personal rectitude. In 1990, these same advisers, this time in the employ of David Peterson, instead suggested manipulating the CBC and Radio Canada networks to make Clyde Wells look like "a spoiled brat who can't be trusted."[22]

As though he had memorized the briefing notes that the federal-provincial relations bureaucrats distributed to Conservative members of Parliament, Denis Pronovost, the deputy speaker of the House of Commons and Tory MP for St-Maurice riding, declared on a local hot-line show in Trois-Rivières: "Clyde Wells is a mental case, several bricks short of a load, a real crank." And for good measure, Pronovost added that with its 40 percent illiteracy rate, "Newfoundland is no more nor less than a Third World country."

In a climate like this, it was impossible to reach an agreement, unless the screws could be put to Clyde Wells. And this is precisely what the federal bureaucrats planned to do. They knew at least one thing about Clyde Wells: that he was emotionally fragile. A few weeks before the final deadline for the Meech Lake Accord's ratification, they decided he was close to cracking. In retrospect, the Newfoundland premier admits he gave way. "Peer pressure, I guess," he says.[23]

Thus on June 9, 1990, he signed a six-page document which expressed the view that Meech should pass "for the good of Canada."[24] He even committed himself to submit the last-minute agreement to his own legislature. (He was gambling that a majority of MLAs, his own Liberals and even a few Tories, would reject it.)

Then why didn't he do so in the end? On the morning of June 22, he had learned that he would lose his gamble and that his own party members, or at least a good half dozen of them, had been so swayed by the speeches delivered in the Newfoundland House by several premiers and by the prime minister, and particularly by desperate appeals from Jean Chrétien, that they planned to "vote for Canada," even if it meant approving Quebec's five conditions. It would have taken only six Liberals to vote against their leader for the accord to be ratified a second time in Newfoundland.

The next evening, in Calgary, when Jean Chrétien, the new leader of the federal Liberal party, embraced his colleague from Newfoundland and told him, "Thanks for everything you've done," he was referring to the massive support he had received from the Newfoundland delegation for his leadership bid. But, as far as the constitutional negotiations were concerned, Clyde Wells was still angry with Chrétien for having been among those who had twisted his arm.

On the morning of June 22, Wells hesitated for a long time before deciding whether to allow a vote in his own legislature. Then, at the last minute, he got a phone call from his only remaining ally in the land. A few minutes before Wells met his caucus for the last time, Elijah Harper called. "I'm going to block the vote in Manitoba," he promised.

Above all, Clyde Wells did not want Newfoundland to be the only province to say no to Quebec. Now that he was assured that Manitoba was in the same boat, he entered the legislature and moved for the adjournment, *sine die*, of the Meech Lake debate.

Thus, three years after he had made it, Richard Hatfield's prophecy seemed closer than ever to being fulfilled: "I believe that independence can only come about in Quebec if it is imposed on Quebeckers by the rest of Canada."

His successor in Fredericton takes the threat seriously. A worried McKenna can only hope that wisdom and calm will prevail.

"I agree that the matter rests with Quebec now . . . Most English Canadians think that Quebec won't react, that it's bluffing. Be it by accident or otherwise, [Quebec separation] is nevertheless what could happen."[25]

CHAPTER ELEVEN

Bourassa's Allies ... In Spite of Him, Eventually!

*The way things are going, it's as though the only
important minister in the Mulroney government is
Robert Bourassa himself.*
> A Mulroney cabinet minister

Between 1970 and 1976, competition between Robert Bourassa's members of the National Assembly and Pierre Trudeau's Quebec MPs was fierce and unrelenting. After that, it was all-out war. Until Brian Mulroney and John Turner came on the scene to lead the two major national parties, the federal members from Quebec were primarily concerned with defending Canada's interests in Quebec, and their own legitimacy in the bargain.

The Conservatives who took over most of the Quebec seats in the House of Commons in 1984 were not members of Robert Bourassa's circle of friends. Essentially they were "*bleus*," the age-old enemies of the Liberals in Quebec. (Quebeckers have traditionally viewed their politics in terms not of left and right, but of red and blue. In general, "*les rouges*" were the Liberals, and the "*bleus*" were the Conservatives and later the Union Nationale.) The "*bleus du Québec*"—Mulroney's Quebec Tories—were in such competition with the Quebec Liberals that at one point they toyed with the idea of creating their own Conservative party on the provincial level. But later, because of the close relationship between the prime minister and his Quebec colleague, Quebec Tories had no choice but to be

Bourassa's allies. Even after some of them formed, with Lucien Bouchard as their leader, a neo-sovereignist party, the Bloc Québécois, all Quebec members of Parliament—with the exception of half a dozen Liberals—kept defending Bourassa's interests in Ottawa . . . in spite of him, eventually!

At the time Robert Bourassa returned to power in Quebec, a contingent of "nationalist" Conservative Quebec MPs—fifty-eight elected in 1984 and sixty-three out of seventy-five in 1988— prepared the ground in Ottawa, and transformed the "party of the English" to the point that its old warhorses could hardly recognize it any more. The transformation also caused the party's traditional Western base to crumble and give in to the siren call from Preston Manning's Reform Party.

If truth be told, Robert Bourassa didn't really have much to do with this historic turnabout in Sir John A. Macdonald's party, which had, let's not forget, established itself in the West by sending Louis Riel to the scaffold. Instead it was Brian Mulroney who had the bright idea to bring into federal politics certain Quebeckers who had, for the most part, been primarily concerned up to then with pursuing their private careers. Once established in Ottawa, these men and women would help Canada discover the modern Quebec.

The traditional profile of the Quebec "*bleus*" did not recommend them to Robert Bourassa at the beginning of the 1970s. They tended to come from the province's hinterlands, not from Montreal. Their families had supported the Union Nationale; their parents had organized elections and run candidates for Maurice Duplessis. Most of them had voted for the first time in 1960, and had broken with their family tradition by throwing in their lot with Jean Lesage and his "*équipe de tonnerre*." But six years later, Daniel Johnson brought them home again to the Union Nationale. Marcel Masse, Johnson's former minister of education recalled: "He [Johnson] promised us the three dimensions of a modern state: economic development, social progress, and cultural sovereignty."[1]

Since they tended to be Quebec nationalists, they were part, though from a certain distance, of the rise of the sovereignist movement. Certainly, a good number of them—including Lucien and

Benoît Bouchard—declined to join Robert Bourassa's team. During the 1970s, while Bourassa was "building," as the slogan had it, they were mostly occupied making money. A lot in some cases, like that of André Bissonnette, who by the age of thirty had become known as "the chicken king" of Quebec for his multi-million dollar poultry operation. Or like Michel Côté, a chartered accountant and part owner of the Quebec Remparts junior hockey team. Or Marcel Masse, who had greased high-level wheels for engineering giant Lavalin through his contracts with provincial Conservative governments. "If we [Lavalin] had a problem with Bill Davis in Ontario, John Buchanan in Nova Scotia, Frank Moores in Newfoundland, or Peter Lougheed in Alberta, we'd send Marcel and he'd fix it."[2]

Others pursued professional careers without paying too much attention to politics. Monique Vézina, for example, who was nicknamed the "silent force" in her native Rimouski, made her way, without a college diploma, into the senior ranks of the Desjardins Credit Union Movement administration as well as the vice-presidency of Quebec's automobile insurance board and the Superior Council of Education. Benoît Bouchard ran a junior college, and like many of Brian Mulroney's future candidates, his interest in politics took him no farther than a seat on the town council of his native Roberval.

In short, when the Quebec "*bleus*" arrived in Ottawa, they were embarking on second careers. This explains why they behaved so differently from the Liberals of the 1960s who, like André Ouellet and Jean Chrétien, had entered politics around the age of thirty, or who, like Marc Lalonde and Francis Fox, had known only the corridors of power in the Prime Minister's Office.

A good many of Brian Mulroney's recruits had studied at Laval University rather than the University of Montreal, the alma mater of most of Pierre Trudeau's closest political associates. The difference is not without significance: in Quebec during the 1960s, the Laval group encountered a different generation of anglophones, people like Peter White, Michael Meighen, George MacLaren, and, of course, Brian Mulroney. Like them, these anglo-Quebeckers were from the regions, from the Eastern Townships or the North Shore, and they were far better integrated into Quebec society than the unilingual and often arrogant anglo-Montrealers. "Unlike a lot of people in the Parti Québécois, I have ties of friendship with anglophones that I formed in my youth,"[3] explained Lucien Bouchard. Benoît Bouchard said it another way:

Our nationalism had nothing to do with the frustrations of people in Montreal who were denouncing unilingual [English] signs. We didn't have that here: our nationalism stems from our sense of belonging.[4]

Speaking of his home region, Lac St. Jean, where the anglos who ran Alcan were considerably less snooty than those who ran the Royal Bank from the upper floors of Place Ville-Marie, Benoît Bouchard would have his knuckles rapped for his candid references to a society "undisturbed" by the English, of the "ethno-cultural purity" of his corner of Quebec where 97 percent of the population is "of Québécois language and race." These were words that the champions of multiculturalism, the Ontario New Democrats, would not soon forget.

It was the referendum campaign, and the economic bankruptcy of the Liberal regime, that led the "*bleus*" into politics, and, by way of the Conservative party, to Ottawa. "Strange as it might seem," said Benoît Bouchard, "the referendum is responsible for my career in Ottawa."[5] Like many others, he felt a "profound humiliation" when he heard Pierre Trudeau on May 16, 1980, at the Paul Sauvé arena, once again exploiting the natural anxiety Quebeckers feel when faced with crucial choices. "I've always thought that Trudeau didn't have to talk like that," says Bouchard, a "Yes" partisan who knew by then that his side had already lost.

The Liberals made a strategic blunder in the 1984 election when they attacked a dozen or so Conservative candidates who had previously been active on the "Yes" side of the referendum campaign. In doing so, they only reinforced—as though it was necessary—the Quebeckers' desire for revenge against the Liberals. Others, mostly businessmen active in their local chambers of commerce or the Richelieu Clubs (a Québécois equivalent of the Kiwanis), had simply had "enough of socialistic Liberal policies."[6]

Thus, by the time they had reached the age of forty, the Quebec "*bleus*" had by and large followed the same trajectory. During the 1960s, they had been stirred by the great social democrats—Robert Cliche, Jean Marchand, and even the pre-October Crisis Pierre Trudeau, who had given federalism a Quebec face, a French voice, and a generous reform program. Lucien Bouchard, who would develop a reputation as a "tough nut to crack" among the public service unions with which he dealt as a chief government negotiator in 1982, had even been on the verge of going to work for the Confederation of National Trade Unions because of Jean Marchand. Finally, they all backed Pierre Trudeau in 1968.

During the 1970s, applying their social democratic instincts to Quebec, they discreetly transferred their sympathies to René Lévesque and his promise of "good government." Then came Pierre Trudeau's referendum speech, and more particularly, the constitutional conference in November 1981, which they regarded as a betrayal. As a result their political instincts were awakened by a hankering for revenge.

During the 1980s, they accepted the "worthy risk" offered to them by Brian Mulroney, "someone who went to Ottawa at the head of a delegation of nationalists. Not fanatics or hyper-aggressives. People with plenty of common sense, who came from the regions, from all over Quebec, with the experience of their personal lives," as Lucien Bouchard put it.[7]

When Guy Charbonneau, Jean Bazin, Michel Cogger, and Mario Beaulieu—all of whom later became senators—put an organization and lots of money at Brian Mulroney's disposal in 1983, they were primarily concerned with the interests of the Conservative party. But in 1984, another team of Quebeckers, people like lawyer Bernard Roy (who went on to be the prime minister's principal secretary), ace adman Rodrigue Pageau (who died shortly after the 1984 breakthrough), or Gary Ouellette and Pierre-Claude Nolin (both of whom became ministerial chiefs of staff), became the head-hunters of the Tory campaign, recruiting local candidates one by one. To those who hesitated, they made a unique proposal:

You're one of those people who wants to change things, but you don't want to do what it takes. We're offering you a platform. We're not telling you you'll succeed, that your riding is assured, but it can be taken.[8]

These Quebeckers felt so far removed from the Conservative party that they all insisted on meeting Brian Mulroney before making up their minds. And it was Mulroney's brilliant idea to offer them a double agenda in which, from all evidence, he sincerely believed: to wash away all traces of the affront inflicted on Quebec by the Liberals in 1981, and to "make Canada work."

The message found a receptive audience. On February 29, 1984, the very day Pierre Trudeau announced his retirement, François-Xavier Bouchard, a personal friend of Robert Bourassa's and a solid Trudeau supporter, confided to his son Benoît: "Mulroney is probably the only man in the country right now who can pick up the pieces ... I'm wondering if I shouldn't vote Conservative next time."[9] Unfortunately, there would be no next time for François-Xavier Bouchard: the old man died two weeks later. But when his son met Brian Mulroney in Laval on May 28 the next year, he undertook to carry the Conservative standard in a riding in which Joe Clark's candidate, with a grand total of 532 votes, had finished dead last in 1980, well behind the Rhinoceros Party candidate. At the time, Benoît Bouchard told himself:

> I'm not going to Ottawa as a guy who lost his referendum. I'm going with the conviction that I have something to give, with my strength as a Quebecker who has confidence in himself. If we have to live in this country, we might just as well take an active role.[10]

Lucien Bouchard would say later:

> Mulroney was very good at reading what was going through his candidates' minds. He had a good understanding of the sense of frustration, revolt, and refusal that a lot of people felt about the political process in Quebec. He figured all that out. And he felt the need to provoke a breakthrough.[11]

During the election campaign, but only in Quebec, Brian Mulroney promised to get Quebec to sign the 1982 constitution. In this respect Lucien Bouchard recalls:

There would be a price to be paid for that. The right of with-
drawal, the notion of peoples, the principle of a "direct," not
just a "privileged" role in international relations. I insisted
that it be in his speeches.[12]

Six months after he become head of the federal government,
Brian Mulroney would reaffirm these principles before none other
than the President of the United States at the airport in Quebec
City. One year later, at the francophone summit meeting in Paris,
Mulroney was the only member of the federal delegation who was
not offended by Robert Bourassa's unexpected incursion into the
field of international affairs. Lucien Bouchard, then the Canadian
ambassador, had prevented his boss from making too much fuss
about it. "It was for rendering such services [keeping Ottawa-
Quebec relations smooth]," said one insider, "that Bourassa
insisted that Mulroney bring Lucien Bouchard into the federal
cabinet."[13]

Thus more than a year before Bourassa's comeback in Quebec, a
team of Quebec nationalists was preparing the ground in Ottawa,
and patiently undertaking the conversion of English Canada. In a
way they were the advance guard of the Meech Lake Accord. By
their behaviour, and by their statements in caucus and cabinet, they
convinced the "party of the English" that Quebeckers were indeed
different. Different in a friendly way.

The Conservatives from English Canada were not difficult to
seduce. There were exactly as many Western Tories as there were
Quebec Conservatives in the parliamentary class of '84. And these
people, like the Newfoundlanders, had, to a certain extent, the same
objective as the Quebeckers: to remove the insult of Liberal policies
(the National Energy policy in particular) and to "make Canada
work."

At best, Brian Mulroney expected to get about twenty or so of his
Quebec candidates elected. On September 4, he found himself with
a list of fifty-seven Quebec Conservative MPs, not counting himself. Few of them, however, were cabinet material. "I'm trying to
get up to ten, but it's not easy," he told an insider while putting
together his cabinet.[14] A number of them would have to content
themselves with junior portfolios. "We couldn't ask for too much

because we were inexperienced and had a lot to learn about the exercise of power," admitted Benoît Bouchard.[15]

A highly unorthodox style of relations between the governments in Ottawa and Quebec soon developed. Lucien Bouchard explains:

> Relations between the two governments went through my office in Chicoutimi, and that's what I did full-time. When the Lévesque government asked me to carry its list of demands to Ottawa, I refused. Instead I got Louis Bernard [then Lévesque's chief of staff] together with Bernard Roy and we went over the list of major items that had to be settled.[16]

For four years after Robert Bourassa's election as premier, and particularly during the Meech Lake negotiations, communications between the two governments depended on the close personal contacts between Bourassa and Mulroney, two Quebeckers who admired each other and who were basically on the same wavelength.

The arrival in Ottawa of a crew of Quebec nationalists, even though they weren't "fanatics," as Benoît Bouchard puts it, nevertheless caused a number of shocks. There was the language shock, for starters. The young MPs, some of whom had never set foot in the federal capital, had trouble, as Gérard Pelletier did when he first arrived in 1965, adjusting to the domination of the anglophones. "Why do you hate us Quebeckers so much?" Chateauguay MP Ricardo Lopez demanded of a patrician deputy minister of energy whose department didn't hire enough francophones. And when the commissioner of the Royal Canadian Mounted Police was summoned to explain his mostly unilingual English practices before the joint committee on official languages, the chairman, Charlevoix MP Charles Hamelin, said in a menacing tone: "If the official languages came under the criminal code, we'd have had to bring you here in handcuffs."

The process of learning how to exercise power was not without pitfalls. "Mulroney didn't cultivate friendships in Quebec for thirty years with the idea that one day he'd let them cash in," insisted Lucien Bouchard.[17] But there were those in the Conservative leader's entourage who still had fond memories of the old ways that were in vogue during the salad days of the Union Nationale. Despite what Bouchard said, a goodly number of Quebec entrepreneurs lined up to "cash in," and a series of scandals decimated the ranks of the Tory rookies from Quebec.

It was a bad time to remind the country of the Quebec politicians' taste for patronage: Robert Bourassa had recently been re-elected premier, and English Canada still had vivid memories of the scandals that had helped bring down his government in 1976. It was generally overlooked that the call for a reform of the federal party financing laws, inspired by the Parti Québécois electoral reform in Quebec, had originated in the ranks of the Quebec wing of the Conservative party. It was the Big Blue Machine in Ontario that had resisted the initiative. Incidentally, the pioneers of this cleanup operation, MPs François Gérin and Louis Plamondon, along with Lucien Bouchard (who came to Ottawa as the Quebec Tory "Mr. Clean"), later formed the foundation of the Bloc Québécois.

But what really bothered some was that after two years of on-the-job training, the Quebec ministers were beginning to assert themselves. Marcel Masse initiated the English-Canadian Conservatives to real nationalism, quoting American authors like Thomas Janeway: "The truly sovereign among a people are those who shape the spirit, the way of thinking, tastes, and principles. We cannot accept having this supremacy exercised by foreigners." Monique Vézina, who was minister of supply and services at the time, rejected the advice of her civil servants and, with the help of Robert de Cotret, who then held the pursestrings at the Treasury Board, gave the lavish contract for the maintenance of the Armed Forces' fighter jets to Canadair in Montreal. Elsewhere, Michel Côté managed to nail down orders for Quebec shipyards. In short, Robert Bourassa could say that "federalism has never before been so profitable."

The Quebec Conservatives felt carried along by the wave of entrepreneurship that was sweeping across Quebec. "When I see Bernard Lamarre, Pierre Péladeau, Paul Desmarais, Pierre Lortie, Michel Bélanger, it gives me strength. It makes me want to hang in there,"[18] said Benoît Bouchard. To the surprise and then alarm of their colleagues from English Canada, the Quebeckers started to bang their fists on the cabinet table. "I don't want Quebec on its hands and knees in Canada," warned Gilles Loiselle, who went on to take over from Michel Côté as the Tories' Quebec City-area strongman. "I want a Quebec that's strong—one that rocks the boat."[19]

Liberals and New Democrats from English Canada were annoyed when this new nationalist crowd started rearing its head in Ottawa. But in the ranks of the Conservative party, these Quebeckers were not only useful, they were becoming downright indispensable. Since 1988 they represented 40 percent of the Conservative parliamentary caucus.

And they had become more and more demanding. Moreover, the example of the Quebec "*bleus*," who weren't shy about speaking up, spread to the two other major national parties. In the NDP, the Quebec wing flexed its muscles during the leadership campaign for Ed Broadbent's successor, blocking the advance of the Western candidate, Dave Barrett, the former premier of British Columbia. On the Liberal side, Paul Martin tried to convert Pierre Trudeau's party in the same way Mulroney had changed the Conservatives. To English Canadians who refused to listen to him, Martin said in 1990: "Quebec will want to stay in Canada the day it is convinced that Canada believes in itself and wants to accomplish great things."[20] But Robert Bourassa's ministers didn't even give Martin credit for trying. Instead, they lined up their provincial organization—particularly in Quebec City and Eastern Quebec— behind Sheila Copps.

Since 1988, storm clouds had been accumulating in Quebec's political sky. The "rainbow coalition"—made up of "*bleus*," "*rouges*," Péquistes, and Socreds—that Mulroney had created in 1984 came unglued during the debate on free trade with the United States. An additional five seats in the Conservative representation from Quebec in Ottawa after the election of November 21, 1988, and the collapse of John Turner's Liberals in Quebec, obscured a profound malaise whose gravity no one wanted to admit, least of all Brian Mulroney or Robert Bourassa.

During the summer of 1988, a group of Tory "dinosaurs" from English Canada regrouped under the banner of what they called the

BBC—the Backbenchers' Club—and rebelled openly against the generosity of the government's official languages reform. Brian Mulroney had to expel them from his party.

The Quebec members began taking stock of their situation, and noticed that despite their leader's honeyed words, the capital was crawling with bureaucrats who were as partial to Ontario as ever. A phantom space agency quietly distributed research contracts to Toronto, while Montreal and Ottawa quarrelled over what would soon be little more than an empty shell. The West and the Maritimes each had its own regional development agency, whose kitty was kept well filled by the federal treasury, while bureaucrats from Ottawa and Quebec fought over commas in an agreement that never materialized.

During Mulroney's second term, Bernard Roy was gone and anglophone bureaucrats—first Derek Burney, a career diplomat, then Stanley Hartt, a lawyer and former associate of Mulroney in Montreal, then Norman Spector—took over the reins in the Prime Minister's Office, and things deteriorated rapidly. "What made me angry when I came into the government [on March 31, 1988]," said Lucien Bouchard, "was to see how much importance these people had taken on."[21] As often happens in Ottawa, Mulroney-the-Quebecker had let himself be taken over bit by bit by what Bouchard called "*la machine*"—the federal bureaucracy. "And I can say that the best speeches Mulroney ever made weren't shown to the "*machine*," he sighs, recalling the good old days.

Quebec Tories were getting less and less comfortable. Long before there was any talk of his resignation, Lucien Bouchard, then the senior Quebec minister in the federal cabinet, openly denounced the "*machine*." Addressing a group of students at the University of Quebec in his home town of Chicoutimi, he said:

> These immense overlapping structures, inextricably linked
> with their so-called decision-making processes, never work
> and always have to be short-circuited to get any decisions
> made.

The Quebec ministers felt cut out of the major economic decisions. "The way things are going, it's as though the only important minister in the Mulroney government is Robert Bourassa himself,"[22] sighed one of them sadly. The Quebeckers listened with evident irritation as they were told by their leader and his assistants that "Quebec shouldn't complain: it has Meech Lake." As though paralyzed by the fear of reviving English Canada's animosity, Robert Bourassa's ministers showed little spine in defending their initiatives.

On the front lines of the increasingly open confrontation with English Canada, the Quebec Conservative members were growing more convinced that they were being had. People were saying that Quebec was "paying dearly for Meech Lake." The chief of staff for one of the ministers with a senior economic portfolio commented: "We can't even give Quebec a pack of cigarettes any more without having it provoke a jealous fit in English Canada."[23]

Lucien Bouchard was barely installed in the federal cabinet—he had been there exactly six months—when he began threatening to quit. Along with several members, who in a year and a half would follow him out the door to form the Bloc Québécois, he solidly supported Robert Bourassa's decision to invoke the notwithstanding clause to uphold the law banning all but French from outdoor commercial signs in Quebec. Gilles Loiselle explained:

> Outside Quebec, there are no immigrants who assimilate into
> the francophone community, while in Quebec, they all want
> to assimilate into the anglophone minority. These people are
> confirming our fears, that we are in the process of disappear-
> ing. But it is because we are in Canada that Quebeckers
> are obliged to put up billboards to say that people should
> speak French. If we weren't in Canada, it would go without
> saying.[24]

In fact, there were more and more warnings from Quebec to which English Canada turned a deaf ear. When Robert Bourassa and Brian Mulroney continued to call publicly on the Manitobans and Newfoundlanders to accept without reservation Quebec soci- ety's distinct character, the Quebec Conservative ministers said to anyone who would listen: "This has gone on for three years, and everything that drags gets dirty." Actually, it became less and less assured that those ministers still wanted Meech Lake.

English Canada preferred to listen to Jean Chrétien's reassuring statements. Quebec, he predicted, "would agitate for a bit as usual, then fall into line." It was an excusable error in that Robert Bourassa never contested this kind of assertion.

Well before the Meech Lake Accord went into its death throes, the Quebec Conservatives were doing little to hide their discomfort in the federal capital, "this porcelain town where, if you move suddenly, things break,"[25] as Benoît Bouchard said. Since 1987, he avowed, he had been "living dangerously close to the edge of situations in which he would become uncompromising." Lucien Bouchard now refused to submit his speeches to the Prime Minister's Office in advance, for fear that they would be censored by the *"machine."* In the discreet surroundings of local chambers of commerce, he was already calling on Quebeckers to join the resistance. An influential member of the federal cabinet and Brian Mulroney's Quebec lieutenant, he put Quebec into something of a state of alert as early as 1989:

> Our timetable will once again bring us close to our breaking point by June [1990]. Everyone should understand and be prepared to take the consequences of his decision. We should not make the mistake of thinking that Quebec's moving forces have been exhausted; we have always lived on our feet.[26]

Benoît Bouchard was more accommodating. During the spring of 1990 he still allowed the unilingual English "machine" in the Federal-Provincial Relations Office to translate the texts of his speeches, all the better to censor them.

> I'm worried about the future of this country. The symbolism of biculturalism, whether it's called Michel Rivard or Laval University in 1960, the October Crisis in 1970, the death of Pierre Laporte, the 1980 referendum: who do I share that with? I want to fight and to convince myself that I belong in Canada. But I tell you, my job isn't easy.[27]

Benoît Bouchard admitted almost pathetically that his own children were advising him to pull out. In 1984, his eldest son, Louis, encouraged him to embark on the federal adventure. "Maybe you should find out if you really want to live in this country, if you want to participate. You won't find out by staying in Lac St. Jean."[28] Six years later, Louis was at the point of breaking with his father. The son felt his father's sadness, his anguish at having been mistaken and having tried right to the end, all for nothing, and his fear of finding himself confronted with a void.

Even the diplomatic and career-minded Gilles Loiselle began to get impatient. Loiselle, who, as Quebec's delegate to London, Paris, and Rome, had had to explain the meaning and implications of "Masters at Home," "Equality or Independence," and "Cultural Sovereignty," was becoming increasingly irritated that the "distinct society" was going down so badly in Ottawa. Or not going down at all. As he said:

> The English Canadians are fully prepared to tell us: "We acknowledge your distinct society, but, for God's sake, don't piss us off. So speak English, unless we're not around." My only determination is to go with Quebec, down whatever road it takes: in Canada, if that's possible. Or elsewhere, if Canada isn't interested."[29]

Despite the confusion, Robert Bourassa still hoped that if they remained faithful to Brian Mulroney, the Quebec Conservatives would continue to defend the interests of their province. Lucien Bouchard "carried the Quebec caucus on his back," he later said. The strategy, Bouchard confirmed, was to save the "integrity of the 1987 constitutional agreement, whatever the cost, because I think it nevertheless brings us forward a bit. Whether we like it or not, there will exist in the history of this country a document called the Meech Lake Accord, bearing the signature of eleven first ministers, in which it will be written that Quebec is a distinct society. The 'worthy risk' at least gave us that."[30]

During the long winter months of 1990, Lucien Bouchard rebuffed all attempts—"and there were several," he claims—to dilute the Meech Lake Accord. But he admits that at the time he was as concerned with protecting his friend Brian Mulroney's electoral interests as he was with enshrining a political accord that Quebec could use in front of the Supreme Court of Canada or the United Nations general assembly. Bouchard explained to the prime minister:

> The first ministers' signatures are there to stay, and they'll protect you in the eyes of history. In constitutional law, these signatures count for something: in a strange sort of way, it resembles a constitutional convention.[31]

It was the same argument he took to Jean Charest, the chairman of the Commons committee assigned to recommend a "parallel" accord to the Meech Lake Accord based on proposals from the three dissident provinces. Bouchard also collared colleagues Gabriel Desjardins and André Plourde to tell them the same thing. But it was all in vain, because behind the closed doors where the Charest committee was meeting, discreet negotiations had already been undertaken with Jean Chrétien (the leading candidate for the Liberal leadership) and Audrey McLaughlin, who had just been elected NDP leader. To Brian Mulroney, unanimity of the three national parties was essential. Though Chrétien was not elected leader yet, "he carried a lot of weight in this debate," Paul Tellier explained to Bouchard.[32]

Alerted by these little dodges, which displeased him immensely, Bouchard became suspicious. The government therefore took advantage of one of his trips as environment minister to Vancouver on March 26, 1990, to introduce the resolution proposed by New Brunswick in Parliament, thereby hoping to slip it through with a minimum of fuss. So it was on television, that same day, that the Conservative leader's Quebec lieutenant learned the contents of the prime minister's ultimate "Address to the nation." In tabling the New Brunswick Resolution in the House of Commons, Mulroney implicitly admitted that the "integrity" of the Meech Lake Accord could no longer be saved and that it had to be diluted with so-called "clarifications" and "additions" proposed by the dissenting provinces.

(According to Jean Charest and to senior advisers to the prime minister however, these were strategic moves aimed at bringing all the first ministers around the table one last time. Lucien Bouchard apparently agreed to the strategy after Mulroney assured him personally that whatever happened at this last conference, the Meech Lake Accord would remain untouched.)

Somehow Lucien Bouchard convinced himself that attempts were being made to isolate the Quebec ministers who were not flexible enough. His personal relations with Stanley Hartt, then Mulroney's chief of staff, didn't help. Bouchard was even tempted to cancel a scheduled trip to Norway where he was to attend an international conference on global warming. When on May 10, on his way to the airport, Mulroney's Quebec lieutenant made his final recommendations to the clerk of the Privy Council—"don't even try to sell the promotion of Canadian duality to the Quebec caucus"—Paul Tellier insisted that he make the trip to Norway. "Maybe they found it convenient not to have me around," he said after the fact.

This last mission as federal environment minister also marked Lucien Bouchard's final personal contact with Brian Mulroney. A few days before his departure he had received the Canadian passport issued to his young son, Alexandre. Lucien Bouchard was so excited that he immediately got on the phone to his old friend Mulroney to let him know how delighted he was for his son to be carrying his first passport—a Canadian one! "Have a good trip to Bergen," is all Mulroney told him, without mentioning his negotiations with Jean Chrétien. In less than two weeks, their twenty-seven-year-old friendship would come to an abrupt end. And Lucien Bouchard, who had boasted two months earlier that he often spoke to Robert Bourassa, would be limited to contacts with Quebec ministers, notably Gil Rémillard and Marc-Yvan Côté, whose prime concern, like his own, was to preserve the integrity of the June 1987 agreement.

On the days following that afternoon of Thursday, May 10, two unrelated developments dovetailed, and allowed English Canada to claim that Lucien Bouchard had planned his exit well in advance, that he was the one who had dug the Meech Lake Accord's grave, and that he was a traitor, as Liberal leadership candidate John Nunziata had branded him a few weeks earlier in Halifax. Officials in the Prime Minister's Office claim that since January 1990, he had been secretly meeting with Parti Québécois officials to plot his resignation. However, this is not at all what Lucien Bouchard says he had planned.

> Unlike Benoît [Bouchard], who had been making noises, I was hoping to stay with Mulroney to the end of the Meech Lake Accord. I was saving my energy for sailing and lying on the beach on June 23, all the better to spend the summer in quiet reflection.[33]

When he left Ottawa, Bouchard took with him a briefcase bulging with "things to do." Thus he came across an invitation from the local Parti Québécois association in his home riding to attend the party's general council meeting that would shortly be held in Lac St. Jean. Bouchard had not renewed his PQ membership card since being named ambassador to Paris in 1985. But in all likelihood the membership lists had not been brought up to date since then. "The invitation, in my riding, on May 20, the tenth anniversary of the referendum . . . embarrassed me a little. I thought it would be polite to send a telegram as a courtesy." He says he informed "the people in Mulroney's office" of his intentions.

The environmental conference turned out to be more problematic than expected. Bouchard was the only one of some forty ministers present in Bergen who opposed a set of resolutions prepared by a group of experts—including the former premier of Quebec, Pierre-Marc Johnson—because he thought the proposals were too timid. On Tuesday, May 15, Bouchard and Johnson had lunch together. They talked about Quebec politics, of course, and Bouchard discussed his intention to send a telegram to his riding's PQ association. "Are you going to talk about Lévesque in it?" Johnson asked. "You're looking for trouble. What do you stand to gain from it?" the former Quebec premier added.[34]

During the afternoon, while one of the Latin American delegates delivered an interminable speech, Lucien Bouchard found himself dozing off. To ward off boredom, he began drafting his telegram. But then he was called away for an urgent message, and he left his notepaper on the conference table. "I looked everywhere, but I never found my draft," he said. Could it be that it was found by a zealous bureaucrat who then hurriedly forwarded it to Ottawa? There are those in Brian Mulroney's entourage who say they were "warned" about the telegram while others deny it. If anybody in the Prime Minister's Office had been notified, why was nothing done to dissuade Bouchard from going through with his plan? Because it was only two days later, and under very special circumstances, that Bouchard would finally write his message to his "Dear compatriots everywhere in Quebec."

On Wednesday, May 16, the minister returned to Paris to join his wife and son. He stayed in the large apartment, often used for official functions, which was occupied by Marc and Patricia Lortie, both diplomats at the Canadian embassy in Paris. Marc Lortie had previously served as Brian Mulroney's press secretary, and maintained close contacts with his former colleagues in the Prime Minister's Office.

In the evening there was a phone call from Camille Guilbault, Mulroney's assistant in charge of liaison with the Quebec caucus. "The Charest report has been leaked to the newspapers," she said. "There may be certain things in there ... "

"Fax it to me right away," replied Bouchard, who immediately understood what was happening. He promised not to make any public statements before he returned to Ottawa.

On the tape of the Lorties' telephone answering machine, messages from Benoît Bouchard and Jean Charest were accumulating. Bouchard did not return any of the calls. The only call he was waiting for, and which never came, was from Brian Mulroney.

The next day, when he read the unanimous report from the Commons committee, and noted that neither Paul Tellier nor Jean Charest had taken his recommendations into account, Lucien Bouchard exploded. "When I reworked the telegram again that day, I decided to give it everything I had. I had a feeling that it was going to shock people a little, but I figured everyone knew me, after all." His press secretary, Micheline Fortin, advised him to sleep on it. "We've got enough trouble as it is," she added.

Reading the telegram over again the next morning, Bouchard nevertheless felt a certain sense of satisfaction. It stated:

The commemoration of the referendum directly concerns us all as Quebeckers. It is another occasion to remember the candor, the pride, and the generosity of the "Yes" we defended along with René Lévesque and his team. The memory of René Lévesque unites us all this weekend, because he made Quebeckers discover their inalienable right to decide their destiny themselves.

Jacques Parizeau created quite a stir when he read Bouchard's message to the Parti Québécois delegates gathered in Alma. Mulroney, sitting in the family room at 24 Sussex, was listening to the speech on Telemedia, the largest private radio network in Quebec, that was carrying it live. "The prime minister was flabbergasted!" says a close associate. "He knew that was it, that it was irreparable." A few hours later, the phone rang again in the Lorties' apartment. Lucien Bouchard was there alone. Without thinking, he answered. It was a furious Paul Tellier, who loudly demanded an immediate explanation of what he meant by his telegram. Bouchard also raised his voice in reply:

> Do you think I'm going to compromise everything I've done for the past five years for the sake of a telegram? I've done a lot worse than that since I've been in the cabinet. The telegram isn't what's important. It's the report, the Charest report, Jean Chrétien's little pile of crap. That's what I want to talk about. On Monday!

Because the notorious telegram to the Parti Québécois had almost succeeded in overshadowing the contents of the report, which even Robert Bourassa had immediately deemed "unacceptable," Lucien Bouchard suspected he was being set up as a scapegoat, that he would be held responsible for a constitutional failure that now seemed inevitable.

Had Brian Mulroney already resigned himself to Bouchard's departure? Or did the Federal-Provincial Relations Office take it for granted? During the course of Saturday, May 19, without even waiting for Bouchard's return, Lowell Murray and Norman Spector proceeded to give Manitoba's Gary Filmon a strategy paper and several legal opinions softening the impact of the clause recognizing Quebec society's distinct character.

When Bouchard landed in Montreal on the Sunday afternoon, he refrained from making any comment. He knew the next day would be difficult: they would try to make him apologize for his show of sympathy towards the Parti Québécois, and, at the same time, bury his opposition to the Charest report, which was essential if the premiers were to get to one final meeting in Ottawa on June 2. Still feeling the effects of jetlag, Bouchard awoke at five o'clock on Monday morning and began drafting his letter of resignation. Mentally he prepared himself for the pressures that his friends would bring to bear on him to convince him to renounce his gesture.

When he arrived at Paul Tellier's office in the early afternoon, Tellier tried to start the discussion by bringing up the problem of the telegram. What bothered him in his position as Privy Council clerk, the guardian of cabinet solidarity in Ottawa, was the reference to the Quebec people's right to self-determination. Ottawa had never consented to give an inch of ground on this question: this at least called for a "clarification." "Your problem is the Charest report," interrupted Bouchard.

After two hours under pressure—"it was coming from everywhere"—Bouchard began to feel tired. He hadn't eaten yet, and he was anxious to get to his office so he could sign his letter of resignation. At about four o'clock, one of his friends, "someone very, very close," asked to see him.

It was a holiday in Ottawa—Victoria Day—and the Langevin Block, which houses the Prime Minister's Office, was deserted. Mulroney was at his official residence on Sussex Drive. Thus it was Tellier who went downstairs to admit the visitor.

Alone in the clerk's office, Bouchard swivelled in his chair, distractedly studying the paintings and photographs on the wall. He was assailed by doubts. "Maybe I'm making too much of it," he mused. "Maybe I'm wrong: everybody else is swallowing this Charest report. Why can't I swallow it?"

Suddenly his gaze lit on a small plaque of the sort that is awarded to the winners of amateur sports tournaments. It was from the employees of the Canadian Unity Information Office who had awarded it to Paul Tellier the day after the referendum. "He was the separatists' favourite target," read the laudatory inscription.

Lucien Bouchard's hands balled into fists. He thought: "Follow your instinct . . . these are Quebec's historic enemies. Remember that. Mulroney, your pal who brought you into politics, isn't listening to you any more. He isn't interested in your speeches any more. He's moved on, he's dealing with the Spectors, the Telliers, Jean Chrétien's friends, the guys who fought against Quebec, who drove it to its knees . . . The guy—it happened to be Bernard Roy—who came up to see me got one hell of an earful," Bouchard recalls.

All that remained was for him to see Brian Mulroney. The two men retired to the small office in which the prime minister had decided a few days earlier to roll the dice one last time on the constitutional conference table. The minister's letter to his boss said it all:

> We have gone a long way together. In less than six months I have fought two election campaigns, both essentially based on the ratification of the Meech Lake Accord and the Free Trade Agreement . . .
>
> I took the gamble that the signatures freshly inscribed on the bottom of the Meech Lake Accord would be respected. But, like all Quebeckers, I have watched with consternation and growing sadness the reactions that have arisen against the accord. Francophones in all parts of the country have seen new displays of intolerance. While the Quebec flag was trampled underfoot, those who supported the "Yes" in the referendum have been accused of racism and treason . . .
>
> And, as the height of irony, the provinces, repudiating their signatures, are coming forth with their claims, with their shopping lists, notably this modification that serves to neutralize the distinct character of Quebec society . . .
>
> As for the rest, my departure cannot help but relieve a certain body of opinion that requires from Quebec's elected representatives in Ottawa an unconditional, not to say sacramental, adherence to the existing federalist formula.

Brian Mulroney was personally hurt. For the next six months, none of his ministers could bring up an important political question without evoking a bitter reference to "Lucien's treason." Even so, Bouchard has never ceased to speak well of his former friend. "Mulroney is quite a tolerant man. He is a very generous man and he deserves to be known much better by Canadians,"[35] he insisted the day of his resignation.

Was it all a dark plot, as the prime minister's advisers claimed, and as Mulroney himself would finally come to believe? Lucien Bouchard's resignation, which had been preceded by those of MPs François Gérin and Gilbert Chartrand, would be followed by three others. Lucien Bouchard had already accepted a series of high-profile speaking engagements for the following few days, and wherever he went in Quebec he was hailed as a hero. Though he had promised not to attack his former party, he was accused of raiding the Quebec Conservative caucus—in vain as it turned out.

It is true that behind the scenes Bouchard used his contacts with ministers like Gil Rémillard and Marc-Yvan Côté and a few members of the National Assembly to exert pressure on Robert Bourassa to avoid "the trap of a last constitutional conference." As it turned out, however, Lucien Bouchard, like René Lévesque in 1967, walked out of his party with only a handful of loyalists behind him. The haemorrhage that some feared would drain the Conservative ranks was stemmed, for better or for worse, by the cajolings of the faithful Benoît Bouchard and by Brian Mulroney's promises.

The sovereignists applauded the creation of the Bloc Québécois, and threw the weight of their grass-roots organization behind Bloc candidate Gilles Duceppe in the August 1990 by-election to replace the late Liberal MP, Jean-Claude Malépart, in the midtown Montreal riding of Laurier-Sainte-Marie. Some time before his death the populist Malépart had also decided to abandon Jean Chrétien's party. The Bloc Québécois was opening a second sovereignist front in Ottawa. Behind the scenes, the PQ encouraged the Bloc to make trouble. "Canada has to go to the dogs before anything can change,"[36] said a party official.

Lucien Bouchard (whom Bernard Lamarre, the president of giant engineering company Lavalin, had derisively nicknamed "Hamlet") told his friends: "For the first time I feel completely at ease with myself." He had perhaps taken a long time to make up his mind, but at the age of fifty, his conviction was overwhelmingly solid. Jean-Roch Boivin, René Lévesque's former comrade in arms, said of Bouchard, "He's a man of rare integrity. He possesses a higher-than-average intellect. Maybe Bouchard hasn't got the right answers yet, but at least he's asking the right questions."

The only disappointment, perhaps, was that he did not succeed in convincing enough of his colleagues in the House of Commons to follow him across the floor to make him leader of a "real" party, recognized under the House rules. "Solitude, when it is imposed and when there is a good number to share it, has a tendency to transform itself into solidarity," he had said, still full of hope in February 1990.[37] In English Canada, people tried to paper over the crisis, to "go on to other things." "Visit the Gaspé Peninsula. Or watch baseball on TV," Jean Chrétien advised them on June 23.

A handful of ministers and a few Quebec Conservative MPs would nevertheless fight one last battle at Robert Bourassa's side, when the Quebec government decided to take one last chance at going "one on one" against the federal bureaucracy. Mulroney was reluctant to reopen a wound that was still too fresh. In fact, opinion was mounting in English Canada against any attempt at bilateral negotiations between Quebec and Ottawa. Once more, Benoît Bouchard dared to say out loud what many increasingly upset Quebec Conservatives were thinking:

> I want to know what English Canada has to tell us. We've been telling them what we want for 123 years, and it has never worked. So now I feel like listening. The Canada of the Reform Party, is that what they want? Ontario in particular seems to be up in the air. But isn't it the province that benefits most from the status quo?[38]

The prime minister gave way, one last time, to the pressure from the Quebec "*bleus*" and created the Citizens' Forum, headed by the colourful Keith Spicer. As for Benoît Bouchard, his outspokenness cost him the little influence he still had in Ottawa and threatened his role as Brian Mulroney's political lieutenant in Quebec.

He had said too much in this "porcelain town" where things break if you move suddenly. And Robert Bourassa had fewer and fewer allies in the federal capital.

CHAPTER TWELVE

Up Against the "Red Power"

*I was afraid it would all end in a bloodbath, that we
would find ourselves with years of terrorist activity,
like Ireland. Because it always starts out like this . . .*
Robert Bourassa

On April 29, 1980, Pierre Trudeau met the chiefs of the First
Nations at the Skyline Hotel in Ottawa. Addressing himself particularly to those who had come from Quebec, he promised them that
a "No" vote in the referendum would clear the way for a wave of
constitutional reform from which they would have much to gain.
"If not," he threatened, "your goose is cooked."[1]
René Lévesque could not resist replying:

It's a funny kind of Quebecker who ardently defends the
"national" rights of the Inuit and the Indians, but who still
has such a total block when it comes to this nation, which is
no less indisputable, called French Quebec.[2]

Unlike Robert Bourassa, Lévesque had always tied a satisfactory
settlement of the native issue to Quebec's accession to sovereignty.
Shortly before his death, he said to a close friend, "Quebec will
never achieve political independence as long as the native issue
remains unsettled."[3]
Relations between Bourassa and the province's native leaders had
never been exactly friendly. To be sure, his justice minister, Jérôme

Choquette, was the first to offer an autonomous justice system to the Quebec Inuit. And the James Bay settlement, with its $225-million compensation package, gave rise to a generation of native entrepreneurs. But for the chiefs, these concessions remained somewhat abstract and were defined too much in terms of white man's "business." The native leaders wanted instead a show of political solidarity from the Quebec government, especially since the native claims and those of the Quebec people were not unrelated. "I live in Quebec," Inuit Chief Amédée Nungak pointed out. "I feel like a Quebecker because I derive strength from the people of Quebec."

One of the little ironies of history is that in 1975, Robert Bourassa set the example for the rest of Canada with the degree of self-government accorded the Quebec Cree and Inuit in the James Bay agreement. Paul Tellier, who at the time was deputy minister of Indian Affairs, recognized that "even if the agreement is imperfect, it remains a model ... There are a lot of comparable elements between the treaties signed by Canada in the nineteenth century and the James Bay agreement."[4]

It was Quebeckers, in any case, who had historically been most receptive to native claims. In 1987, Decima research established that two-thirds of them were ready to give native groups jurisdiction over education, health, social services, hunting and fishing, and renewable resources.[5] The more perceptive observers in English Canada recognized this. "Almost without exception, comparisons show that native people live in better circumstances in Quebec than elsewhere in Canada."[6] "Concerning the native people, if I may say so in passing, we have no lessons to learn from anyone," concluded René Lévesque.

The Inuit and Indian leaders had always been suspicious of constitutional conferences. They opposed patriation of the Canadian constitution, because it would cut the historic tie they had with the British crown, a tie that had existed even before there was such a thing as Canada.

In 1981, thanks to Saskatchewan's efforts, the Inuit, Indians, and Métis at least succeeded, unlike Quebec, in protecting their acquired rights. In effect, the federal government and the nine signing provinces recognized that the new constitution "shall not be construed so as to abrogate or derogate from any aboriginal, treaty or other rights or freedoms that pertain to the aboriginal peoples of Canada." The constitutional agreement also provided for three constitutional conferences—there would finally be four—dedicated exclusively to the native question.

But there really wasn't just *a* native question; instead there were as many problems to address as there were native peoples. The half million Indians officially registered with the Department of Indian and Northern Affairs spoke fifty-two languages spread among ten distinct linguistic groups; they were divided into 596 bands living on no fewer than 2,284 reserves. Non-status Indians and Métis were living off the reserves in increasing numbers; three-quarters of them cited English as their mother tongue. Of the 28,000 Inuit, on the other hand, 74 percent spoke Inuktitut, and lived primarily in the Northwest Territories and northern Quebec. So, in as much as language, culture, or territory was concerned, the issue was extremely complex—as the first ministers would discover during the three first constitutional conferences on native issues.

The fourth and last of these conferences was scheduled to open in Ottawa on March 26, 1987. Everybody knew that since March 6, Quebec had concocted its own constitutional agreement with Ottawa and the governments of the English provinces. Between meetings on the native question, the bureaucrats spent two days in Ottawa discussing "the Quebec agenda."

"Quebec's message is going over well," they said when they emerged. So well that Brian Mulroney decided to invite his colleagues to Meech Lake on April 30. The native leaders took note. They too had an interest in seeing the Quebec question settled as quickly as possible. On March 9, the federal negotiators had submitted to them a "consensus document" proposing explicit constitutional recognition of their right to self-government.

But the three Western provinces—which incidentally had been created on the backs and the lands of the Métis and Indians—opposed the enshrinement of native self-government. Any constitutional amendment was therefore doubly dependent on Quebec's participation: to make up the magic number of seven provinces and the required 50 percent of the Canadian population.

Federal negotiator Norman Spector went so far as to raise hopes—falsely—among the native leaders by letting them think that Quebec's participation at the March 26 conference wasn't absolutely necessary if the province committed itself to ratifying later any agreement reached by six other provinces.[7]

The native question was so closely linked with the Quebec question that on March 25, during a private dinner, the first ministers discussed settling both simultaneously. However, there was one empty chair at the table in the dining room at 24 Sussex Drive: Robert Bourassa's. His absence would have serious consequences.

Quebec's premier had delegated his Canadian intergovernmental affairs minister, Gil Rémillard, to represent him at the Ottawa conference. But instead of interesting himself in the native issue, Rémillard engaged in some subtle bargaining to advance his own cause. When all eyes among the native leaders turned to him for a *"beau geste,"* Rémillard said simply:

> The premier of Quebec must reaffirm that the constitutional situation imposed on him [by the 1982 repatriation] is unacceptable. He can therefore make no gesture that would normalize such a situation.[8]

Brian Mulroney did nothing to alleviate the ambiguity of such a statement. "Quebec's absence imposes a burden on all the other provinces that cannot be ignored. We cannot possibly continue without Quebec," he said.[9]

"We've had enough of being held hostage by Quebec's demands," the native leaders declared bitterly. Unnoticed in the crowd at the time was the parliamentary secretary to Manitoba's minister of northern affairs, Elijah Harper.

In the end, Newfoundland joined the three Western provinces in opposing the recognition of any form of native self-government. Therefore Quebec's participation became a theoretical point only. Four Conservative governments had scuttled five years of constitutional negotiations.

By way of justifying itself, English Canada let on that the Indians, the Inuit, and particularly the Métis were too assimilated, that they were already too far removed from sovereignty to assume self-government. In other words, native communities would not be economically viable. Was this not the argument that had been thrown at Quebeckers during the 1960s, when they were excluded from senior management in industry and finance? On the contrary, Gil Rémillard used the failures of others to assure his own victories. "It has been proven that the constitution cannot be amended without Quebec present at the bargaining table," he declared. This kind of blackmail, applied by Quebec to demonstrate the need to reach an agreement at Meech Lake five weeks later, did not go unnoticed.

A few feet away from Rémillard, one of his own advisers murmured into a journalist's ear: "Let's hope Quebec doesn't get a taste of the same bitter pill of constitutional failure in the negotiations that start officially next April 30 in Ottawa."[10]

Five weeks before the Meech Lake Accord was signed, Rémillard and Mulroney's boasts had convinced the native leadership, with or without good reason, that Quebec had dropped them, or worse, that it had used them as a stepping stone to advance its own cause. The native people were basically under the impression that Quebec had done a number on them. "In 1870 and 1885 we could count on support from Quebec when we needed it," protested the leader of the Manitoba Métis, himself a descendant of Gabriel Dumont, Louis Riel's lieutenant at the Battle of Batoche. "It saddens us that Quebec isn't there today."

No one should therefore have been surprised at their anger thirty-five days later when they saw the first ministers shaking Robert Bourassa's hand and wishing him "Welcome to Canada." The native people had just spent five years and four constitutional conferences trying in vain to attain a form of hybrid "autonomous government." In eleven hours of closed talks, Quebec had obtained powers that Robert Bourassa claimed were "unlimited."

The Western first ministers left the native leaders on March 27 without even promising to continue the dialogue. But then they had just been guaranteed a constitutional conference on Senate reform for the following year.

Quebec had regained its right to self-determination—or at least its premier was saying so. But the amending formula negotiated at Meech Lake subjected the rights of the Inuit and the Dene nation to the approval of ten provinces. In a way it became easier for Quebec to get out of Confederation than for the native people to get in.

What's more, the clause defining the "fundamental characteristics
of Canada" spoke of the presence of French-speaking Canadians
and English-speaking Canadians, without any reference to Canada's aboriginal peoples.

For three years, Quebec and Ottawa took no more notice of the
opposition from native representatives than they did of Frank McK-
enna and Gary Filmon's concerns. And the Supreme Court
appeared to back them up on June 2, 1988, when it refused a
hearing to the Northwest Territories government, which was con-
testing the validity of the Meech Lake Accord.

In May 1990, the members of the Charest committee knew that
their proposals would not satisfy the native chiefs. "Natives have no
veto right,"[11] Liberal André Ouellet reassured members of the
committee. So it wasn't surprising that Brian Mulroney deliberately
ran the risk of holding off a "last-chance conference" on the Meech
Lake Accord until the last minute. His advisers simply forgot to tell
him about the repeated warnings from the premier of Manitoba.
Frank McKenna said later:

> Sharon Carstairs and Gary Doer warned me weeks in advance
> that they'd have problems with their own caucuses, including
> Elijah Harper. In fact, the three Manitoba party leaders
> warned us: everybody knew very well that there was a native
> member of the legislature who could use procedure to block
> the ratification.[12]

"What's in the Meech Lake Accord for us?" asked the Manitoba
Métis leader. "We've got nothing to lose, with or without Meech
Lake." His own people, who had after all founded Manitoba, had
been driven from their lands by Loyalist farmers from southern
Ontario. In 1990, 85 percent of the Manitoba Indians were living on
welfare. What indeed did they have to lose?

In June 1990, Elijah Harper finally furnished the native leaders
with a means for revenge. "Don't tell me Quebeckers feel humiliated," said Inuit chief John Amagoalik. "They still don't know
what the word means. Us, we've been living with it for three hundred years."[13]

In the crowd massed on the front steps of the Manitoba legislature on the morning of June 22, 1990, there were more whites than native people. Without being fully aware of it, the native people were being manipulated once more, by English Canada this time. By saying no to Quebec, the ethnic communities in the Western cities in particular were justifying the refusal they would one day use on their own native communities. "Manitoba thinks it has a clear conscience because it has been so democratic with the native people," exploded Lucien Bouchard. "What hypocrisy! Canada is a veritable tangle of hypocrisy."[14]

Indeed, it was not Elijah Harper's gesture that would bring the native question to the forefront of constitutional reform. His vote was lost amid the shambles of June 22. There were so many people crowding into the Meech Lake firing squad that Elijah Harper would never know which shot had found its mark—his own, or Clyde Wells's, or Sharon Carstairs's, or Pierre Trudeau's, or Jean Chrétien's.

On July 12, 1990, when English Canada had begun to forget the Meech Lake saga and Quebeckers had retreated to their summer cottages, the native question surfaced once more with a vengeance. The day before, the Quebec provincial police had tried to clear a barricade that four months before had been thrown up by Mohawks across a little-used dirt road at the Kanesatake community near the town of Oka.

This ill-prepared action was intended to allow the Oka city councillors to get on with enlarging their golf course. Instead, the action ended in spectacular failure, and Police Corporal Marc Lemay lost his life in the fusillade that erupted when the police stormed the barricade. Afterward, the Mohawk Warriors helped peaceful Mohawks from Kanesatake set up solidly reinforced barricades around their village; others blocked off the Kahnawake reserve and closed one of the bridges linking the Island of Montreal to the south shore of the St. Lawrence.

Mixed as it was with the demands of a few profit-minded cigarette smugglers, the Oka incident would trivialize the claim of territorial sovereignty by a distinct people, and allow experts of all sorts to bring back the ultimate argument for blocking all attempts by Quebec to achieve separation: the fact that its own territorial integrity was not assured.[15]

"I hope these are not reprisals against those who are being held responsible for the failure of the constitutional negotiations," Quebec native representative Konrad Sioui said slyly. First Nations leader George Erasmus went one better: "To assure their survival, Quebec's aboriginal people had to ally themselves with the English, at whose side they fought on the Plains of Abraham."

The MP for Western Arctic, Ethel Blondin, herself a member of the Dene nation, was in Israel on a parliamentary mission when the crisis broke out. "The uprising against the Meech Lake Accord was our *intifada*," she declared upon her return to Canada. "We are all united now."

As it turned out, all the native leaders would exploit the Oka crisis. In a few days, English Canada would feel a lot less guilty for having refused to recognize Quebec society's distinct character.

During a two-hour news conference (televised without an offer of equal time for reply) by the CBC's Newsworld channel, Erasmus declared that Quebec had for years been carrying out a campaign of "genocide worthy of the Third Reich." And the Quebec police, he added, were no better than "Hitler's SS." Public opinion in English Canada was deliberately stoked to a white heat against Quebec by the English media. And Robert Bourassa, with whom the Canadian security and intelligence service finally deigned to share information they had been accumulating for three years, feared for the worst. As Bourassa said later:

> I was afraid it would all end in a bloodbath, that we would
> find ourselves with years of terrorist activity, like Ireland.
> Because it always starts out like that: a core of activists could
> have been created, and Quebec would have paid very dearly
> for a hasty gesture by a head of government who wanted to
> play the macho, to make like Tarzan. Even Mr. Parizeau was
> demanding a strong-arm intervention.[16]

Robert Bourassa waited for thirty-eight days before calling in the army and "giving them instructions to avoid all provocation and not to give in to provocation by others." By then he had no choice, the situation was getting out of hand: two provincial ministers, John Ciaccia, who was responsible for native affairs, and Sam Elkas, the public security minister, had already submitted their resignations. And a few hotheads in Chateauguay had resorted to acts of vandalism.

"The situation was on the verge of exploding," Bourassa recalled. "It was more serious than Meech Lake . . . But in the end there were neither heroes nor martyrs." [17] And what would he have to say of the exploitation of the events in English Canada? "One day I'll explain it to them and they'll understand," he said, shrugging his shoulders.

But the explanation might come too late. On August 17, the day Robert Bourassa officially appealed to the army, a senior federal bureaucrat commented:

> From now on it's going to be difficult for the Quebec government to claim any form of sovereignty when it has had to call in the Canadian army to oppose the same claims by the Iroquois. [18]

"The principal victim of Oka could well be Quebec independence," said Roy McMurtry, former Ontario justice minister, who had started a new career as a lawyer for a number of native groups.

At the federal Department of Indian and Northern Affairs, it was decided, from August 8 on, and well before the first barricade was dismantled, to reopen discussions concerning the land claims of Quebec native groups only. As a federal official said:

> Before the fall, by means of the discussions on the native question, the federal government will remind Quebeckers that a large strip of land, which cuts the province in two and extends along the banks of the St. Lawrence, running from James Bay to the U.S. border—that perhaps this strip of land simply doesn't belong to them. [19]

In 1976, after the election of the Parti Québécois, a Toronto lawyer named James Arnett had been preoccupied with the question of a sovereign Quebec's territory. "It would be much smaller than the territory of the province of Quebec," he concluded. "More than half its territory was accorded to it on the assumption that it would stay in Canada." [20]

Elijah Harper had not, of course, foreseen all this when he shook his head one last time on June 22 to prevent Manitoba's ratification of the Meech Lake Accord. But the haste with which the Oka crisis was exploited spoke volumes about the true intentions of those who applauded him that day.

The Mohawk crisis will long remain a painful episode in Quebec history. A few days after the end of the Meech Lake episode, an extraordinary St. Jean Baptiste day celebration took place. On June 25 the people went on the march, the police at their side. Quebeckers were nearly unanimous in the confidence they had in their head of government. But they did not have time to measure the force of this exceptional solidarity before English Canada turned on them, calling them fascists. Humiliated, they ended up doubting their leader who nevertheless, alone with his wife, knew he was showing the ultimate courage: to be prepared to risk one's life in the best interests of the state.

For at the beginning of August, the irate citizens of the suburb of Chateauguay which borders on the Kahnawake reserve, had, in turn, blocked roads and a bridge over the seaway. "When is the government going to act? When is Bourassa going to clear the bridge?" cried the mob. "I'd like it too if we could reopen the bridges," Bourassa told his wife, Andrée. "I could go get myself treated [for cancer] like everyone else ..."[21]

CHAPTER THIRTEEN

Separate Rooms or Divorce

*The referendum means that the two major political
parties in Quebec are getting closer. But if the two
parties are not finally in agreement, we'll have to
think twice about it. Because it is a heavy responsibility to call a referendum without being sure of
winning it.* [1]

Robert Bourassa

"They were moments I wouldn't like to relive."

January 1991. Robert Bourassa was back in his Montreal office
on the seventeenth floor of the Hydro-Quebec headquarters building on what is now René Lévesque Boulevard. On the coffee tables
in the reception room were weeks-old newspapers. This was a
highly unusual situation for a premier who likes to get the early
editions of the next day's papers delivered to his home late the night
before. It was as though life had stopped around Robert Bourassa.

"There's nothing there," Dr. Rosenberg at the Bethesda Institute in Maryland finally told him. "All we have to do is a follow-up
every three or four months. In Montreal if you want."

Freed from his personal anguish over the skin cancer on his back
that had been diagnosed the summer before, the political leader
resurfaced. He calculated, weighed his options, thought of the
future. "The future is what lasts the longest," he said smiling.
Robert Bourassa went back to observing, with a certain indifference
and without illusions, the waves that were upsetting public opinion.

At the beginning of the summer of 1990, two Quebeckers out of
three were convinced he was doing a good job defending Quebec's

interests, better than Jacques Parizeau. By fall, he was widely condemned. People freely predicted that his party would come apart at the seams. Already people were handicapping the chances of his potential successors. But by December, Quebeckers had regained their affection for their fragile leader, who was now disillusioned by the past and uncertain about the future. So much like themselves, in the end.

On the beaches of Florida, hawkers would offer bottles of suntan lotion to Canadians fleeing the northern winter. "Better be careful," Quebeckers would tell each other. "Look what happened to our premier." "Our" premier, they called him. Once again Quebeckers had adopted him, ready to follow where he might lead. And this is what worried Robert Bourassa.

> My preoccupation in the next few months, and the next few years—because this will take some time—will be to make sure that Quebeckers don't make a mistake about their future.[2]

He felt a responsibility to calm his people's political fever, which— what with the Oka crisis, the recession, and the looming war in the Persian Gulf—was not abating, but rising. "I'm trying to stay cool and collected," he said at the time. "Even though I share the emotion."[3]

The man had indeed demonstrated his sang-froid. And an uncommon level of sang-froid at that! In May 1990, his political entourage had noted that he was in a foul temper. Was it the Charest report, which he had rejected out of hand and in astonishingly brutal fashion, so unlike his normal, cautious manner? Or was it Lucien Bouchard's resignation, which couldn't have come at a worse time, on the eve of an important constitutional conference that might be the last for Quebec?

There was also the brown spot on his back that looked like a large beauty mark, which he couldn't see and which had developed without his being aware of it—although his family was starting to ask questions about it. His doctor had told him at the end of May that perhaps it would be better to remove the spot—"a little five-minute operation." But Bourassa told himself, "It can wait."[4] He was more preoccupied with the working dinner for the first ministers scheduled for Sunday, June 3. He'd see to it later.

But the Ottawa meeting dragged on interminably, and it kept him in Ottawa for a full seven days. Then there were the endless phone calls to colleagues in other provinces, and to Mulroney and Parizeau, first to try to save the Meech Lake Accord, and then to deal with its failure.

It wasn't until the first week of July that Bourassa was finally able to start thinking about his holiday in Maine. "But before that," his wife insisted, "you're going to have that spot removed."

"We'll run some tests and have some news for you in August," his doctor told him after the treatment.[5]

·But the premier didn't go on holiday that summer. On July 11, the Mohawk crisis erupted. "It'll be over in a few days," he told himself. On July 14, while celebrating his fifty-seventh birthday with his family, he talked about his intended vacation again.

Then came some alarming information from Ottawa: the Warriors, dug in behind their barricades in Oka and Chateauguay, were armed, it was said, with heavy weapons, maybe even rocket launchers. Andrée Bourassa wound up going to the cottage the family had rented near Bar Harbor by herself.

As for Bourassa, he slipped back into his premier's habits in times of great decision. Isolating himself on the roof of his Grande Allée bunker, he plotted strategy. Visitors who were summoned were exposed to the last rays of the sun sliding gently down towards the river and Île d'Orléans.

On top of the Oka crisis, he had begun negotiating the formation of an expanded National Assembly committee on Quebec's political and constitutional future. He moved quickly to enlist Lucien Bouchard, as though to neutralize him and to nip in the bud the idea of an "Estates General," of which he had heard talk. With something like that he could well lose control of the "post-Meech" process.

Between two meetings with his crisis management team, the premier paused to reflect:

> There is, to be sure, the question of process: should we establish sovereignty first and then regroup afterward? Or do we

regroup without being sovereign to keep a part of sovereignty?[6]

In July 1990, Robert Bourassa already seemed to have made a rendezvous with the people of Quebec. "The referendum?" he said during a wide-ranging conversation. "If I announce it in public, everyone is going to take a neutral position." Jacques Parizeau in one corner. Probably Lucien Bouchard in another. And himself, backed into the federalist camp? The premier pondered his options. And when the conversation turned to the "quiet power of the great wave of blue flags that had unfurled over Montreal,"[7] he listened attentively. "Quebeckers have a lot of confidence in me as far as their constitutional future is concerned," he said. Having been alternately swept into office and widely detested over a period of twenty-four years, he was in a good position to know how fleeting such confidence could be. From 1967 to this afternoon in 1990, from profitable federalism to the distinct society, from "marrying for money"—because there couldn't be any question of love—to separate rooms, he and the province had kept to the same trajectory. "It all has to be brought up to date," Bourassa told himself, thinking of the Bélanger-Campeau commission which he was going to set up. Which meant taking the Meech Lake failure into account.

But, in a few days, he would become the "commander-in-chief" of the Quebec army. An army borrowed from Ottawa.

One day early in August he got the phone call he'd been dreading. The "brown spot" that his family had been worrying about since spring was a malignant form of melanoma—a melanosarcoma. In other words, he had skin cancer.

"You have to be operated on," insisted his doctor.

"How do you expect me to do that?" sighed Bourassa. "I'm responsible for the army in Quebec. If I wind up on a hospital bed, the people we're confronting will say, 'We've brought down the government.'"

The doctor tried in vain to convince Bourassa of the gravity of the cancer that was growing quietly within him, but Bourassa refused to let himself be influenced by his personal problems. "Above all, I wanted to be sure that all the decisions made in the Oka crisis would be made in the interest of Quebec, whatever it cost me.'"[8]

The Oka crisis dragged on and on, while Bourassa's wife Andrée, the only person he had told about the seriousness of his illness, was growing increasingly impatient. "There are limits," she told him. "You have a right to get yourself treated like anyone else." In fact, Bourassa would have preferred to rush to the hospital. But, right or wrong, he was concerned that moving too rapidly against the heavily armed and well-entrenched Warriors would be a mistake.

Robert Bourassa's personal physician had studied and practised at the Bethesda Institute in Maryland, near Washington, which had an excellent reputation for its research on skin cancers. He advised Bourassa to go to Washington, where he would come under the care of Dr. Rosenberg, who had also treated President Reagan. "When the [Mercier] bridge is open," Bourassa promised.

But when the barricades were finally cleared from the bridge on September 5, Robert Bourassa was still not free to go. Now he had to be in the National Assembly to oversee the debate on Bill 90, authorizing the creation of the expanded constitutional committee. Thus, it was not until September 10 that he left for Washington, shrouding his trip in such secrecy that it embarrassed his spokesmen and generated all sorts of rumours.

But Robert Bourassa was still worried about the Warriors. "I said I was taking a few days of rest instead of a vacation so as not to mislead people. But I couldn't say I was in the hospital. They would have said, 'We've broken the government.'"[9]

But he had waited too long by then; the melanoma had spread to the lymph glands in his groin. On September 12, Dr. Rosenberg declined to make a categoric diagnosis. He could say only that he believed all the cancerous cells had been removed and proposed to perform exploratory surgery before making a final judgement.

"In a month," he suggested.

"Can't it wait until the Christmas holidays?" asked Bourassa.

"It would be better at the beginning of November," the doctor insisted.

But like the first operation, this one too was delayed. The negotiations with the leader of the Parti Québécois about the chairmanship of the proposed commission were more difficult than expected, and the opening of its hearings, for which Bourassa wanted to be present, did not take place until November 6.

When the premier returned to Washington on November 13, the speculation about his health became even more rampant, and some of those who coveted his job found it hard to control their impatience.

The doctors explained to Bourassa that if new cancer cells had appeared since September, they would "close up very quickly." On the other hand, the longer the exploratory surgery lasted, the more encouraging it would be for him. Thus, when he woke up afterward, the first thing he asked his wife was: "What time is it?"

The operation had lasted for more than three hours, and all was for the best. Or almost ... There was an intestinal problem, and Bourassa had to go on the operating table a third time. "For a minor adjustment," Dr. Rosenberg assured him.

But the summer of 1990 didn't bring only bad news and worries for Robert Bourassa. On August 28, at 6:45 p.m., he learned from his son François that his daughter-in-law had just given birth to a son and that he was now a grandfather. "It was like a moment of pure joy in the midst of that dark month," he said in January 1991.

Mathieu Bourassa will barely be emerging from childhood at the turn of the twenty-first century. With the birth of his grandson, a whole new horizon opened up for the premier, who, at the age of fifty-eight, had just had a brush with death, and risked seeing his political career come to an abrupt end.

When he got back to Montreal in December, Bourassa still kept out of sight. Reduced to a liquid diet for two weeks, he had lost a lot of weight and did not want to ignite a new spate of rumours about his health. But those who were in direct contact with him had no doubt that he had regained his form. "This time I'm going on a real holiday," he said. And with a note of regret in his voice, he added: "I'll have to be careful of the sun from now on." His convalescence was already well under way: "Ah, the joy of being a grandfather; François comes by with the little one every day," he confided.

Robert Bourassa was a changed man, and not only because of his illness. To be sure he fell back into many of his old habits, devouring the morning papers the night before, and avidly following the hearings of the Bélanger-Campeau commission. But every day, like a call to order, his young grandson would come to give him a new reason for keeping up the fight—and for taking care of himself. Remembering that his ambitions and career plan during the 1960s had prevented him from spending time with François and Michelle, he added in a sombre voice: "At the age when you become a grandfather, you're also closer to the end of the line."

As party leader, Bourassa was already immersed in strategic calculations. "There's a lot of positioning going on around me, and I don't know to what point the party has evolved. But clearly it has evolved."[10] In fact, there was so much "positioning" going on in the Liberal party that panic began to seep into the federalist ranks. The public hearings of the Assembly commission on Quebec's constitutional future had been dominated by expressions of sadness, indignation, and anger at English Canada's behaviour in rejecting Quebec's demands after signing the Meech Lake Accord. The conclusions drawn by co-chairmen Jean Campeau and Michel Bélanger were unequivocal:

> Quebec's relationship with the rest of Canada, within the current political regime and the reigning constitutional order, has reached an impasse . . . Quebec had a constitutional straitjacket imposed on it in 1982, and, in 1990, a rejection of its plea for full and freely consenting integration . . . The refusal to recognize Quebec as being different is a clear refusal of the Quebec people's right to be different.[11]

The province's business circles in particular felt abandoned by the Liberal party. Claude Ryan, on whom they had counted heavily, refused to intervene in an effort to change the flow. Perhaps he too felt such a wave of indignation and anger could not be stopped.

Despite his illness, Robert Bourassa had kept a close ear to the business community's growing anguish, particularly the message from the Quebec Chamber of Commerce, which he said had inspired him greatly. Indeed, there were traces of that message to be found in the commission chairmen's analysis:

The population of Quebec benefits, along with the rest of
Canada, from a common economic space which has contributed to the attainment of an enhanced quality of life . . . Canada's domestic market, its monetary and fiscal framework,
constitute assets which, if called into question in a clumsy
manner, would involve considerable costs for both parties.[12]

Everything was in place for Robert Bourassa, who had concluded
in December that the two commissions currently studying Quebec's constitutional options, the expanded Assembly commission
and an internal Liberal party task force, were "related to each
other."[13] And since the report from the task force, headed by lawyer
Jean Allaire, would be ready before the Assembly commission
report, the Liberal leader insisted that his party align itself with the
two main thrusts Bélanger and Campeau had promised him would
be the basis of their analysis: Quebec's right to be different, and the
preservation of a common economic space with the rest of Canada.

Finding the right strategy was the major problem facing Robert
Bourassa when he returned to full active duty in January. He had
never liked being tied to a government program, nor to precise
timetables. But when he took party affairs in hand once more, no
one asked him if a referendum should be held. The question now
was *when*.

"Eleven years after the first referendum, more than a year after
the failure of the Meech Lake Accord, after six months of study by a
commission with unprecedented scope, what's the rush?"[14] Lucien
Bouchard asked the friends he had cultivated in the Liberal party.

To make sure that Bourassa would not temporize one more time,
the "sovereignists" on the Bélanger-Campeau commission quietly
created the Mouvement Quebec 91 and, as they said, put Bourassa
"under house arrest." This group was distinctly removed from the
Parti Québécois, a fact that allowed its members to suggest:
"Bourassa should listen to us. We're not an opposition party looking to defeat him tomorrow morning."[15]

To buy some time, and to calm the federalist wing of his party,
which was afraid of such a prospect, Bourassa timidly suggested that

the Allaire committee recommend a referendum on sovereignty be held some time within the government's current mandate. "1992 is pretty near the end of the mandate," he said on January 24. The night before, a meeting of regional party leaders and key members of his caucus, which had gone on until two in the morning, had confirmed that he would get what he wanted most: more time.

For Bourassa, make no mistake, was not yet converted to sovereignty. "As Mackenzie King said, not necessarily, but if necessary,"[16] he said of the possibility that he might someday become head of a sovereign state. But the polls were telling him that Quebeckers wanted him to concern himself more with the economy, the environment, and, above all, demographic trends.

> [Demography] is the problem that concerns me most, because it's tied to Quebec's cultural security. Every month they bring me alarming demographic statistics, and I tell myself that if things keep on that way, we can do all we want on the economic level, but lose out on the essential someday because we're facing a rapid aging of our population.[17]

Robert Bourassa's immediate concern therefore was to "settle the problem of Quebec's identity without upsetting the current structures, with all that implies in terms of negotiations and delays." But after 1971, 1976, 1990, after three failures spread over a quarter century of his political career, was Quebec still prepared to give Robert Bourassa a mandate as its negotiator? Lucien Bouchard certainly wasn't. As he said:

> It would be illegitimate, perverse, and against Quebec's interests, an attempt to divert Quebec's democracy. Bourassa no longer has a mandate to negotiate anything with the federal government. The sovereignists will cut him off at the knees. It'll be guerilla warfare: if they have to fill the Olympic stadium in Montreal in May, if they have to have a parade of 400,000 people instead of 200,000 on St. Jean Baptiste Day, they'll do it.[18]

It would be the people, therefore, who would determine his course of action, but then that was the way Bourassa liked it. He had never governed otherwise, had never taken any important decisions unless he felt—for better or worse—carried along by an irresistible movement.

He would therefore use all his political clout—and he still had a lot—to convince Quebeckers that English Canada wasn't yet ready to negotiate seriously. "We have to make sure that the referendum makes a big impact. It's a lever we have to use at the right moment: this delay for reflection is not very long."[19]

The objective of such negotiations would be, as the Allaire report suggested, Quebec's accession to the status of a sovereign state, unless it acquired exclusive powers over social programs, education, housing, family law, employment, health care, communications, regional development, research, income security, and so forth. In all, twenty-three areas of exclusive jurisdiction.

The polls, along with the hysterical reaction to the Allaire report in parts of English Canada, seemed to prove Bourassa's point that Canada needed more time. Before even knowing what Quebec's demands were, the rest of Canada, by a massive 62 percent majority, indicated it would prefer the federal government to reject them, even at the risk of having the province separate. Quebeckers, on the other hand, preferred—or perhaps hoped—in the same two-to-one proportion, that Canada would accept them.[20]

The reaction of the anglo intellectuals, or at least those who read the Quebec press, like the *Globe and Mail*'s Jeffrey Simpson (who also has a weekly column in *Le Devoir*), spoke volumes. Simpson said:

> The Allaire report is an insult and a joke . . . As soon as pos-
> sible, Canada should rid itself of the Quebeckers who lead
> the national parties, and those with a senior role in the federal
> public service, and find appropriate representatives for the
> negotiations with Quebec in its own midst.[21]

For Jean Chrétien, who had been proclaiming Canada's virtues to Quebec for twenty-eight years; for Brian Mulroney, who was elected Conservative leader largely because he was a Quebecker; for Paul Tellier, whose role as a senior adviser to the federal government was greatly appreciated by English Canada during the 1980 referendum, Simpson's dismissal of Quebec's leaders was a slap in the face.

The reaction finally revealed the true face of those who, six months earlier, had been ardently defending the vision of a tolerant and generous Canada. Simpson even had the nerve to suggest in *Le Devoir* that "a Canada amputated from Quebec would be unilingually English."

After the publication of the Allaire report, Robert Bourassa stepped up his phone calls to his friends in the East and the West—for he still had a good many left—suggesting that they declare themselves as well, and soon. Because if Brian Mulroney's credibility was doubtful, even in Quebec, Bourassa desperately needed an encouraging sign from English Canada to justify his "pause for reflection," and to push the date of the referendum as far back in his mandate as possible.

Bourassa especially pressured Ontario Premier Bob Rae to speak up on Quebec and in Quebec more often. He waited impatiently for his colleague from New Brunswick, Frank McKenna, to come forward with his idea for a national referendum on ways to amend the constitution. And above all, he hoped that the Western provinces would spell out their list of constitutional demands, a list that was easily as long as Quebec's.

> Quebec will not be alone with its list of demands, and I don't
> know how Canada will deal with that. The ideal thing would
> be to hold a national referendum on the broad outline of a
> new constitution. That way Quebec would know where it
> stands.[22]

What several provinces (and Ottawa) wanted, in effect, was for Canadians to declare themselves once and for all on the great principles of Confederation, like bilingualism, equalization payments, the degree of autonomy they are prepared to offer native peoples, the role of the provinces in monetary policy, and so forth. And within this framework, these "parameters" as McKenna and Bourassa called them, the premiers and their experts could draft a new constitution.

Brian Mulroney hoped his Conservatives on the special joint Senate-Commons committee on how to amend the constitution (which was chaired by Senator Gérald Beaudoin, a noted constitutional authority in his own right, and Alberta MP Jim Edwards) would come up with a recommendation for a question to be used in a referendum to be held in the fall of 1991.[23]

But the problem with referendum questions is that the answer depends as much on the popularity of the government that asks the question as the actual content of the question itself. Frank McKenna added:

> I don't think Brian Mulroney has any credibility left at all in
> constitutional matters. The general feeling is that all he
> thinks about are Quebec's interests, or his own political
> interests.[24]

Indeed, the Citizens' Forum, under Keith Spicer, confirmed that "there is a fury in this country" over the prime minister's leadership.

One thing was certain: many elements of the Allaire report found favour with the other provinces, notably those in the West. The Cassandras of the *Globe and Mail* and the Saint John *Telegraph-Journal* must have forgotten that in October 1976, Peter Lougheed, in the name of all his provincial colleagues, claimed a good third of the powers now sought by the Quebec Liberals. And that in September 1980 seven provinces—including Newfoundland, signed a joint provincial policy position paper drafted by the Parti Québécois government. Many of the points contained in this "common position" were not incompatible with the Allaire report.

Quebec has always had a lot of support in the West. "And connections too," added Grant Devine, pointing out that his former deputy minister, Norm Riddell, was now one of Robert Bourassa's principal advisers. Devine also said:

> The stakes will be higher in Quebec, but they'll be high here
> too. We have our list of things we want, which could go as
> long as twenty-five items. But we'll keep doing business
> together. Lavalin and Bombardier will still have contracts
> here, and I'm going to sell my uranium all over North
> America.[25]

This was the kind of realism that appealed to Robert Bourassa. But the time he had bought threatened to turn against him. If the

Meech Lake Accord failed to survive three years of negotiations because three provincial governments were voted out during the period, the political situation would be even more unstable during the eighteen months that Bourassa was giving himself to propose "Quebec's accession to the status of a sovereign state."

Concerned that it would not be enough again to bring English Canada to the negotiating table, Bourassa raised the stakes once more and tabled Bill 150, which calls for a referendum on sovereignty to be held in June or October 1992. He looked like a man loading his gun, bullet after bullet: first the Allaire Report, then the Bélanger-Campeau commission, now Bill 150.

As usual, Bourassa did it in a way that would not shake up the political environment nor the economy. The day Bill 150 was passed, Moody's credit rating service confirmed Quebec's rating while lowering that of Ontario. And on St. Jean Baptiste day, there were no riots in the streets of Montreal, nor did the sovereignists "cut him off at the knees," as Lucien Bouchard had predicted.

"Not that bad, eh?" Bourassa said on a hot summer evening in July 1991, while American and European tourists were flooding the streets in Quebec City. It was ten o'clock at night, and in room 308C of the premier's office on Grande Allée, Bourassa was all by himself, with no secretaries around, flipping through cabinet documents for the meeting he was going to chair the following morning. With a late visitor, he was counting his bets and reviewing his plans for the following twelve months.[26]

"Not a very long time for such a crucial negotiation," the visitor said.

"So what?" Bourassa replied. "Didn't Camp David last only two weeks?"

He was counting on other leaders to help him get a "credible" offer, something he could sell to his fellow Quebeckers. "Rae is conscious of the seriousness of the situation," he explained. "Getty is determined. Filmon is not the one to stand alone in the way of an agreement. And as far as the three Maritime premiers are concerned [Bourassa always ignores Newfoundland's Clyde Wells], they'd better look at the map: with Quebec right in the middle, one tends to forget that one of Quebec's major trump cards is its geographical situation in Canada. So you see," he concluded, "these people realize that I won't go through with it unless they make a credible offer."

Somewhat desperately, Bourassa was hoping he would never have to enforce Bill 150 and call a referendum. "When I look at the situation in Yugoslavia, I ask myself, 'What more do we want?' The army? I could call it, whenever I want. I did it last summer in Oka. You sign a form, and that's it. A whole unit moves from Valcartier, they are all Quebeckers, under my command. On the international scene, we are on our own in dealing with French-speaking countries. And why bother to be 189th in the world when, through Canada, we are part of the seven most industrialized countries. The army, the international clout: we have all the attributes of sovereignty. The rest is plumbing."

Robert Bourassa was optimistically assuming that night that everything would go well, and in the time-frame he had determined himself. "If it doesn't," he said, "I will go across English Canada and read them Bill 150: they will have to decide if they want to take such a risk."

Now that Bourassa had loaded his constitutional gun, he had no choice but to pull the trigger if Canada didn't move. Would he do it? "I have been in politics for twenty-five years, my country has reached the most important moment of its history, and I could say, 'This is too big for me, I pass.' Don't worry: this time I won't cop out."

So said Bourassa in July 1991, facing a national government with which he pretended to be negotiating exclusively but which looked paralysed, as if it held a minority position, since English Canada was questioning the legitimacy of the prime minister and of the nine Quebec ministers who sat beside him in the federal cabinet. That government could lose its majority for real if enough of its Quebec members crossed the floor to sit with the Bloc Québécois, or refused to stand as candidates in the next election, or again, if enough Tories from English Canada decided that Brian Mulroney was leading them to defeat.

Largely unfamiliar with English Canada, Robert Bourassa underestimated the extent to which that society had questioned its own language, lifestyle, and its own symbols—the flag, bilingualism, tolerance, and even the RCMP uniform—all in the name of the Charter of Rights and Freedoms.

Maybe it was this Canada that Benoît Bouchard was thinking about when he anxiously asked Ontarians to tell him if the country they were going to propose to him was the Canada of the Reform Party and Preston Manning.

Paul Martin also had his doubts about a country that no longer tried to develop its sense of identity, and about Canadians who no longer expressed any desire to belong to it: "A Quebecker succeeds in France and he's still a Quebecker on the international scene," he said. "But an English Canadian leaves Canada for the international scene and becomes an American."[27]

Westerners, Maritimers, Newfoundlanders: Canadians tended more and more to define themselves in terms of their corner of the country. Robert Bourassa secretly hoped that the "Canada-under-the-gun" game would force them to regroup according to their regional affinities (or solidarities). "Having five regions (the Maritimes, Quebec, Ontario, the Prairies, and British Columbia) seems to me to be a desirable and defensible formula," he said, insisting he had been inspired in this respect by Father Georges-Henri Lévesque, the revered father of Quebec social science.[28]

But Quebec's "frontiers" were already being contested by native Canadians and anglo-Quebeckers, whereas in the West they were not fully evident. "Alberta and British Columbia, both relatively rich and with similar economies, draw closer together. And Manitoba is split between Saskatchewan and Ontario."[29] Even Grant Devine seemed visibly disturbed by his own province's possible isolation.

The rise of "provincialism" (Pierre Trudeau's word), inspired by Quebec's example, and of individualism, encouraged by the Charter of Rights and Freedoms, had fractured all the institutions Robert Bourassa wanted to reform. Quebec alone knew what it wanted. And it wanted more than the others.

Robert Bourassa, like most Quebeckers, would never settle for a federal system that did not give Quebec "somewhat different powers."[30] It was the "right to be different" that the Bélanger-Campeau commission was endorsing. But the Canada envisaged by Jean

Chrétien and by Audrey McLaughlin, among others, unanimously rejected this kind of asymmetry, except perhaps for the administration of Quebec museums, libraries, and schools.

Sometimes orthodox federalists claimed to know better than the majority of Quebeckers what kind of political system was best suited for Quebec. "Canada has protected Quebec against its interior demons," Pierre Trudeau had insisted. "Quebec has grown within Canada," Jean Chrétien was still saying. And it is true that it was thanks to Ottawa, and at times despite its own government, that Quebec was able to develop a good number of its social institutions, like the universities and health services.

But it is also true that Quebeckers pulled themselves out of the great darkness of the Duplessis years without Ottawa's help, and after having entered the twentieth century sixty years late, they were preparing to enter the twenty-first as well prepared as English Canada, if not better.

There was therefore some good as well as bad in the federal system. And Jean Chrétien's reasoning resembled that of a father saying to his son: "You've grown up in my house, so now you'll have to spend the rest of your life under my roof."

Robert Bourassa, as a well-brought-up young man, did not want to walk out. "All his life he's remained the little boy who wanted to please his mother,"[31] said his childhood friend Jacques Godbout. Even in 1990, he gloried in having absorbed English Canada's insults and bad faith without flinching. As Bourassa said after the failure of the Meech Lake Accord, "I stayed to the end, without banging my fist on the table, without slamming the door, right up to the point at which the others said, 'No,' as if they had said, in a way: 'You're now free to go.' "[32]

Bourassa didn't want to use that freedom right away, for he wanted to give Canada "time for reflection." While this time was passing, he was pondering Robert Normand's advice more and more. A former adviser to the Quebec government, now publisher of Quebec City's *Le Soleil* and a member of the Spicer commission, Normand had been predicting for some time that the synthesis of special status, neo-federalism, and "confederalism"—which was basically what Bourassa was after—"could never see the light of day or be accepted by the rest of Canada unless Quebec has the courage to announce, calmly and serenely, its intention to declare independence unilaterally in case of a refusal."[33]

Canada Under the Gun...
and Quebec to the Wall[1]

*There are those who claim that if we scare the Eng-
lish enough, we can get what we want without going
as far as independence . . . I admit that it's funny to
see English-language politicians getting jittery. But
it also has its consequences: there is nothing meaner
than a poltroon who has overcome his fear.*[2]

Pierre Elliott Trudeau

Sovereignty? "I have no prejudices one way or the other," Robert
Bourassa insisted. "In politics I always worked at the Quebec level.
But in terms of economics, there are advantages for Quebec if it
stays within a Canadian community."[3] In the final analysis, it was
up to Quebeckers to decide. But the economist in Robert Bourassa
advised him to preserve a system with which he was familiar; locked
into this federalist scenario, he refused to envisage, even hypotheti-
cally, a sovereign Quebec.

The politician in him no doubt would have preferred to lead a
sovereignist government than to lose power prematurely. In fact, a
lot of people suspected that deep down Bourassa thought it would
be in Quebec's best interests to allow him to make the transition to
sovereignty rather than submitting the province to the vicissitudes
of a Péquiste government. Had not the Allaire report said that it
would be the government formed by the Liberal party—and whose
leader therefore was Robert Bourassa—that would propose Quebec's accession to the status of a sovereign state?[4]

The only certainty in Robert Bourassa's political future, the only action he could take by himself, was to call a referendum on the sovereignty of the state of Quebec. For, as Robert Normand suggested and as a clear majority of Quebeckers seemed to think, English Canada had to be forced to take Quebec seriously.

Robert Bourassa, like Brian Mulroney, envisaged only an "in-depth" reform of the existing federal system. At best, and in very vague terms at that, they evoked the scenario of a "reconfedera-tion" of Canada as four or five regions. But, be it as a province or a region, Quebec always ran the risk of trivialization, of finding itself in the end with a government "like the others," having lost its right to be different.

No matter how he looked at it—whether he saw Brian Mulroney's proposals as a dangerous and time-consuming "last-chance attempt," or whether he felt that English Canada was simply refusing to negotiate—Robert Bourassa had no choice but to be prepared to behave like a "sovereignist" party leader and head of government.

Besides, with Bill 150, had he not launched Quebec into a pre-referendum campaign in June 1991? Whether Bourassa liked it or not, the "rest of Canada" (which included federal institutions in Quebec) and probably the United States, were already entering a "transition" phase. It would be underestimating the wisdom of major corporations to think that they have been waiting for a referendum on sovereignty to begin reorganizing. They probably began long ago: the Quiet Revolution, the turbulent 1970s, and the election of the Parti Québécois no doubt required substantial adjustments on their part. It is unthinkable that Bell Canada, for example, has not already built a corporate framework that would withstand any brutal break up in the event of a "reorganization of the Canadian political structure."

American companies have also taken note of the process that has been under way north of the 45th parallel for some time. They know that it will neither stop in its tracks nor go backwards, and that they had better get used to the idea. In 1976, the day after the election of the Parti Québécois, California's Stanford Research Institute put out a series of guidelines to the clients of its Business Intelligence Program.[5] "The question that should be asked," suggested the Institute, "is not *if* Quebec will separate from Canada, but how, to what extent, and when."

If English Canada has not yet come to the same conclusion, it is because its political leaders—notably those from Quebec—have never stopped telling them that Quebeckers are nothing but a "wretched little race of blackmailers" (Pierre Trudeau), who "bluffed" (Jean Chrétien) and who have let themselves be swayed by the "dream merchants" (Brian Mulroney).

The transition is also under way on the international scene. It is not merely limited to speculations by the State Department in Washington and the Quai d'Orsay in Paris, but it is probably a given in the computers at the Pentagon and at NORAD, the Canada-United States alliance for the defence of the high northern frontier. It is hard to believe that in the plans for deploying Canadians and Americans, in the organization of the northern "line of defence," in the plans for situating fighter bases (and their maintenance facilities) and naval ports, and, most important, the assignment of troops, there is not somewhere a parameter called "Quebec-Canada."

In fact, everyone is preparing for Quebec sovereignty—except the Quebec government itself. Whether it happens in 1991 or 1992 or shortly thereafter, the day after the referendum will be no time for improvising . . .

Though Robert Bourassa has never liked showdowns, there is one concrete fact he cannot escape: English Canada may deploy the lockout technique and refuse to bargain even before Quebec has begun rolling out its negotiating artillery.

Since the 1982 patriation, Quebec has been locked into the Canadian system. The question of international support thus becomes paramount, because the self-determination process, democratic as it may be, cannot be made legitimate within the Canadian federation. There are those, for example, who take France's support for granted. But that remains to be seen. In the case of Lithuania, President François Mitterand has been notably circumspect.

Quebec, therefore, has a reason, right off the bat, to identify potentially friendly capitals in which it can systematically undermine the Canadian federation, and particularly its so-called "central" government. There is nothing revolutionary about such a proposal: in 1980-81, Quebec and no fewer than seven English provinces openly contested the Canadian government's constitutional program at the Westminster Parliament in London. Pierre Trudeau was beside himself, and Margaret Thatcher was very embarrassed. But the operation was a success: Canada was obliged to return to the bargaining table.

Robert Bourassa could even summon back from Ottawa, immediately if he tried hard, the principal artisan of that diplomatic dust-up, Gilles Loiselle. He would no doubt be more useful back home than tabulating the deficits at the federal Treasury Board.

Since Robert Bourassa's return to power, a new situation has arisen, one that did not exist at the time of the 1980 referendum: the absence of political goodwill in English Canada—except for the bravado of certain Western political leaders who declared themselves ready to "let Quebec go"—to cooperate with any process leading to Quebec sovereignty.

Between 1976 and 1980, during the course of talks on constitutional repatriation and other negotiations (dealing with fiscal agreements, for example), Quebec's "good government" and some of its representatives, like Jacques Parizeau and Claude Morin, made some important friends among the English-Canadian establishment, its bureaucratic class in particular. It required an enormous effort by Pierre Trudeau's administration to discredit Quebec to the point at which it could be isolated in November 1981.

All that understanding, that sympathy, has now evaporated. The campaign against the Meech Lake Accord, the reaction to Bill 178, and the Oka crisis in the summer of 1990 have had their effect. That public opinion in English Canada has been turned against Quebec is a fact that Robert Bourassa seems unaware of.

Robert Bourassa seems to think that Quebec's future, even under sovereignty, will always depend on the goodwill of the rest of Canada. Whether he wants to negotiate a reinforcement of the Canadian economic union or to preserve the Canadian economic space in the

event of separation, he always has to count on English Canada's
good faith.

The whole dynamic of the negotiations would change if Bourassa
finally realized that for reasons of security or economic stability, the
United States—which was ready to strike a deal with Mexico, and,
country by country, with the rest of the Americas—could be interested in negotiating a province-by-province agreement with Can-
ada.⁶ One can just imagine how the premier of Ontario would react
to a sovereign Quebec taking the lead in negotiating with the Americans. There would be a shoving match in Washington to see who
could get through the door first. Naive as it may be for Quebeckers
to imagine that support from certain countries is guaranteed in
advance, it is also presumptuous of English Canada to believe that
the Americans' ultimate interest is to preserve Canadian unity at all
costs.

Finally, if it comes to that—and assuming that it doesn't come to
civil war—Robert Bourassa and Jacques Parizeau possess, through
the Bloc Québécois, the ultimate weapon: the capacity to paralyse
the federal Parliament. If the "rainbow coalition" was able to bring
Brian Mulroney to power, what might it accomplish with Lucien
Bouchard?

At the very worst then, Quebec has to be prepared, during the
months preceding a referendum on sovereignty, to undermine English Canada's credibility in foreign capitals and to paralyse federal
institutions.

The most urgent task is to draft, starting immediately, the constitution of a sovereign Quebec. This document would allow Robert
Bourassa not merely to ask a question in his referendum, but to
formulate a response. All that would interest Quebeckers would be
the first article of such a constitution, which would read, "Quebec
is a sovereign state." For the rest, the choices about the shape of
Quebec society could be made from the political programs of its
political parties.

The advantage of such a referendum, which would confirm an
existing situation rather than timidly asking a question, is that it
would confront Canada with a fait accompli. Because lockout or no

lockout, the negotiations will be vicious. English Canada will fall into line when Quebec touches its most sensitive nerve: money.

The right of the people's representatives to levy taxes is, after all, at the heart of American democracy. The National Assembly could therefore do the same. Economist Georges Mathews has brilliantly demonstrated how, by taking into account the province's contribution to the federal deficit, Quebec is at a billion-dollar disadvantage in its current relationship with Canada.[7] Without getting back into the "war of figures," which no one will ever win, the analyses suggest that Quebec could unilaterally "patriate" all taxes—and its share of the federal deficit—without any great effect on transfers to individuals and corporations. Corporate taxes could be a problem. But there are more and more corporate citizens, just as there are more and more people on the streets, who favour sovereignty. Quebec wouldn't have to negotiate all of its corporate taxes with Ottawa.

One question remains: is Bourassa ready to launch a tax strike? There is good reason to bet that such an action must have tempted his finance minister, Gérard D. Lévesque, and some of his colleagues. When Maurice Duplessis opened the way in 1954, with his "Act to secure the province the revenues necessary for its development," the Quebec government had repatriated 15 percent of its federal taxes. Even Pierre Trudeau, who may have detested Duplessis, saying he negotiated "like a thug," wound up approving *Le Chef*'s initiative.

Robert Bourassa could test Quebeckers' enthusiasm then and there by repatriating the taxes Quebec requires for:

> . . . exercising henceforth its full sovereignty in the areas of jurisdiction that are already exclusive to it (such as social affairs, education, housing, family law, employment policy, and health care), and in the sectors not specifically enumerated in the Canadian constitution, that is to say residual powers, as well as in certain areas now under shared jurisdiction (such as communications, regional development, research and development, income security) . . . [8]

He might be surprised by the response.

But then it might not have to come to that. Under the nose of Clyde Wells, Quebec has just recently patriated $332 million and the seventy civil servants who administer immigration programs involving Quebec—and this without having the Maritime provinces fall off and sink into the Atlantic Ocean.

English Canada may be hoping to work in a little blackmail when it comes time to divide the assets. Indeed, it is usually the distribution of effects in a divorce that provokes the bitterest recriminations. But this does not take into account the fact that over the previous seven or so years the Conservative government in Ottawa has already privatized a considerable portion of the government's assets, like Air Canada, Petro-Canada, and some airports and railways. One could argue that with Brian Mulroney at least, the division will be easier. And if English Canada really wants to keep its assets, Quebec could, with a clear conscience, leave it its debts as well.

Among other things, Robert Bourassa is deeply concerned about economic stability. It is one of the main reasons why he wants to avoid "structural upheavals" and to negotiate diplomatically instead.

There is nothing to prevent the Quebec premier from immediately reassuring Canada and Quebec's partners that commercial and defence treaties will be respected. The Americans in particular do not dissociate the two because their national security depends on their supply of strategic materials. They would soon see the advantage of negotiating James Bay electricity exports with Quebec, instead of with Quebec and the National Energy Board. Among other things, they could be reassured that the St. Lawrence Seaway would remain open.

In sum, the National Assembly could very well adopt an immediate resolution stating that Quebec, once it has been recognized as a sovereign state by the United Nations, would consider itself bound, until their eventual renegotiation, to all international treaties signed in its name by the government of Canada. Such an assurance of stability, endorsed by the two major parties, would encourage many countries to accelerate Quebec's entry into the ranks of the United Nations.

★

It is a good bet that Robert Bourassa will talk a lot about currency. He has been doing so since 1967, and Jacques Parizeau loves debates among experts. But Quebec's insistence on talking about "monetary union" has convinced English Canada that the young sovereign state would be the "petitioner," and therefore vulnerable and sensitive to all manner of extortion.

Why did the two major parties insist so steadfastly on limiting their options to the Canadian dollar? Quebec could start enlarging its horizons right away by envisaging the possibility of a "zone dollar," which would involve the American dollar, the Mexican peso/dollar, and, if it deigned to agree, English Canada's dollar. By seeking a monetary union with Canada at any price, Quebec is tying its fate to the currency of an enormously indebted country. In the era of global markets, the value of the "Bourassa buck" should be determined in relation to a currency index that also includes the Japanese yen, the German mark, the English pound, and the French franc.

No doubt Jean Chrétien wants to involve himself in the negotiations by talking about the famous Canadian "passport." Apparently Quebeckers are quite attached to it. But Robert Bourassa, who is familiar with Europe, can point out to them that the red European Community passport was such a success that many French citizens no longer carry their old blue passports. The important thing is not issuing passports, but rather a nation's right to recognize citizenship. There could be a common passport bearing the Canadian coat of arms if it really mattered so much to Jean Chrétien. The only thing left to do would be to choose from the spectrum of colours.

The *Montreal Gazette* will probably brandish the threat of a massive brain drain. The reorganization of corporate headquarters previously installed in Montreal has removed the possibility of a fresh flight of capital and an eventual replay of the "Brinks affair" of 1970. Instead, there might be talk of a Canadian Airlines affair this time, because these people will be in such a hurry to flee to Ontario, they won't even trust Via Rail.

Granted, there would be an exodus. But one also has to take into account the influx of francophones from outside Quebec—and these are often highly-trained newcomers—who could very well establish a positive migratory balance for a sovereign Quebec.

The most difficult aspect of the negotiations will no doubt be the part dealing with territory. There can be no sovereign state without borders.

English Canada will not hesitate to use native land claims as a pretext to redraw Quebec's borders. Its task will be made even easier by the fact that native peoples receive better press at the United Nations than Quebec does. Canada could pose as the ultimate defender of the rights of its aboriginal peoples in order to make allies on the international scene. As for the English majorities in Montreal's West Island and Pontiac County in western Quebec, they can be counted on to claim their little corners of territory. Up Outaouais way there is loose talk of a "Duchy of Pontiac."

Quebec, with its 15.6 million square kilometres, is larger than any single one of the United States (with the exception of Alaska). It is a tempting chunk of territory, and it's a good bet that Canada will try to impose some form of partition on Quebec, as in Ireland. Some eminent professors have gone on record to say that international law will assure Quebec its existing territorial integrity at the moment it achieves sovereignty. But we live in an age when states, particularly young states, must be prepared to defend their borders. If not by force of arms, then by the threat of arms.

Robert Bourassa has had some experience in this area: on two occasions during his career as premier of Quebec, he has called in the army. A record, no doubt, for a leader of a non-sovereign government. The neo-federalists—and even the sovereignists—may have been jumping to conclusions when they suggested that defence and territorial security could be shared with Canada.

An army is first and foremost the ultimate symbol of territorial sovereignty. It can also be an instrument of diplomacy. What right would Canada have had to speak at the United Nations during the Gulf War had it not contributed to the allied effort with three warships, twenty-six fighter-bombers, as well as a military field hospital?

And above all, the army is a powerful engine for industrial development. Purchasing policy for a Canada-Quebec army would always be decided by an English majority, an experience Quebec might not want to prolong. Quebec already has its Bombardier. Why couldn't it have a company like Saab? If Sweden has an automobile industry, it is no doubt due in part to the fact that it has its own armed forces who buy its fighter planes.

1971. 1976. 1990 . . . Robert Bourassa's long political career, beginning with his election to the National Assembly for the first time in 1966, is definitive if at times absurd proof that English Canada's political will to negotiate with Quebec has tended to diminish the closer Quebec moves to the sovereignty option. But there is a wave that even the Berlin Wall could not contain: the collective will of a people who are convinced, determined, resolute, and unshakeable.

Determined, resolute, and unshakeable: Robert Bourassa has shown he can be all these things. All that's left for him is to convince himself that Quebeckers are just like him.

Ottawa, July 1991

NOTES AND REFERENCES

CHAPTER 1

1. Robert Bourassa, interview with the author, July 1990.
2. The *Globe and Mail*, June 12, 1990.
3. Robert Rumilly, *Histoire de la province de Québec* (I: George-Étienne Cartier), Montreal, Bernard Valiquette, 1940, p. 20.
4. Robert Rumilly, op. cit., p. 27.
5. Ibid., p. 35, 39-40.
6. See *Débats Parlementaires*, Quebec, 1865, and *Les années Bourassa*, interviews with Raymond Saint-Pierre, Montreal, Héritage, 1977.
7. Lucien Bouchard, letter to the Rt. Hon. Brian Mulroney, May 21, 1990.
8. Robert Bourassa, interview with the author, June 1989.
9. Hershel Ezrin, interview with the author, June 1987.
10. Lucien Bouchard, telegram from Paris, May 19, 1990.
11. Robert Bourassa, interview with the author, July 1990.
12. Ibid.
13. Frank McKenna, interview with the author, July 1990.
14. *Western Report*, July 2, 1990.
15. Lucien Bouchard, interview with the author, July 1990.

CHAPTER 2

1. Ian Macdonald, *From Bourassa to Bourassa*, Montreal, Primeur/Sand, 1985, p. 236.
2. Confidential interview.
3. Ian Macdonald, op. cit.
4. Monique Roy, *Chatelaine*, November 1988.
5. Pierre Bourgault, *Le plaisir de la liberté*, conversations with Andrée Lebel, Montreal, VLB Éditeur, 1987, p. 196.

6. *Le Quartier latin*, November 29, 1956, p. 4.

7. Ibid., December 3, 1953, p. 1.

8. Ibid., December 17, 1953.

9. Ibid.

10. *Les années Bourassa*, conversations with Raymond Saint-Pierre, Montreal, Héritage, 1977, p. 282.

11. Jean-Louis Gagnon, *Apostasies III: Les palais de glace*, Montreal, La Presse, 1990, p. 167.

12. Ibid.

13. *Le Quartier latin*, February 1956.

14. Monique Roy, op. cit.

15. Confidential interview.

16. Ibid.

17. Michel Arsenault, *Saturday Night*, February 1989, p. 19.

18. Monique Roy, op. cit.

19. Ibid.

20. Robert Bourassa, interview with the author, July 1990.

21. CBC, *Cross Canada—The Observer*, April 21, 1966.

CHAPTER 3

1. Robert Bourassa, *Le Québec dans le Canada de demain*, Montreal, Le Jour, p. 168.

2. René Lévesque, *Attendez que je me rappelle* . . ., Montreal, Québec-Amérique, 1986, p. 299.

3. Daniel Johnson, *Égalite ou indépendance*, Montreal, Éditions de l'Homme, 1965.

4. See in particular Pierre Godin's book, *Les frères divorcés*, Montreal, Éditions de l'Homme, 1986.

5. Charles de Gaulle, press conference, in *La politique étrangère de la France*, Paris, (official edition) 1967, p. 168.

6. Charles de Gaulle, cabinet statement, July 31, 1967, op. cit., p. 56.

7. Daniel Johnson, official statement, July 29, 1967.

8. Daniel Johnson, Confederation of Tomorrow Conference, opening statement, November 27, 1967.

9. Charles de Gaulle, op. cit., p. 179.

10. Lester B. Pearson, cabinet statement, July 25, 1967.

11. Robert Bourassa, interview with the author, July 1990.

12. René Lévesque, op. cit., p. 288.

13. André Laurendeau, *Journal*, Montreal, VLB Éditeur, and Succession André Laurendeau, 1990, p. 67.

14. Ibid.

15. Robert Bourassa, interview with the author, July 1990.

16. Ibid.

17. Robert Bourassa, in *Le Devoir*, October 3, 4 and 5, 1967.

18. Charles de Gaulle, op. cit., p. 146.

19. René Lévesque, op. cit., p. 297.

20. René Lévesque, *Le Devoir*, October 5, 1967.

21. Robert Bourassa, interview with the author, July 1990.

22. Ibid.

23. The report of the Liberal party's constitutional affairs committee was published in *Le Devoir* October 11, 12, and 13, 1967.

24. Report by Michel Roy and Paul Cliche, in *Le Devoir*, October 16, 1967.

25. Ibid.

26. Robert Bourassa, interview with the author, July 1990.

27. Ibid.

28. Ibid.

29. Ibid.

30. Ian Macdonald, *De Bourassa à Bourassa*, Montreal, Primeur/Sand, 1985, p. 236.

31. Jean Louis Gagnon, *Apostasies, Tome III: Les palais de glace*, Montreal, La Presse, 1990, p. 167.

32. Robert Bourassa, *Bourassa Québec*, Montreal, Éditions de l'Homme, 1970.

33. Ibid.

34. Robert Bourassa, interview with the author, June 1989.

35. Ibid.

CHAPTER 4

1. *Les années Bourassa*, interviews with Raymond Saint-Pierre, op. cit., p. 64.

2. Pierre Godin, *La poudrière linguistique*, Montreal, Boreal, 1990.

3. *Les années Bourassa*, op. cit., p. 50.
4. Royal Commission on Bilingualism and Biculturalism, Preliminary Report, Supply and Services Canada, 1965.
5. Royal Commission on Bilingualism and Biculturalism, record of 83rd meeting, February 27, 1971, Ottawa, Information Canada.
6. Stephen Fogarty, *Resume of Federal-Provincial Conferences (1927-1980)*, Ottawa, Library of Parliament, 1980.
7. For more information on Robert Bourassa's first mandate and his relationship with Pierre Trudeau, see Michel Vastel, *The Outsider: The Life of Pierre Elliott Trudeau*, Macmillan of Canada, 1990.
8. *La Presse*, October 3, 1970.
9. Robert Bourassa, interview with the author, June 1989.
10. Ibid.
11. Ibid.
12. Ibid.
13. *Les années Bourassa*, op. cit., p. 53-55.
14. Stephen Fogarty, op. cit.
15. *Les années Bourassa*, op. cit., p. 53.
16. Canadian Press, February 10, 1971.
17. *Le Devoir*, May 13, 1971.
18. *Journal de Montréal*, May 19, 1971.
19. *Les années Trudeau*, Montreal, Le Jour, 1990, p. 307.
20. *Les années Bourassa*, op. cit., p. 60.
21. Robert Bourassa, interview with the author, June 1989.
22. *La Presse*, June 21, 1971.
23. *Les années Bourassa*, op. cit., p. 52.
24. Ibid., p. 61.
25. Ibid., p. 64.
26. Lucien Bouchard, interview with the author, February 1990.
27. *La Presse*, March 8, 1976.
28. *Les années Bourassa*, op. cit., p. 152.
29. Canadian Press, June 29, 1976.
30. Francis Fox, interview with the author, August 1989.
31. Robert Bourassa, interview with the author, June 1989.
32. Robert Bourassa, interview with the author, June 1989.
33. Ibid.
34. *Les années Bourassa*, op. cit., p. 265.
35. Ibid.

36.   René Lévesque, *Attendez que je me rappelle* . . . , op. cit., p. 357.
37.   Robert Bourassa, interview with the author, July 1990.

CHAPTER 5

1.   Gilles Loiselle, interview with the author, January 1991.
2.   *Forbes*, March 1975.
3.   *Les années Trudeau*, Montreal, Le Jour, 1990, p. 390.
4.   Charles Lynch, Morningside.
5.   *Les années Bourassa*, op. cit., p. 282.
6.   Graham Fraser, *PQ: René Lévesque and the Parti Québécois in Power*, Toronto, Macmillan, 1984, p. xiv.
7.   *Les années Bourassa*, op. cit., p. 265.
8.   René Lévesque, *Attendez que je me rappelle* . . . , op. cit., p. 374.
9.   Robert Bourassa, interview with the author, July 1990.
10. Ibid.
11. Ibid.
12. Confidential interview.
13. Robert Bourassa, interview with the author, June 1989.
14. Robert Bourassa, "L'union monetaire et l'union politique sont indissociables," Montreal, Liberal Party of Quebec (Referendum documents), 1980.
15. Pierre Bourgault, interview with Claude Lévesque, Radio Canada FM, October 21, 1988.
16. Quebec Government, "Quebec-Canada: A New Deal," Government Printing Office, Quebec, 1979.
17. Claude Morin, *L'art de l'impossible*, Montreal, Boreal, 1987.
18. Robert Bourassa, interview with the author, July 1990.
19. *L'Actualité*, September 15, 1990.
20. Robert Bourassa, *Forces* [Hydro-Quebec quarterly magazine], Spring 1987.
21. Corinne Cote-Lévesque, Jean-Roch Boivin, interviews with the author, July 1989.
22. Robert Bourassa, interview with the author, June 1989.
23. *L'Actualité*, November 1983, p. 48.
24. See *L'Actualité*, January 1982 and *The Outsider*, op. cit., p. 257-274.

25. Robert Bourassa, interview with the author, July 1990.
26. *Les années Trudeau*, op. cit., p. 395.
27. *L'Actualité*, May 1982, p. 15.
28. *Les années Trudeau*, op. cit., p. 324.
29. Pierre Trudeau, interview with Jack Webster, Vancouver, CHAN-TV, November 1981.
30. *Les années Trudeau*, op. cit., p. 394-396.
31. *Les années Bourassa*, op. cit., p. 56.
32. Lucien Bouchard, interview with the author, July 1990.
33. Reprinted in Jean Louis Gagnon, *Les Apostasies*, Vol. III, Document G, Montreal, Les Editions La Presse, 1990, p. 237-246.
34. Robert Bourassa, interview with the author, July 1990.
35. Robert Bourassa, interview with the author, June 1989.
36. Ibid.
37. Ibid.
38. Robert Bourassa, interview with the author, July 1990.

CHAPTER 6

1. *Chatelaine*, November 1988, p. 50.
2. Confidential interview.
3. Robert Bourassa, interview with the author, June 1989.
4. *L'Actualité*, May 1989, p. 37.
5. Robert Bourassa, interview with the author, June 1989.
6. Ibid.
7. Confidential interview.
8. Robert Bourassa, interview with the author, July 1990.
9. Lucien Bouchard, *Le Devoir*, September 21, 1985.
10. Lucien Bouchard, interview with the author, July 1990.
11. Lucien Bouchard, interview with the author, February 1990.
12. Raymond Garneau, press statement, July 1984.
13. Lucien Bouchard, interview with the author, February 1990.
14. Gil Rémillard, *Le Federalisme Canadien*, Vol. II, Montreal, Québec-Amérique, 1985, p. 434.
15. Robert Bourassa, interview with the author, July 1990.
16. Constitutional committee of the Quebec Liberal Party, *Une Nouvelle Federation Canadienne*, Montreal, PLQ, 1980, p. 13.

17. Task Force on Canadian Unity, *Se Retrouver* (Observations and Recommendations), Ottawa, Department of Supply and Services, 1979, p. 92.
18. Macdonald Commission Report, Vol. 3, Ottawa, Department of Supply and Services, 1985, p. 383.
19. Robert Bourassa, interview with the author, July 1990.
20. Gil Rémillard, speech at Mont-Gabriel conference, May 1986.
21. Lucien Bouchard, interview with the author, July 1990.
22. Grant Devine, interview with the author, July 1990.
23. Ibid.
24. *Le Devoir*, April 22, 1987.
25. Hershel Ezrin (chief of staff to the premier of Ontario) interview with the author, April 1987.
26. Grant Devine, interview with the author, July 1990.
27. Robert Bourassa, interview with the author, July 1990.
28. *Le Devoir*, May 9, 1987.
29. *Le Devoir*, May 14, 1987.
30. Michel Roy, in *The Outsider*, op. cit., p. 243.

CHAPTER 7

1. Robert Bourassa, interview with the author, July 1989.
2. Pierre Elliott Trudeau, Lettre ouverte aux Québécois, July 15, 1980.
3. Robert Bourassa, interview with the author, July 1990.
4. Joint Senate-Commons committee on the Constitutional Agreement of 1987, August 27, 1987, p. 14:128.
5. *National Assembly Debates*, June 18, 1987, p. 8708.
6. Robert Bourassa, interview with the author, July 1990.
7. Michael Bliss, brief delivered to the Senate-Commons committee on the constitutional agreement of 1987.
8. Robert Bourassa, *National Assembly Debates*, June 18, 1987, p. 8709.
9. *Senate Debates*, 1987, p. 2997.
10. Roy Romanow, interview with the author, December 1989.
11. Gilles Loiselle, interview with the author, May 1990.
12. Gilles Loiselle, interview with the author, January 1991.

13. Robert Bourassa, interview with the author, July 1990.
14. *Senate Debates*, 1987, p. 3017.
15. *Saturday Night*, December 1985.
16. Claude Morin, *Les lendemains piégés*, Montreal, Boréal, 1988.
17. Southam News, May 30, 1990.
18. Confidential source—one of the premiers who was present.
19. Frank McKenna, interview with the author, July 1990.
20. Robert Bourassa, interview with the author, July 1990.

CHAPTER 8

1. William Davis, interview with the author, February 1981.
2. Claire Hoy, *Bill Davis*, Agincourt, Methuen Publications, 1985. p. 309.
3. David Peterson, interview with the author, July 1987.
4. Statistics Canada, 1986 census.
5. David Peterson, interview with the author, July 1987.
6. Ibid.
7. Jacques Hebert, in *Les années Trudeau*, op. cit., p. 155.
8. David Peterson, interview with the author, July 1987.
9. David Peterson, interview with the author, May 1983.
10. David Peterson, interview with the author, July 1987.
11. David Peterson, "Ontario's Future in a Changing Canada," August 10, 1990.
12. David Peterson, interview with the author, December 1989.
13. Robert Bourassa, interview with the author, July 1990.
14. *Forces* [Hydro-Quebec quarterly magazine], spring 1987.
15. David Peterson, "Ontario's Future in a Changing Canada," op. cit.

CHAPTER 9

1. *Inside Outer Canada*, unpublished study quoted by David Kilgour, Edmonton, Lone Pine Publishing, 1990.
2. Preston Manning, interview with the author, March 1988.
3. Grant Devine, interview with the author, July 1990.
4. Ibid.

5.   Ibid.
6.   *Forces* [Hydro-Quebec quarterly magazine], spring 1987.
7.   Statistics Canada, 1986 census.
8.   Grant Devine, interview with the author, April 1988.
9.   Grant Devine, interview with the author, July 1990.
10. Bill Vander Zalm, interview with the author, October 1987.
11. Ibid.
12. Ibid.
13. Howard Pawley, interview with the author, December 1987.
14. Gary Filmon, interview with the author, March 1988.
15. André Laurendeau, op. cit., p. 68.
16. Claude Rompré, interview with the author, June 1990.
17. Ibid.
18. Howard Pawley, interview with the author, December 1987.
19. *Le Devoir*, February 2, 1988.
20. Preston Manning, interview with the author, March 1988.
21. *Le Devoir*, April 14, 1988.
22. Ibid.
23. Confidential source (one of the businessmen present).
24. Gary Filmon, interview with the author, April 1988.
25. Jake Epp, interview with the author.
26. Robert Bourassa, interview with the author, July 1991.
27. Grant Devine, interview with the author, July 1990.
28. Frank McKenna, interview with the author, July 1990.
29. Grant Devine, interview with the author, July 1990.
30. Claude Morin, *Les lendemains pièges*, Montreal, Boreal, 1988, p. 365 and 372.
31. Grant Devine, interview with the author, July 1990.
32. Ibid.

CHAPTER 10

1.   *Forces* [Hydro-Quebec quarterly magazine], spring 1987.
2.   Frank McKenna, interview with the author, July 1990.
3.   Frank McKenna, interview with the author, June 1988.
4.   Ibid.
5.   Frank McKenna, interview with the author, July 1990.

6. Ibid.
7. Ibid.
8. Statistics Canada, 1986 census.
9. Confidential interview.
10. Frank McKenna, interview with the author, July 1990.
11. Ibid.
12. Frank McKenna, interview with the author, November 1987.
13. Ibid.
14. Frank McKenna, interview with the author, July 1990.
15. *Forces*, spring 1987.
16. Frank McKenna, interview with the author, June 1988.
17. Frank McKenna, interview with the author, July 1990.
18. Ibid.
19. *The Outsider*, op. cit., p. 251.
20. Ibid., p. 122.
21. Frank McKenna, interview with the author, July 1990.
22. Southam News, June 1990.
23. *Saturday Night*, January 1991, p. 34.
24. Frank McKenna, interview with the author, July 1990.
25. Ibid.

CHAPTER 11

1. Marcel Masse, interview with the author, October 1985.
2. Confidential interview.
3. Lucien Bouchard, interview with the author, February 1990.
4. Lucien Bouchard, interview with the author, February 1987.
5. Ibid.
6. André Bissonnette, interview with the author, November 1984.
7. Lucien Bouchard, interview with the author, February 1990.
8. Benoît Bouchard, interview with the author, February 1987.
9. Ibid.
10. Ibid.
11. Lucien Bouchard, interview with the author, February 1990.
12. Lucien Bouchard, interview with the author, July 1990.
13. Confidential interview.
14. Ibid.

15. Benoît Bouchard, interview with the author, February 1987.
16. Lucien Bouchard, interview with the author, July 1990.
17. Lucien Bouchard, interview with the author, February 1990.
18. Benoît Bouchard, interview with the author, February 1987.
19. Gilles Loiselle, interview with the author, April 1990.
20. Paul Martin, interview with the author, April 1990.
21. Lucien Bouchard, interview with the author, July 1990.
22. Confidential interview.
23. Ibid.
24. Gilles Loiselle, interview with the author, April 1990.
25. Benoît Bouchard, interview with the author, February 1987.
26. Lucien Bouchard, unpublished speeches, Val d'Or and Moncton, November 1989.
27. Benoît Bouchard, interview with the author, February 1987.
28. Benoît Bouchard, interview with the author, February 1987.
29. Gilles Loiselle, interview with the author, April 1990.
30. Lucien Bouchard, interview with the author, February 1990.
31. Ibid.
32. Lucien Bouchard, interview with the author, July 1990.
33. For the events between May 10 and 20, 1990: Lucien Bouchard, interviews with the author, July 1990 and January 1991; Benoît Bouchard, interview October 1990; Jean-Roch Boivin, interview, November 1990; and various confidential interviews, June 1990.
34. Pierre-Marc Johnson, interview with the author, June 1991.
35. Lucien Bouchard, news conference, May 22, 1990.
36. Confidential interview.
37. Lucien Bouchard, speech at *Le Devoir*'s 80th-anniversary celebration.
38. Benoît Bouchard, interview with the author, October 1990.

CHAPTER 12

1. Robert Sheppard and Michael Valpy, *The National Deal*, Toronto, Fleet Books, 1982.
2. René Lévesque, *Attendez que je me rappelle* . . . , op. cit., p. 490.
3. Confidential interview.
4. Paul Tellier, interview with the author, June 1982.
5. *Le Devoir*, March 10, 1987.

6. John Price, *Indians of Canada*, 1979, quoted by René Lévesque, op. cit., p. 490.

7. Norman Spector, briefing for journalists, March 9, 1987.

8. *Le Devoir*, March 27, 1987.

9. Ibid.

10. Confidential interview with the author, cited in *Le Devoir*, March 28, 1987.

11. André Ouellet, interview with the author, May 1990.

12. Frank McKenna, interview with the author, July 1990.

13. *Maclean's*, July 2, 1990.

14. Lucien Bouchard, interview with the author, July 1990.

15. See in particular story by Luc Chartrand, *L'Actualité*, December 15, 1990.

16. Robert Bourassa, interview with the author, January 1991.

17. Ibid.

18. Confidential interview, August 1990.

19. Ibid.

20. *L'Actualité*, op. cit., p. 34.

21. Robert Bourassa, interview with the author, January 1991.

CHAPTER 13

1. Robert Bourassa, interview with the author, January 1991.

2. Ibid.

3. Ibid.

4. Ibid.

5. Robert Bourassa never regarded it as an "operation," even less a hospitalization, because he was away from the affairs of state for only an hour. (The author has adhered strictly to the premier's version because it was not the details of his illness which were important, but rather his courage at this time and his capacity to carry on his functions under difficult circumstances.)

6. Robert Bourassa, interview with the author, July 1990.

7. Benoît Bouchard, interview with the author, June 1990.

8. Robert Bourassa, interview with the author, January 1991.

9. Ibid.

10. Robert Bourassa, interview with the author, December 1990.

11. *La Presse*, January 25 and 28, 1991.
12. Ibid.
13. Robert Bourassa, interview with the author, December 1990.
14. Lucien Bouchard, interview with the author, January 1991.
15. Ibid.
16. Robert Bourassa, interview with the author, January 1991.
17. Robert Bourassa, interview with the author, July 1990.
18. Lucien Bouchard, interview with the author, January 1991.
19. Robert Bourassa, interview with the author, January 1991.
20. Gallup Canada, poll taken January 2 to 5, 1991. The proportion of Canadians prepared to see Quebec separate varied from 63 percent in the Maritimes, to 70 percent in Ontario, to 78 percent on the prairies to 79 percent in British Columbia.
21. *Le Devoir*, February 4, 1991.
22. Frank McKenna, interview with the author, July 1990.
23. Confidential interview.
24. Frank McKenna, interview with the author, July 1990.
25. Grant Devine, interview with the author, July 1990.
26. Robert Bourassa, interview with the author, July 1991.
27. Paul Martin, interview with the author, April 1990.
28. Robert Bourassa, interview with the author, January 1991.
29. Grant Devine, interview with the author, July 1990.
30. Robert Bourassa, interview with the author, January 1991.
31. Jacques Godbout, interview with the author, December 1990. Robert Bourassa said one day: ''The Péquistes can howl, but the mothers like me.''
32. Robert Bourassa, interview with the author, July 1990.
33. Robert Normand, speech to the Americas Society, published in *Le Soleil*, October 11, 1990.

EPILOGUE

1. This epilogue is in part based on the author's contribution to a forum on sovereignty organized by the Parti Québécois in Montreal, September 7-8, 1990.
2. Pierre Elliott Trudeau, *Federalism and the French Canadians*, Macmillan of Canada, 1968.

3. Robert Bourassa, interview with the author, January 1991.
4. Quebec Liberal Party, *Un Québec libre de ses choix*, 1991, p. 90.
5. William Waters, *Quebec Separatism*, SRI, 1977.
6. See in particular, Jean François Lisée, *In the Eye of the Eagle*, Toronto, HarperCollins, 1990, especially the remarkably pragmatic analyses by the State Department in the book's appendix.
7. Georges Mathews, *L'Accord*, Montreal, Le Jour, 1990, pp. 158-61.
8. *Un Québec libre de ses choix*, op. cit., p. 71.

INDEX